Philosophical Perspectives on Play

Philosophical Perspectives on Play builds on the disciplinary and paradigmatic bridges constructed between the study of philosophy and play in *The Philosophy of Play* (Routledge, 2013) to develop a richer understanding of the concept and nature of play and its relation to human life and value. Made up of contributions from leading international thinkers and inviting readers to explore the presumptions often attached to play and playfulness, the book considers ways that play in 'virtual' and 'real' worlds can inform understandings of each, critiquing established norms and encouraging scepticism about the practice and experience of play.

Organized around four central themes – play(ing) at the limits, aesthetics, metaphysics/ontology and ethics – the book extends and challenges notions of play by drawing on issues emerging in sport, gaming, literature, space and art, with specific attention paid to disruption and danger. It is intended to provide scholars and practitioners working in the spheres of play, education, games, sport and related subjects with a deeper understanding of philosophical thought and to open dialogue across these disciplines.

Malcolm MacLean studied anthropology and history with a PhD from the University of Queensland, Australia, and is Reader in the Culture and History of Sport and Associate Dean, Quality and Standards at the University of Gloucestershire, UK. He has taught history in New Zealand and worked as a policy analyst and historian in the New Zealand Ministry of Justice. His publications deal with cultural boycotts and sports-related anti-apartheid protests, the cultural politics of settlement colonies, and discourses of indigeneity associated with sport, body, and movement cultures. He is actively involved in international sports studies networks and was Chair of the British Society of Sports History. He is an editor and author of *Philosophy of Play* (Routledge, 2013), 'Sporting nations without states' (2014) and 'The sports club in history: International aspects' (2013).

Wendy Russell is a Senior Lecturer in Play and Playwork at University of Gloucestershire, UK and a consultant on children's play and playwork. She has worked in the UK playwork sector for over 35 years, first as a playworker on adventure playgrounds, then in play development, research, and education and training. She has worked on development, strategic, evaluation and research projects for local authorities, the private sector and local, national and international voluntary organizations. Key publications include, co-authored with Stuart Lester, *Play for a Change* (2008) and *Children's Right to Play* (2010). She co-edited *Philosophy of Play* (Routledge, 2013) with Emily Ryall and Malcolm MacLean. She is on the editorial board of the *International Journal of Play*.

Emily Ryall is a Senior Lecturer in the Philosophy of Sport at the University of Gloucestershire, UK. She is an editor and author of *Philosophy of Play* (Routledge, 2013). She is also Chair of the British Philosophy of Sport Association, book review editor for *Sport, Ethics and Philosophy* and on the editorial panel for the *Journal of the Philosophy of Sport*. She has written and published widely on philosophical issues related to sport.

Philosophical Perspectives on Play

Edited by Malcolm MacLean,
Wendy Russell and Emily Ryall

LONDON AND NEW YORK

First published 2016
by Routledge
2 Park Square, Milton Park, Abingdon, Oxon OX14 4RN

and by Routledge
711 Third Avenue, New York, NY 10017

Routledge is an imprint of the Taylor and Francis Group, an informa business

© 2016 M. MacLean, W. Russell and E. Ryall

The right of M. MacLean, W. Russell and E. Ryall to be identified as the authors of the editorial material, and of the authors for their individual chapters, has been asserted in accordance with sections 77 and 78 of the Copyright, Designs and Patents Act 1988.

All rights reserved. No part of this book may be reprinted or reproduced or utilized in any form or by any electronic, mechanical, or other means, now known or hereafter invented, including photocopying and recording, or in any information storage or retrieval system, without permission in writing from the publishers.

Trademark notice: Product or corporate names may be trademarks or registered trademarks, and are used only for identification and explanation without intent to infringe.

British Library Cataloguing-in-Publication Data
A catalogue record for this book is available from the British Library

Library of Congress Cataloging in Publication Data
Philosophical perspectives on play / edited by Malcolm MacLean, Wendy Russell and Emily Ryall.
   pages cm
   Includes bibliographical references and index.
   1. Play (Philosophy) I. Maclean, Malcolm, 1960– II. Russell, Wendy. III. Ryall, Emily.
   B105.P54P54 2015
   128'.4–dc23   2015009368

ISBN: 978-1-138-84143-7 (hbk)
ISBN: 978-1-315-73221-3 (ebk)

Typeset in Galliard
by Wearset Ltd, Boldon, Tyne and Wear

To Rudy (a player from the outset), Rupert and Hayley –
the only three of a kind (Malcolm)
To Vera and Gerry (Wendy)
To Daisy, Poppy-dog and Hilary the cat (Emily)

Contents

List of figures   x
Notes on contributors   xi
Acknowledgements   xvi

Introduction   1
MALCOLM MacLEAN, WENDY RUSSELL AND EMILY RYALL

PART I
Playing at the limits   11

1 Exile and utopia as liminal play: a cultural-theoretical approach   13
   MIHAI I. SPARIOSU

2 Playing war – playing with fire: about dark games   27
   HENNING EICHBERG

3 Games and evil   42
   CARL DAVID MILDENBERGER

4 Posthuman nature: life beyond the natural playground   53
   STUART LESTER

PART II
Play, aesthetics and performance   69

5 A disavowal of games   71
   CHRIS BATEMAN

viii Contents

6 Lessons in playing: Robert Morris's *Bodyspacemotionthings* 2009 as a biopolitical environment 84
TIM STOTT

7 Oasis of happiness – the play of the world and human existence: Eugen Fink's multidimensional concept of play 95
NÚRIA SARA MIRAS BORONAT

8 Homer and competitive play 107
DANIEL A. DOMBROWSKI

PART III
Metaphysics and ontology 121

9 *Homo ludens* in the twenty-first century: towards an understanding of Caillois's *paidia* in sports 123
IMARA FELKERS, ELLEN MULDER AND MALCOLM MacLEAN

10 Locating rhythms: improvised play in the built environment 136
DANI ABULHAWA

11 Weltentzug und Weltzerfall (world-withdrawal and world-decay): Heidegger's notions of withdrawal from the world and the decay of worlds in the times of computer games 152
MATHIAS FUCHS

12 The paradox of rules and freedom: art and life in the simile of play 166
DAMLA DÖNMEZ

PART IV
Ethics of work in play and play in work 177

13 Philosophy, play and ethics in education 179
SANDRA LYNCH

14 Entangled in the midst of it: a diffractive expression of an ethics for playwork 191
WENDY RUSSELL

15 'Excess is truly the key': community, flow and the play of
   control in the picture books of Thomas King   205
   HELENE STAVELEY

   Index   218

Figures

2.1	'Uncle Toby playing war'	28
2.2	Playing soldiers, German children's book, nineteenth century	28
2.3	Play 'pulling the cow to the grass'	37
10.1	Image from *Unknowable*, performed in Sheffield, 2014	137
10.2	Image from *Unknowable*, performed in Sheffield, 2014	138
10.3	Film still from *Alice in Plymouth*, Plymouth city centre, 2009	148
11.1	*Assassin's Creed® Unity*, screenshot	153
11.2	Ramadi, Iraq, US soldiers with tank; screenshot from Arma 2	157
11.3	Ramadi, Iraq, militia in the Ta'meem district; screenshot from Arma 2	158
11.4	Gamers in front of a game world that has been 'put up'	158

Contributors

Dani Abulhawa is a performance artist and senior lecturer in performance at Sheffield Hallam University. Her research is located within the mixed-modal discourse of play, public space and gender, which she has presented in different formats throughout the UK, as well as in continental Europe and North America. Since 2006, and following a history of involvement in the British skateboarding subculture, she has developed practices that respond creatively, playfully and often subversively to the built environment.

Chris Bateman is a game designer, outsider philosopher and author who has worked on over 40 game projects and became the first person to attain a doctorate in game aesthetics (2013). His research explores neurobiological distinctions between different play styles and preferences. His trilogy of philosophy books concerns the role of imagination in human life: *Imaginary Games* (2011) examines imagination in games and art, asking if games can be art or whether all art is a kind of game; *The Mythology of Evolution* (2012) explores the role of imagination in the sciences, asking if it is possible to present the story of life without distorting it; *Chaos Ethics* (2014) explores the role of imagination in morality.

Núria Sara Miras Boronat is a Postdoctoral Research Fellow at the University of Barcelona. She teaches German and English in Lleida, Spain. In 2009 she obtained her PhD in Philosophy at the University of Barcelona with a thesis on *Wittgenstein and Gadamer: Language, Praxis, and Reason*. She has been Postdoctoral Research Fellow and Associate Instructor at the Universität Leipzig (2009–13), Guest Research Fellow at the Humboldt-Universität zu Berlin (2003–7) and Guest Research Fellow at the Institute of Philosophy of the Spanish National Research Council (CSIC, 2000). She has written essays on pluralism, philosophy of language, hermeneutics, phenomenology, American pragmatism, philosophy of film and feminism. She is currently working on a project on the history of philosophy of play in the first decades of the twentieth century. She has also translated science fiction and philosophy books from German into Catalan and Spanish.

Daniel A. Dombrowski is Professor of Philosophy at Seattle University. He is the author of 17 books and over 100 articles in scholarly journals in philosophy, theology, classics and literature. He is the author of *Rethinking the Ontological Argument: A Neoclassical Theistic Perspective* (2006). He also studies authors in the philosophy of sport: Johann Huizinga, Paul Weiss and Randolph Feezell. His latest work is *Contemporary Athletics and Ancient Greek Ideals* (2009).

Damla Dönmez is a graduate student at Boğaziçi University, Istanbul and a research assistant in the Humanities and Social Sciences Department at Istanbul Technical University. Her main areas of interest are philosophy of art, moral philosophy and political philosophy. She is writing her PhD thesis on the concept of the sublime and its ethical implications. Since she also works as an actress in an amateur theatre group, she is interested in the questions of philosophy of art in many contexts and their effects on the practical life.

Henning Eichberg is a Professor, cultural sociologist and historian at the University of Southern Denmark, Institute of Sports Science and Clinical Biomechanics, in the field of body culture studies and the study of play. His research has dealt with the history and cultural sociology of body culture and sport, the anthropology of movement culture, the cultural ecology of movement, early modern military technology, Indonesian studies, and democracy, movement and identity. His present fields of research are international comparative studies of body cultures, of sport for all, and of sports policies, and his books include *Idrættens tredje vej* ('The third way of Danish sports', 1994), *Body Cultures* (1998), *The People of Democracy* (2004) and *Bodily Democracy: Towards a Philosophy of Sport for All* (2010).

Imara Felkers is Lecturer in Philosophy at the HKU University of the Arts Utrecht. She has developed cross-over teaching methods in the fields of play and art. She runs a company, Art&KC, working in play in sports and daily life design, including research into these areas.

Mathias Fuchs is a pioneer in the artistic use of game engines in game art installations. He is a writer and theoretician on Game Art, Serious Games and Philosophy of Games. He started the first European Masters Programme in Creative Games at the School of Art and Design at the University of Salford in Greater Manchester. He is Professor at Leuphana University in Lüneburg, Germany, where he directs the Gamification Lab at the Centre for Digital Cultures. He has conceived and designed work for ISEA94 and ISEA2004, resfest, ars electronica, PSi #11, futuresonic, EAST and the Greenwich Millennium Dome. He has built creative games for museums, urban planning and theatre performances.

Stuart Lester is a Senior Lecturer in Play and Playwork/Professional Studies in Children's Play at the University of Gloucestershire and an independent trainer and consultant. Key research interests focus on the nature and value of children's play, playful production of time/space through everyday encounters and the conditions under which children's (and adults') playfulness may thrive. Published work includes *Play for a Change* (2008) and *Children's Right to Play* (2010) (both with Wendy Russell), as well as contributions to a number of play and playwork publications. Ideas presented in this chapter are drawn from a current PhD thesis that draws on Deleuzian and posthuman philosophy to interrupt dominant narratives of play, childhood and indeed the process of life itself.

Sandra Lynch is a moral philosopher, Professor and Director of the Institute for Faith, Ethics and Society at the University of Notre Dame, Australia, and a former teacher. Her research interests lie in the areas of ethics, especially professional ethics; the self; friendship, philosophy and literature; critical thinking; and values education. Her publications include: 'Friendship ethics and democracy' in *Append* (2003); *Philosophy and Friendship: Thinking about Identity & Difference* (2005); *Strategies for a Thinking Classroom* (with Gregory Leaney, 2008); 'Professional healthcare education: Ethical competence and emotional intelligence as aspects of care' (2011); and 'Giving voice to values: An undergraduate nursing curriculum project' (with Bethne Hart and Catherine M. Costa, 2014).

Malcolm MacLean studied anthropology and history with a PhD from the University of Queensland, and is Reader in the Culture and History of Sport and Associate Dean, Quality and Standards at the University of Gloucestershire. He has taught history in New Zealand and worked as a policy analyst and historian in the New Zealand Ministry of Justice. His publications deal with cultural boycotts and sports-related anti-apartheid protests, the cultural politics of settlement colonies, and discourses of indigeneity associated with sport, body, and movement cultures. He is actively involved in international sports studies networks and was Chair of the British Society of Sports History. He is an editor and author of *Philosophy of Play* (Routledge, 2013) and author of 'Sporting nations without states' (2014) and 'The sports club in history: International aspects' (2013).

Carl David Mildenberger studied economics in St. Gallen, Boston and Witten and philosophy in Paris and St Andrews. He holds a PhD in economics and is the author of *Economics and Social Conflict* (2013), in which he makes extensive use of data from the massively multiplayer online role-play game 'EVE Online' to establish the need for a concept of evil in economics. Having lectured in Germany in both economics and philosophy, he is working towards a second PhD in philosophy at the University of St Andrews. In his thesis, he answers the question of what it takes to make a market exchange just.

Ellen Mulder is a former professional volleyball athlete. She is a trainer in personal development, coaches athletes and teaches meditation and qi gong. She runs a company, Art&KC, working in play in sports and daily life design, including research into these areas.

Wendy Russell is a Senior Lecturer in Play and Playwork at University of Gloucestershire and a consultant on children's play and playwork. She has worked in the UK playwork sector for over 35 years, first as a playworker on adventure playgrounds, then in play development, research, and education and training. She has worked on development, strategic, evaluation and research projects for local authorities, the private sector and local, national and international voluntary organizations. Key publications include, co-authored with Stuart Lester, *Play for a Change* (2008) and *Children's Right to Play* (2010). She co-edited *The Philosophy of Play* (2013) with Emily Ryall and Malcolm MacLean. She is on the editorial board of the *International Journal of Play*.

Emily Ryall is a Senior Lecturer in the Philosophy of Sport at the University of Gloucestershire. She is an editor and author of *Philosophy of Play* (2013). She is also Chair of the British Philosophy of Sport Association, book review editor for *Sport, Ethics and Philosophy* and on the editorial panel for the *Journal of the Philosophy of Sport*. She has written and published widely on philosophical issues related to sport.

Mihai I. Spariosu, Distinguished Research Professor and Academic Director at the Institute for European Studies at the University of Georgia, is a leading cultural historian and theoretician in Western philosophy, literature and science. He has published on intercultural and global studies; European studies; literary and theory criticism; history of ideas; philosophy and literature; literature and science and humanities. His 1989 book *Dionysus Reborn: Play and the Aesthetic Dimension in Modern Philosophical and Scientific Discourse* was seen as groundbreaking in its exploration and presentation of these closely linked concepts. Other publications include *The Wreath of Wild Olive: Play, Liminality and the Study of Literature* (1997) and *God of Many Names: Play, Poetry, and Power in Hellenic Thought from Homer to Aristotle* (1991). He is also a theoretician of Intercultural Knowledge Management, as seen in *Global Intelligence and Human Development: Toward an Ecology of Global Learning* (2005) and *Remapping Knowledge: Intercultural Studies for a Global Age* (2006).

Helene Staveley completed a PhD on elements of play and game in Canadian fiction in 2008. Her research interests involve expressions of ludicism in Canadian fiction, children's literature, contemporary fiction, postmodernism and postcolonialism. She teaches English literature at Memorial University in St. John's, Newfoundland, Canada.

Tim Stott is Lecturer in Art History and Theory at Dublin Institute of Technology and Associate Researcher at the Graduate School of Creative Arts and Media, Dublin. He has a BA (Hons) in Drawing and Painting (2003) and an MSc in Contemporary Art Theory (2004), both from Edinburgh College of Art, and a PhD in contemporary art criticism from the Department of Visual

Culture at NCAD. He has published widely on contemporary art in journals such as *Afterall*, *Art Review*, *Circa*, *Frieze*, *Printed Project* and *Variant* and is preparing a monograph on the use of play and games in contemporary art and co-editing a collection of essays revisiting modernism through the lens of complex systems theory.

Acknowledgements

We would like to give great big thanks to our co-workers inside and outside the University of Gloucestershire who helped organise the second 'Philosophy at Play' conference in April 2013, run in conjunction with the British Philosophy of Sport conference. This book is the product of 'Philosophy at Play 2' and we are indebted to Hilary Smith, Leonie Labistour, Francis Barton, Kelly Conibere and Gillian Hartley. The conference could not have happened without the support of the University of Gloucestershire, in particular Mike Cogger and Jane Cantwell. Our biggest thanks are to those who contributed to this book; in the case of authors, your timeliness, goodwill, good humour and tolerance has made our jobs so much easier; in the case of Simon Whitmore and Will Bailey at Routledge, your support, guidance, patience and tolerance has been invaluable and eased the process in immeasurable ways.

Malcolm MacLean, Wendy Russell and Emily Ryall
February 2015

Introduction

Malcolm MacLean, Wendy Russell and Emily Ryall

> It's advantageous for the community to have a number of people available who practice childishness as a job, or a vocation, and may even get paid for thus playing with words and generating imaginary problems and equally imaginary solutions.... So much more useful, I will add, the less it crystallizes, the more possibilities it explores, the crazier stories it tells.
>
> (Bencivenga, 1994: 43)

In this extract from Bencivenga's *Philosophy in Play*, Angelo is, of course, talking about philosophy itself. He goes on to draw more parallels between philosophy and play, calling it 'a continuous exploration of novelty which refuses in principle to settle down, which defies by vocation all rules' (ibid.: 46).

There is much in this snippet that is paradoxical: the importance of non-utility that may perhaps eventually yield something of use, but with no guarantee; the apparent futility of creating non-existent problems in order to solve them; the identification of defining features of philosophy – understood as rules of engagement – that includes rule-breaking. And of course Angelo's fellow dialoguers are keen to differ, to present alternative perspectives on philosophy, to point out the inconsistencies in his argument, such as his certainty about the value of uncertainty. Philosophy here is seen as activity, and dialogue 'the most lively, most valid aspect of doing philosophy' (ibid.: ix).

It was an interest in these and other paradoxes and a desire for dialogue that was behind our approach to two international *Philosophy at Play* conferences hosted at the University of Gloucestershire. They sought to build disciplinary and paradigmatic bridges between scholars of philosophy and of play, and to provide a space for such playful dialogue. The first of these conferences, held in 2011, generated the essays in *The Philosophy of Play* (Ryall *et al.*, 2013); the second, held in 2013, gave rise to those in this volume.

The first conference and book were likened to 'dipping the toe in the ocean of philosophical play and playful philosophy' (p. 2). Contributors drew on a range of (mostly) Western philosophical traditions to ask metaphysical, epistemological, ontological and ethical questions about the phenomenon of play. One paradox that came to light, explored in our introductory chapter in the first volume, was the potential for play both to highlight and to dissolve the tensions between mimesis and alterity, between our 'yearning for the true real' that can be accurately represented and our desire to 'reinvent a new world and live new fictions' (Taussig, 1993: xvii). Or, to put it slightly differently, the mimicry and mockery of our current worlds within a frame that allows for temporary respite from both the dull and alienating routines of daily life and the ontological anxieties of an uncertain world (Sutton-Smith, 1999). From here, it is a mere hop, skip and a jump to Hakim Bey's (1985) notion of a Temporary Autonomous Zone (TAZ), with its attendant meanings of, *inter alia*, fleetingness; territory, borders, liminality and interstices; disorder, resistance and freedom.

What emerged from our editorial discussions for this volume was a related paradox that can be found in many of these chapters, that of play's freedoms and its rule-boundedness. The connection arises from play's ambiguous positioning as both apart from and a part of what might be seen as 'not-play' – whatever that might comprise: 'real' life, seriousness, the struggle for survival, alienation – depending on your philosophical bent. A zone, however temporary or autonomous, presumably has a border even if this is symbolic, dynamic, porous or soluble; it is contained, held, embedded within a frame (Bateson, 1972/55) or what Huizinga (1955) calls a magic circle. This frame is what sets play apart from 'not-play'. It may be a metaphorical boundary, but it has material effects too, both in terms of scholarship and practice. Furthermore, the TAZ (for which Bey resisted giving a tight definition, saying it spoke for itself), as *autonomous*, is – by definition – a law unto itself, but still a law nonetheless.

For Bateson (1972/55), the frame allows players to share the understanding that what takes place within it is playful and therefore, in some sense, not 'real' but 'as if'. The playful nip between play-fighting dogs both is and is not what it connotes. It is not a 'real' bite, since its intention is not to hurt, but to continue engagement in the bonding activity of rough and tumble play. Its incompleteness communicates that this is a play fight; in this sense it is a 'real' action. Additionally, its referent is real enough, and all players are aware of what it both mimics and mocks. In this understanding, the frame does not entirely separate play from not-play, and the rules of the game are that this is pretend fighting and all players need to abide by that in order to prevent the frame from falling apart. The shared agreement that 'this is play' is the foundational rule for all play regardless of whether it has structured, constitutive or regulatory rules over and above this one. It is the decision to play that produces play and produces the space (the TAZ) within which it occurs.

The power of such a rule is that, for many but not all play forms, there is a lack of 'real' consequences. The purpose is to mimic or mock the conventions of society in a way that offers a sense of power through an inconsequential subverting of the rules of daily life, in the manner of the pantomime, the charivari, the carnivalesque. Of course, if your choice of play is adrenalin sports or gambling, then real consequences may well apply, but for many other forms of play, particularly rationalized forms of *agon* and *mimesis*, the argument is that they do not. Yet we must take care not to assume the frame is hermetic in metaphysical, ontological or ethical terms. The metaphysical problem of defining play requires that we create a conceptual boundary round it in order to distinguish it from not-play, yet it is never entirely separate. As Mary Midgley (1974) notes in her important but often underused paper 'The Game Game', players bring themselves to the game – they do not become a *tabula rasa* when they enter the field of play. Furthermore, reducing play to a specific activity bounded by time and space does not allow for those more fleeting moments of playfulness that arise in the midst of not-play. Neither does the frame entirely separate 'as if' from 'real'. Children giggle when reciting rude rhymes precisely because these are taboo words; the Shakespearian fool can speak truth to power in a way that formal advisors would not dare; performances of power within the play frame can reflect as well as refract those outside. Mimicry, mockery and subversion rely on having something that ordinarily should not be mimicked, mocked or subverted.

The frame around play, play's delimitation, its magic circle, can offer a suitable metaphor to consider play's marked-off-from-seriousness, but our use of the term 'boundary', no matter how indeterminate we might insist the frame or boundary to be, implies some sort of demarcated space with ontological distinctiveness. In making this case for a fluid, porous, leaky boundary we are restating a view that we expect is widely held in play studies, but we would take the notion of a frame a step further. Thinking of a frame not as a thing, a metaphorical or material line on the ground, but as a relationship suggests a very different status for the enframed. Bey's TAZ, as useful as it is to help conceptualize the phenomenological space of play, still leaves largely taken for granted the borders of the zone. The literature (and cultural studies) scholar John Frow (1982) can help us distinguish this delineation with his notion of the literary frame that draws on work by Erving Goffman and Mikhail Bakhtin. Frow's case focuses on aesthetic – literary or similar – texts, objects or processes, which have a frame or frames (the plural is important) that are peculiar in each case. We have noted earlier that the framing of play is often the product of play; the decision to play produces its TAZ, yet it is not the source of the frame that matters, but its role and function.

Rather than seeing the frame of an aesthetic work as its limit, demarcating it from its context, Frow argues that it concurrently delimits the work from its context *and* provides the bridge between the enframed and the wider/ contextual/'real' world. There may be multiple frames: a picture may have an ornate or plain wooden or metal frame; if it hangs in an art museum it will carry a different meaning than if it hangs in a dealer gallery or auctioneers, which again carries different meanings than if it hangs in a private residence or workplace. In Frow's words 'we could think of the "edge" of [a piece of] work as a series of concentric waves in which the aesthetic space is enclosed' (1982: 25).

Whereas we may tend to see a frame as if it were a fixed and solid barrier between text, object or process and context, Frow's argument is that this 'barrier', as well as being multiply layered, is more osmotic than impermeable. The frame is therefore neither and both inside and outside the text, object or process it frames; it is a component of both the structure of the text and of the situation in which the text exists such that 'the text is closed and suspended' (1982: 27). In this vision, a frame is more complex and more nuanced than a simple barrier, symbolic, dynamic, porous, soluble or otherwise: it is internal to the text's, object's or process' closure *and* allows the text, object or process to signify difference. Looking at this in terms of play, therefore, play itself signifies what it excludes: we see both play and the limits of play. As Frow suggests, 'the energy of the frame thus radiates in two directions simultaneously' (1982: 27). This two-way radiation allows and conducts into the play-space elements or traces of the excluded, non-play-space, meaning that play becomes constructed by its internally produced limit. Frow's frame therefore helps us make play into an autononomous, self-producing (autopoietic) thing.

What this does not necessarily allow, or rather, does not necessarily make obvious, is play's subversion – and that is where we come back to 'rules' and also to ethics. As noted, rules make play, but as some of our contributors point out (Bateman; Mildenberger; Felkers, Mulder and MacLean; Dönmez), players need to choose to abide by those rules so the 'rule' that we are playing is the one that forms the frame(s), that both hails those frames into existence and makes them disappear. No matter how simple or complex the constitutive, regulatory, eligibility or implicit rules of the game might be, without the basic decision to submit oneself to the rule that we-are-playing, that is, without a 'lusory attitude' (Suits, 1978), none of the rest has any significance. Without the frame, play is nothing; but in the spirit of Frow's frame, play is not to be sanctioned off, sidelined to the trivial, the infantile or as an element of bread and circuses amusement: it is an essential element of the 'real' world leaching into it and being leached into. It is also the fundamental ontological basis of this 'let's play' rule that means that we are not attempting to define play, but to highlight the fluidity and duality even of its delimiting component.

In the introduction to our previous collection, we noted that when play becomes 'the *subject* of study ... it takes on a new hue that allows it to be seen as an element of the everyday' (Ryall *et al.*, 2013: 1–2), but that retains a relatively low level of subjecthood. For many of the essays in this collection, play's subjectivity is more profound. It is not a subjecthood of the banal but one of the rule, generating freedom by, for example, working within the rules to make distinctive performances (Dönmez), or finding moments of freedom in the gaps that performing play forces between the rules of the game (Felkers *et al.*) or in play's rule-created liminality (Spariosu). This emphasis on subjecthood, often more implicit than explicit, shifts the terms of play's distinctiveness from its autotelic form (play for itself) to its autochthony (play of itself) as linked to its impermanence and transience. As a playful aside, in the very first draft of this introduction, a typo meant that 'transience' became 'intransigence' – and perhaps this is also an aspect of play's subjectivity. We are, however, cautious about taking this notion of play's subjecthood much further towards subjectivity (or even this far) given the tendency, in late capitalism, for the subjectivity of the immaterial to become materialized, reified and then commodified (Simon,

2013), thereby destroying the use value that lies in its very impermanence, transience and indeed intransigence.

The frame-as-bridge, as both demarking and linking to the 'real' world, suggests a need to rethink the magic circle of play. As a metaphor, it worked for the era of modernity with its culture of separation (Caraça, 2012) – of work and home, ontology and epistemology, economy and society, culture and science, culture and nature – but in an increasingly fluid era of postmodernity (Harvey 1990) or liquid modernity (Bauman, 2000) Huizinga's magic circle risks marking territory that is unsustainable. This poses further questions for subsequent investigation about the meaning of 'enframing but not separating' in the context of play as the subject of analysis. Accepting play as *the* subject of analysis does not mean making play *a* subject and crucially does not grant it subjectivity. Play's subject~ness/~hood exists for analytical purposes only, as a heuristic device. As Gadamer (2000) reminds us, play must have players. Although play plays the players, it is not autonomous of the act of playing – the *idea* of play is, the *actuality* of play is not; play without players is a performative and ontological contradiction. These players must be faithful to the *idea* of play. Without that fidelity, players are not playing. This disposition, or lusory attitude, marks play's specific situationality, autotelia and autonomy; it is play of the here and of the now. Play, therefore, cannot be contained within its frames because it has no independent existence from its players. Play as a subject, without performers (that is, granting play subjectivity), risks isolation from the material conditions of its existence. From this, idealization and reification can ensue, rendering play the subject of nostalgia for a golden age of playing that no longer applies (if it ever did), and subsequent attempts to pronounce on the ethics of playing or what constitutes 'good' play.

The frame we have used to provide an order and structure to these essays takes account of this danger of granting play subjectivity. The four chapters in Part I, 'Playing at the limits', disrupt and unsettle both ideas of discrete boundaries for play and many of the romanticized visions of play as innocence, as the activity of children and as a safe place to experience ways of being. They do this through explorations of play as on and of the margins of existence, of war, of evil and as both a part of and apart from social context. In the opening essay, Mihai Spariosu sets the scene for much of what is to come through positioning play itself as liminal, with mimetic association to both exile and utopia as forms of ludic liminality. The exiled person, at the margins of both the place exiled from and that exiled to, can, despite evident constraints and difficulties of enforced exile, imagine a space of freedom for creating forms of agonistic play that have a power beyond the control of exilers. Such forms of resistance to convention enter into the myths and stories of most times and cultures, being particularly prevalent in twentieth-century Western literatures of exilic, utopic and dystopic imagination. Henning Eichberg delves further into this question of the marginal, the limits of play(ing), making the case that considering war as play (for one strand of post-Nietzschean thinking, war is the favoured form of play) challenges the morals of play research with its tendency towards romantic idealization. Equally important in his case is the argument that war-play takes place in a space of heightened negative freedom while also suggesting a constantly moving situation where rules cannot anticipate every eventuality, meaning that the fluidity of the theatre of war grants considerable opportunity for free play to exist. This identification of play in paradoxical settings links to Carl Mildenberger's Kantian discussion of the consequences of play, where its rules institutionalize its agreed morality and in creating the play-world delimit its boundaries. This imbrication of rules and morality mean that in creating a play-world, it is the rules of the game that determine good and evil. Maintaining the integrity of the play-world means that banal evil, the result of players' compliance with bad rules, is not possible, nor is evil as a result of bad rules themselves; the only source of evil in a specific play-world determined by a specific set of world-making rules is human frailty. Finally in this part of the book, Stuart Lester challenges modernist separations and the notion of limits through a critique of the primitivist construction of both childhood and play as natural, pre-social and pre-rational. His critique asserts that the vitality of play as a practice co-creates a social space that contains both 'nature' and 'culture' but that also disrupts the boundary between them. As a result, he contends that as the rules construct the space-of-play, the play itself makes the world-in-transience into a liveable place: consequently play is profoundly and dynamically ontological and ethical.

Moving from chapters that disrupt notions of play and question many of the banal presumptions that are often embodied in discussions of it, Part II, 'Play, aesthetics and performance', turns to ideas of fluidity, dynamics and balance in the performance, enactment and anticipation of possible worlds in play. Chris Bateman explores the prospects for defining a game as a series of aesthetic tropes and traits. In doing so he provides a powerful counterpoint to many discussions of freedom, rules and resistance in the moral economy by asserting a dynamic and relational approach. Crucially for this discussion, Bateman's 'game' does not require any specific necessary condition, but provides an interactive and relational definition that gets beyond the limitations of more formalist approaches. Tim Stott extends this problematization of rule-based approaches through his consideration of Robert Morris's installation *Bodyspacemotionthings*, an interactive piece shown at the Tate in 1971 and 2009 with each showing shifting the balance between governance and voluntary participation to explore in a specific instance ways that play may be understood as what he calls an 'unnatural freedom'. This poses challenging questions about governance and autochthonous rules, regulation and practice and suggests important ways that rules are inherent in the praxis of play. Núria Sara Miras Boronat's chapter retains an emphasis on the experience of play but shifts focus to make a forceful case, drawing on phenomenological approaches, for an understanding of play as a subject. Her discussion of Eugen Fink's work makes sense of play as a practice that 'does things' through its internal aspects rather than a practice that allows things to be done. In this analysis, play relies on symbolic projection and the production of the possible to disrupt the distinction between real and fantasy worlds, and in doing so makes clear that while there are extrinsic elements that are a product of play, play's subjecthood means that it should be understood as a thing that does. Finally in this part of the book, Daniel Dombrowski draws on works by Homer to explore that most regulated form of play, namely sport, to consider a moral approach to both sport and play generally, identifying play/sport as serious-nonseriousness. While there is a significant ontological element to this chapter, defining sport as competitive play, the case turns on a moral imperative to avoid excess and extreme action in favour of a greater balance between physical and moral excellence, with a weighting in favour of moral excellence.

The ontological orientation initiated in Dombrowski's chapter then become a focus of Part III, 'Metaphysics and ontology'. In the opening chapter, Imara Felkers, Ellen Mulder and Malcolm MacLean also focus on sport as competitive play in their re-evaluation of elements of key twentieth-century play texts by Huizinga and Caillois. They argue that efforts to understand and make use of sport and play in public policy risks over-emphasizing formalized, rational instrumental approaches, Caillois's *ludus*, at the expense of the lustful tumultuousness of *paidia*, thereby downplaying fun and joy. In making this case, they also propose a revision of Caillois's analysis to pay greater attention to the presence of *paidia* in sport as regulated play, arguing that although *ludus*-structures regulate sport, *paidia* continues to exist at the interstices of the artefacts that impose *ludus*. Dani Abulhawa's essay draws on spatial analyses by Henri Lefebvre and on her practice-as-research work to explore playful disruptions of city-space and the occupation of liminal, marginal, banal urban elements. She positions these as cases that disrupt conventional flows and movement, resulting in spatially created communitas. In this discussion, play-praxis-as-rule-making is considered as a case of freedom within spaces that are constrained by aspects of their formation. Taking us back to gaming, Mathias Fuchs' contribution takes for granted that rules create game-worlds. Drawing on Heideggerian phenomenology, he explores the character of that world's mimetic relations to the 'real' world as the world outside the boundaries of game-world. His case turns around three Heideggerian tropes – *world-withdrawal* (where the reference point at the time of an artwork's creation no longer exists), *world-decay* (the withdrawal of a reference point from the current experience) and *worlding* (the place of players beyond the magic circle of play), and through a discussion of rules, explores the ontological character of the world being created. Concluding this part of the book, Damla Dönmez retains a focus on rules-in-play, adapting Huizinga's classic analysis to explore rules as a source of freedom and art as a subset of play. In doing so she unravels the paradoxical relationship between an ethos of freedom in art/play and institutionalization through rules as a form of constraint ('unfreedom') to argue that voluntary submission to rules is a way to create freedom.

The final three chapters in Part IV, 'Ethics of work in play and play in work', consider discussions of playful philosophy in the classroom, the ethics of adults working with children at play and the work of fictional 'worlding'. Sandra Lynch considers the Philosophy in Schools programme as a case of playful pedagogy where pupils have the freedom to try out ideas and practices, to develop higher-level critical and reflection skills and to learn the fuzzy aspects of ethics that are not rule based. While most of the other chapters in the collection have brought philosophy to bear on play, Lynch has inverted the relationship to remind us of the importance of playfulness, of a playful disposition, to doing and teaching philosophy, echoing perhaps our opening ideas from Bencivenga (1994). Wendy Russell returns us to the issue of rules: not the rules of play but the rules of work. She unpicks paradoxes in the 'rules' of professional practice in play-work to explore the morality and ethics of playwork practices as not inherent within playworkers and players as people but in the relations between them. This is a case in favour of an ethics of openness to alterity and being comfortable with uncertainty, arguing that the rules of deontology are useful when it comes to professing an ethics of playwork, but less so when it comes to supporting children's play. Finally, Helene Staveley analyses trickster play through a series of picture books focused on Coyote as a trickster figure throughout Native American and Aboriginal Canadian thought. She considers Thomas King's Coyote stories as tales of god-games, excess and fun, ego and world-making, unintended consequences and communitas to build both powerful moral tales and moments of pleasurable resistance through Coyote's refusal to accept what is. This is a fitting and powerful conclusion to the collection that disturbs again romantic notions of play and the idea that play has no consequences in the real world. This last is seen most obviously in the idea that Columbus ended up colonizing the Americas as a result of Coyote summoning him and his crew up because she wanted someone to play baseball with.

In presenting this collection in this way with a structure based in play's limits and margins, in aesthetics and performance, in metaphysics and ontology and in ethics we are aware that we have imposed one of many possible structures on this group of essays. An equally important series of tropes runs through the collection, and readers might benefit from paying attention to, for example, issues of freedom as an ethos of play, rules as the means of play's institutionalization, resistance and play practice and morals as a mode of community-marking in play. No one organizational mode, however, holds the Truth of the collection. Readers are encouraged to build their own narratives and connections between the chapters, to playfully disrupt our attempts to disrupt play's place in the cultures of separation, to transcend the liberal ethos of play as a space of socialization and acculturation and see play as disruptive, as a means of meaning-making in the here and now and as continuing to see play, as we suggested in our previous collection, as a means of mimetic anticipation (Ryall *et al.*, 2013, p. 8).

Our previous collection paid close attention to play's autotelicity, its *for-itself-ness*, which has in this collection become almost taken for granted in a philosophical understanding of play. As such this has created a space for much more testing of the limits of play, and in doing so has allowed the contributors to pose new questions, propagate uncertainty and demand that their readers think anew about what we thought we knew about play. Such is the practice of philosophy; as Frédéric Gros recently observed, 'in philosophy there is no inherent search for a result … we aren't looking for a result outside of thought through the pursuit of philosophy but … we privilege the very thought process itself' (Gordon-Farleigh, 2014: 16). Returning to our opening thoughts from Bencivenga (1994: 43), we can see how 'playing with words and generating imaginary problems and equally imaginary solutions' might describe the rationale of this collection, complete with its crazy, uncrystallized stories. These essays build on our proposition that play should be the subject, not the object, of study and that philosophical practice can illuminate that subject, but not in ways to proclaim singular truths that become reified, fixed and demarcated. Whereas we previously dipped our toe in the sea of philosophical consideration of play wondering if there were monsters in its uncharted regions, this collection says that this may well be the case, alongside emergent archipelagos whose occupants remain unclear and partial.

References

Bateson, G. (1972 [1955]) *Steps to an Ecology of Mind*, Chicago: University of Chicago Press.
Bauman, Z. (2000) *Liquid Modernity*, Cambridge: Polity Press.
Bencivenga, E. (1994) *Philosophy in Play: Three Dialogues*, Indianapolis: Hackett.
Bey, H. (1985) *T.A.Z.: The Temporary Autonomous Zone, Ontological Anarchy, Poetic Terrorism*, New York: Autonomedia.
Caraça, J. (2012) 'The separation of cultures and the decline of modernity', in Castells, M., Caraça, J. and Cardoso, G. (eds) *Aftermath: The Cultures of the Economic Crisis*, New York: Oxford University Press, 44–55.
Frow, J. (1982) 'The literary frame', *Journal of Aesthetic Education*, 16, 25–30.
Gadamer, H.-G. (2000) *Truth and Method* (2nd edn), transl. Weinsheimer, J. and Marshall, D. G., London: Continuum.
Gordon-Farleigh, J. (2014) 'Interview: Frédéric Gros', *STIR*, 6, 16–19.
Harvey, D. (1990) *The Condition of Postmodernity: An Enquiry into the Origins of Cultural Change*, Oxford: Blackwell.
Huizinga, J. (1955) *Homo Ludens: A Study of the Play Element in Culture*, Boston: Beacon Press.
Midgley, M. (1974) 'The Game Game', *Philosophy*, 49, 231–53.
Ryall, E., Russell, W. and MacLean, M. (eds) (2013) *The Philosophy of Play*, London: Routledge.
Simon, J. (2013) *Neomaterialism*, Berlin: Sternberg Press.
Suits, B. (1978) *The Grasshopper: Games, Life and Utopia*, London, Ontario: University of Ontario Press.
Sutton-Smith, B. (1999) 'Introduction: What is children's folklore?' in Sutton-Smith, B., Mechling, J., Johnson, T. W. and McMahon, F. R. (eds) *Children's Folklore: A Source Book*, Logan: Utah State University Press.
Taussig, M. (1993) *Mimesis and Alterity: A Particular History of the Senses*, London: Routledge.

Part I
Playing at the limits

1 Exile and utopia as liminal play
A cultural-theoretical approach[1]

Mihai I. Spariosu

In the past century, numerous studies have focused on exile and utopia as independent concepts, but have largely ignored the close correlation between them and have only rarely placed them in a general cultural-theoretical or philosophical framework. In what follows, I shall argue that what brings these two concepts together is the fact that they are both forms of ludic liminality. In order to support my argument, I shall first review the ways in which the concepts of play and liminality have been employed in cultural theory, as well as my own use of them. Elsewhere (Spariosu, 1997), I explore at length the relation between play and liminality in general. Here I shall briefly consider these two concepts in the specific context of their relevance to exile and utopia.

Play in contemporary cultural theory

In his classic study, *Homo Ludens*, Huizinga defines play as a 'voluntary activity or occupation executed within certain fixed limits of time and place, according to rules freely accepted but absolutely binding, having its aim in itself and accompanied by a feeling of tension, joy and consciousness that it is "different" from "ordinary" life' (Huizinga, 1950: 13). Play is a 'free' activity not only because it stands outside ordinary life, but also because it is not connected with any material interest or work, and 'no profit can be gained by it' (Huizinga, 1950: 13). It is being carried out for the sake of pure pleasure and, although it is not 'serious', it absorbs the player 'intensely and utterly' (Huizinga, 1950: 13).

This general definition captures the essential features of play but also its highly ambivalent nature. Huizinga, like many other cultural theorists before and after him, invariably defines play as the primary or secondary term in a number of binary oppositions, such as play and work, play and seriousness, play and utility, play and reality, and play and culture. Within the concept of play itself, Huizinga and other scholars have generated such binary oppositions as play versus games, higher versus lower play, rational versus irrational play, violent versus nonviolent play, primitive or natural versus civilized play, true versus false play, fair versus foul or perverted play, and so forth.

For example, Huizinga states that 'in the twin union of play and culture play is primary' (Huizinga, 1950: 46), but then seeks to draw a distinction between primitive or natural play and cultural or higher play in terms of rationality and irrationality. According to him, the higher cultural forms of play are much easier to describe, whereas in interpreting the 'more primitive play of infants and young animals', one immediately encounters 'that irreducible quality of pure playfulness' which is 'not amenable to further analysis' (Huizinga, 1950: 7). For Huizinga, primitive or irrational play lies at the foundation of culture, but within culture itself, rational play gains primacy. In turn, by irrational cultural play he means first and foremost violent and/or destructive play, or what the ancient Greeks called violent *agon* (contest) or *eris* (competition).

A closer look, however, reveals that the distinction between natural and cultural play does not hold water, generating a number of ambiguities. These ambiguities become especially apparent when Huizinga attempts to present his cultural theory of play in historical terms. According to him, in the course of human history,

> the play-element gradually recedes into the background, being absorbed for the most part in the sacred sphere. The remainder crystallizes as knowledge: folklore, poetry, philosophy, or in the various forms of judicial and social life. The original play-element is then almost completely hidden behind cultural phenomena.
>
> (Huizinga, 1950: 46)

Thus, his concept of play becomes a 'golden age' fiction (a form of utopia) of the Totality of Being, from which culture perpetually regresses.

It is from the perspective of this golden age fiction that Huizinga carries out an extensive critique of modernity in 'The play-element in contemporary civilization', the last chapter of his book. According to him, contemporary culture, despite its emphasis on games and sports, has lost the 'child-like' quality of 'original' play. Among other examples, he mentions modernist art, which, despite appearances, has lost its play-quality, because 'when art becomes self-conscious, that is, conscious of its own grace, it is apt to lose something of its eternal child-like innocence' (Huizinga, 1950: 202).

On the other hand, elsewhere in the book Huizinga describes this pre-historical or 'original' play as being irrational and associates it with war and violence. Irrational play can reassert itself in history by arresting the same historical processes that it has initiated. As he puts it, 'at any moment, even in a highly developed civilization, the play-"instinct" may reassert itself in full force, drowning the individual and the mass in the intoxication of an immense game' (Huizinga, 1950: 47). In all likelihood, this is a veiled reference to the mass-intoxication of Nazi Germany, which Huizinga, however, roundly condemns at the very end of his study as false and perverted play. For obvious ideological and political reasons, he is reluctant to characterize the Nazi war 'as a noble game' (even though some of the Nazis themselves saw it that way).

Huizinga himself is aware of this contradiction. Yet, in typical modernist fashion, Huizinga tries to find his way out of this dilemma by falling back on the binary oppositions of play and seriousness, fair and foul play, disinterested and utilitarian play, thereby generating more ambiguities:

> Only through an ethos that transcends the friend–foe relationship and recognizes a higher goal than the gratification of the self, the group, or the nation, will a political society pass beyond the 'play' of war to true seriousness.... Civilization will, in a sense, always be played according to certain rules, and true civilization will always demand fair play. Fair play is nothing less than good faith expressed in play terms. Hence the cheat or the spoil-sport shatters civilization itself. To be a sound culture-creating force this play-element must be pure.... True play knows no propaganda; its aim is in itself, and its familiar spirit is happy inspiration.
>
> (Huizinga, 1950: 209–10)

Here, Huizinga privileges the rational concepts of play that have been operating in philosophy and cultural theory at least since Plato. In fact, the Dutch scholar clearly draws his inspiration from Plato's *Republic* and *Laws*, where Plato gives play a major role not only in the education of the citizens of his utopian State but also in his theology and ontoepistemology. Like Plato, Huizinga attempts to distill a 'pure' and 'disinterested', rational play out of violent contest and to separate it from the idea of power, even though he knows all too well that the archaic ludic concepts associated with war (as they appear, for example, in Homer's *Iliad*) are equally 'pure' and 'disinterested', being manifestations of power for its own sake (Spariosu, 1991: 28–40).

Nevertheless, to conclude my discussion of Huizinga's idea of play, I should like to point out that despite his theoretical ambiguities, his most important contribution to a theory of culture as play is to have drawn attention, in the wake of Nietzsche, to the fact that violent contest, such as war, is a favoured cultural form of play in Western civilization.

Indeed, one may add that power in general has always conceived of itself – and manifested itself – as a form of agonistic play. Furthermore, even though in the archaic period this agonistic ludic concept was unashamedly declared to be at the root of all culture (for example, in passages from Homer, Heraclitus, the Sophists and other Presocratics), it slowly became tamed and concealed under the veneer of rational, 'civilized' play to such an extent that the play concept itself has gradually become entirely separated from the concept of violent contest and power (Spariosu, 1991). Hence all of the theoretical confusions and ambiguities present in most, if not all, Western theories of culture as play ever since Plato.

Liminality and contemporary cultural theory

Like play, liminality has received an ambiguous treatment in Western thought, and largely for the same reasons. And like play, the concept of liminality has a long history within (and outside) Western civilization. In modern times, Arnold van Gennep (1909) was the first to employ the term in anthropology, in relation to the rites of passage characteristic of small-scale societies. According to van Gennep, a passage rite comprises three stages that the young initiand must successfully complete in order to become a full-fledged member of his community: the first stage involves the separation of the young man from his community; the second, or transitional, stage, which van Gennep calls 'liminal', involves the erasure of all social marks that may identify him as a member of his community; and the third stage involves his reintegration in that community (Gennep, 1909).

'Liminality', however, covers much more semantic ground than van Gennep's narrow, technical term seems to imply. Its etymology has a very long multicultural history, stretching over thousands of years: the word *lmn* (vocalized, e.g. in Hebrew as *lmyn* or *lymyn*) was already present in Mediterranean cultures (Greek, Hebrew, Aramaic) in the early Bronze Age and originally meant 'harbor', that is, a place where land and sea meet (Lubetzki, 1979: 158–80). For thousands of years, harbors have been cosmopolitan places of intersection of various cultures and languages, where material goods and artifacts are exchanged alongside with ideas, customs, foods, religious practices and so forth.

In Latin, *limes* meant the borders or confines of the Roman Empire. In turn, *limen* meant 'threshold' or 'passage' denoting a space or place in-between. By extension, *limen* came to mean any transitional space, state, or situation and has given the term *limbo* (Latin, *limbus*) in Catholic theology; it is occasionally also associated with Purgatory and it means a 'half-way station' between Heaven and Hell, where the souls of those who died 'in the friendship of God' (such as many pagan philosophers) await salvation at the hands of Jesus Christ.

The concept of liminality is present in other religious doctrines as well, for example in the Pythagorean view of metempsychosis, that Socrates mentions in Plato's *Republic*, when the old sage recounts the myth of Er. According to Er, who was allowed to come back to the world of the living and report what he saw in the land of the dead, the souls of recently deceased people meet at a middle station, where they are allowed to choose their next lot.

A similar idea appears in Tibetan Buddhism, under the name of *bardo*, which signifies 'gap' or a space 'in-between'. As Chögyam Trungpa Rinpoche explains, *bardo* is 'a kind of landmark which stands between two things' and could denote the 'experience that stands between death and birth. The past situation has just occurred and the future situation has not yet manifested itself, so there is a gap between the two' (Trungpa, 1987: 10–11).

In turn, in the Zoroastrian faith, *hamistagan* denotes a transitional state, after death, in which the soul of a believer, who during his lifetime was neither good nor evil, awaits Judgement Day. Finally, the idea of liminality is equally present in Islam, where *barzakh* describes a transitional state between the moment of death and the day of resurrection, during which sinners are punished, while the righteous repose in peace and comfort. We can thus say with some confidence that this idea is universal, being present, explicitly or implicitly, in both large-scale and small-scale communities, and denoting a transitional state, whether it is a rite of passage during this life or to the next one.

Starting from van Gennep's anthropological study, Victor Turner develops the concept of liminality into a full-blown theory of culture, especially in his book *From Ritual to Theater* (1982). In the first and most important chapter of this book, 'Liminal to liminoid in play, flow, and ritual', Turner argues that liminality is a key notion in understanding the differences between small-scale human societies and large-scale, more complex ones. According to him, the second, transitional stage of van Gennep's rite of passage can be described as an 'anti-structure', because it temporarily reverses or suspends the normal social structure or order of the community. Citing Brian Sutton-Smith's paper on 'Games of order and disorder' (1972), Turner further argues that the liminal stage of a passage rite is a game of disorder, out of which a new order emerges. He then extends this insight to liminality in general, contending that any liminal process or state may be seen as a ludic time-space par excellence. Turner regards such ludic-liminal time-spaces as 'seeds of cultural creativity' that generate new cultural models and paradigms. In turn, these models and paradigms 'feed back into the "central" economic and politico-legal domains and arenas, supplying them with goals, aspirations, incentives, structural models and *raisons d'être*' (Turner, 1982: 28).

Turner eventually retraces his steps to van Gennep's passage rites, however, and confines the liminal to the small-scale societies. According to him, in large-scale societies, the term 'liminality' can apply only metaphorically, and for this reason he proposes the concept of 'liminoid' to describe certain cultural phenomena specific to modern, industrial societies. Although they are not identical with ritual liminality, liminoid phenomena are either like it or related to it. Among such phenomena Turner includes postmodernist theatre and art in general, film, television, opera, rock concerts, carnivals, festivals, pilgrimages, and even social revolutions.

According to Turner, the main difference between the liminal and the liminoid stems from the different social structures of tribal and large-scale communities. The traditional tribal structure is monolithic, concerning the entire community, and thus more rigid and serious than that of modern societies; consequently, tribal liminality assumes the same characteristics of rigidity and seriousness. By contrast, modern social structures are more diverse, loose and flexible, allowing for a great variety of liminoid creativity and innovation. As Turner puts it, 'One *works* at the liminal, one plays with the liminoid' (Turner, 1982: 55).

Here it becomes obvious that Turner's distinction between the liminal and the liminoid breaks down, because it goes against his earlier contention that the liminal space is a ludic space par excellence. Furthermore, this distinction now depends on the opposition between play and work, or play and seriousness, which earlier he had criticized as an unfortunate development of the industrial society, contrasting it to the 'play-work ludergy', or the 'serious play', characteristic of liminal phenomena in both tribal and preindustrial large-scale cultures (Turner, 1982: 43).

In this respect, Turner returns to the theoretical ambiguities already present in Huizinga's definition of play. Like Huizinga, he attempts to have his cake and eat it too, deploring, on the one hand, the historical involution of play into work in industrial societies and, on the other hand, praising the innovative, 'progressive' and 'open' nature of these modern societies. The consistent position would be that while both the liminal and the liminoid can manifest themselves as play, the difference between them resides not in their degree of seriousness, but in their degree of freedom.

In fact, given the ubiquity of liminal phenomena in most cultures (large or small, ancient or modern, Eastern or Western) throughout the recorded history of humankind, one may be better off dispensing with the distinction between the liminal and the liminoid altogether. Instead, one can simply say that in some small-scale communities liminality is put to uses different from those in some large-scale communities and that, moreover, these uses may vary from period to period and from community to community. What gives specificity to these functions is the degree of sociocultural flexibility and imaginative freedom, or *play*, which a particular community – large or small – allows itself at a given time.

On the other hand, it would be useful, in the context of the present discussion of exile and utopia, to introduce a distinction between the liminal and the marginal. Turner unwittingly implies this distinction, when he observes that meaning in culture 'tends to be *generated* at the interfaces between established cultural subsystems, though meanings are then institutionalized and consolidated at centers of such systems' (Turner, 1982: 41, italics in the original). This is an excellent description of the interplay between centre and margin that is characteristic of any power-oriented world. But, as Turner himself points out, the *limen* as threshold can be 'protracted' and become a 'tunnel'. In other words, the liminal can also turn into the 'cunicular' (Turner, 1982: 41), leading away from the centre, rather than back to it, in which case, the liminal can also transcend, not just reenact, the agonistic dialectics of margin and centre. This potential for 'truancy' inherent in liminality is already present in van Gennep's anthropological account, because the initiands who enter the liminal stage of the rite of passage are also beyond the rules of society, with a risk that they may not return.

In my view, then, marginality implies an agonistic relation between the centre and the margins of a structure, system or subsystem, whereas liminality implies a *neutral* relation, such as obtains, for example, in a no-man's-land between two or more state borders. Marginality cannot provide access to or initiate new worlds, whereas liminality can do both. In this sense, a margin can be liminal, but a limen cannot be marginal. Therefore, liminality can both subsume and transcend the dialectics of centre and margin.

To conclude this subsection, I should like to point out that Turner is the first Western thinker (at least to my knowledge) to have realized the close relationship between the concept of liminality and that of play. Although Huizinga's definition of play which I discussed in the previous subsection involves the idea of liminality, the Dutch scholar is not aware of, and, consequently, does not employ the term. Huizinga describes the ludic as an activity that takes place outside, and quite apart from, the everyday world, with its own time, space, and set of rules. Therefore, even in his definition, play appears as a form of liminal experience in which elements of everyday reality are reorganized and transfigured into a different reality.

Finally, I would like to draw a distinction between the ludic and the liminal that will be of use later on in my argument. Just as the liminal and the marginal are not one and the same thing, the ludic and the liminal are different categories. Indeed, the liminal has the same relationship to the ludic that it does to the marginal. Play is a form of liminality, but not all liminal activities or experiences are ludic – in other words, liminality contains, but is not contained by, the ludic. For example, dreams, illness, death are liminal, but not ludic, experiences. And, again, my distinction here ought to be understood not in terms of seriousness, but in terms of freedom.

The liminal, in its most radical form, points to boundless freedom or 'stillness' – what Zen Buddhism calls the 'luminous void', out of which all structure emerges and into which all structure is dissolved. In turn, play is an *active* principle – a creative activity that draws upon this luminous void continuously to generate, reconfigure or dissolve structures. If we were to translate these notions into Western philosophical terms, play is the perpetual process of setting and resetting limits, while radical liminality is what Anaximander probably referred to as the *apeiron* (the boundless) and the Pythagoreans as the 'unlimited'.

Aristotle's discussion of the Pythagoreans in *Physics* and *Metaphysics* is illuminating in this regard. He claims, for example, that Philolaus and the Pythagorean circle around him borrowed Anaximander's notions of *apeiron*, the boundless or unlimited, and *to peiron*, the limited, and that the Pythagoreans identified the void with the unlimited:

> And the Pythagoreans say that there is a void, and that it enters into the heaven itself from the infinite air, as though it [the heaven] were breathing; and this void defines the natures of things, inasmuch as it is a certain separation and definition of things that lie together; and this is true in the first case of numbers, for the void defines the nature of these.
>
> (Guthrie, 1987: 300)

The Pythagoreans equally believed that the cosmos or the order of the universe arises, like the continuum of numbers, in the play of the unlimited and the limited, or emptiness and structure. When the limited 'breathes in' the boundless, the undifferentiated whole of the *apeiron* becomes a living whole of interconnected parts, which are both separated and upheld by the void in-between. It is precisely this 'void' that I call radical liminality.

I may add that the authors of Genesis in the Old Testament largely share the same cosmic view. The account of the Creation *ex nihilo* involves the idea of radical liminality, conceived as undifferentiated darkness and void:

> And the earth was without form, and void; and darkness was upon the face of the deep. And the Spirit of God moved upon the face of the waters.
>
> (Genesis 1.2)

Out of this dark and undifferentiated void (much like Anaximander's *apeiron*) the cosmos, comprising the heavens and the earth, emerge through a divine ludic act. This act consists of the interplay between the boundless and the limited, as God 'breathes in' the void, separating, circumscribing and setting limits to it. Thus, he divides and circumscribes the heavens from the earth, light from darkness, dry land from the seas, and so forth. As the text repeatedly suggests, the Divine Artificer is at play, enjoying and taking satisfaction in his creations: like a true artist, he constantly surveys his work and judges it to be 'good' and 'very good'.

According to certain Cabbalistic readings, God himself is conceived both as Ayin, Absolute Nothingness or No-thing, and as En sof, Absolute All (things). In turn, the cosmos can be conceived as the playground of God, with various versions of this ludic concept of the Creation being part of what is commonly known as *theologia ludens*.

Exile as ludic liminality

In light of the foregoing discussion, I should now like to suggest that exile and utopia could be seen as cultural forms of ludic liminality. Although they are obviously not interchangeable concepts, exile and utopia share certain liminal and ludic features, imparting to them that air of 'family resemblance' which Wittgenstein discerns in the relations obtaining between discrete, yet kindred, concepts (Wittgenstein, 1953: 9–10). Above all, they can both reenact and transcend the dialectics of centre and margin that is associated with a mentality of power.

Whereas probably few scholars will object to describing exile as a liminal experience, its ludic character may not be readily apparent, because the individual who is forced into it will, understandably, perceive it as a highly negative experience; therefore, exile seems to be devoid of at least two basic characteristics of a ludic activity: it is not voluntary or free, and it is not enjoyable. But, if one remembers that contest or *agon* is one of the most common ludic forms and that power, particularly in its archaic guise, often sees and manifests itself as agonistic play, then one can begin to understand exile as a (violent) power *game*.

At the most obvious, immediate level, exile is a power instrument through which an individual or a group can be removed from the community for a number of reasons, be they political, religious, ethical or even physical – indeed, more often than not, because of a combination of such factors. The expelled person or group is temporarily or permanently marginalized and neutralized, with the intention of preventing him from having further impact on the affairs of the community.

In traditional small-scale communities, common reasons for exile involve the transgression of various taboos, including homicide, and exile often results in the speedy death of the expelled individual, who finds it very difficult to survive outside his community. In the city-states of ancient Greece, exile was a common way of dealing with individuals who transgressed against the laws and the traditional customs of their community. A classic example is that of Oedipus, who, we recall, was at first cast away as a baby by his father, the king of Thebes, and then, much later, exiled at Colonus because of his involuntary parricide and transgression of the incest taboo. But exile was also a way of dealing with those who were over-eager in playing the political power contest. Thus, in addition to the routine exile of those who opposed or tried to change the political status quo, there was the political instrument called ostracism, used predominantly in democratic city-states such as Athens: ambitious, overreaching leaders such as Themistocles, Alcibiades or Critias (Plato's uncle) were deemed too dangerous for the well-being of the community and were temporarily removed from it by a majority of votes in the citizens' assembly.

In modern times, exile has often been used for the same political purposes, even though it has become increasingly 'diversified'. For example, internal exile was very common in large countries or empires, such as Russia, where many members of its recalcitrant intelligentsia were sent to Siberia, a practice that was continued under the communist regimes as well. In the British Commonwealth, recalcitrant or dissatisfied members of British society were often sent, or decided on their own to move, to the colonies, such as North America, Australia and New Zealand. In addition, the category of voluntary self-exile has become rather common in modern times and has often merged with that of immigrants, political and economic refugees, and business and cultural 'expats' in the age of globalization. All of these categories have greatly expanded the notion of exile, but have not necessarily changed its cultural and emotional connotations, which have remained largely negative.

Despite the fact that exile may often be perceived as an expedient political instrument of neutralizing or eliminating one's adversaries, as well as an unpleasant, constraining experience for the individuals who must undergo it, the exilic condition can also be fraught with ambivalence and unintended consequences. Thus, it may actually have the opposite effect of providing a free space or playground at the intersection of various cultures and political systems. Once the exiled person leaves his country, he is no longer at home anywhere, including his own land, should he be able to return there subsequently. He is literally 'in no-man's-land', between cultures, languages, social structures and so on. This ambivalent, in-between position gives him a vast amount of freedom or 'free play', and it is up to him to learn how to leverage it. In this sense, exile can be called a ludic-liminal experience.

Viewed in this light, exile becomes also a form of *utopia*, if one uses this term in the sense of 'an imaginary place' or 'nowhere' (a meaning of utopia highlighted in Samuel Butler's anagrammatic title of his novel, *Erewhon*). The neutral playground or liminal space opened by exile can then be used to effect changes on both the expelling and the receiving political systems or cultures. Once the exiled person becomes aware of his liminal condition, he can use it in at least two ways: he can engage in the power game of turning his marginal position into a central one, through political contest – this is the case of the majority of political exiles throughout the ages, from Alcibiades in Sparta, to the popes in Avignon, to Napoleon on Elba, to Lenin in Switzerland, to General de Gaulle in Great Britain. Or he can go even further in transcending his exilic condition by opting out of the power game of margin and centre altogether and engaging in other kinds of utopian play.

The view of exile as a form of liminal play, then, allows us to value it as a potentially positive cultural experience. Claudio Guillén is among the first prominent contemporary scholars who have drawn attention to this positive nature of exile, even though he does not speak of it in ludic-liminal terms. In his brilliant essay, 'The sun and the self: Notes on some responses to exile', Guillén draws a distinction between a 'literature of exile' and a 'literature of counterexile'. For him the prototype of a literature of exile is Ovid's *Tristia*: the Latin poet remains forever an alien among 'barbarians', with his eyes perpetually fixed on Rome, his homeland, idealized as both an immobile centre and a lost paradise (Guillén, 1990, 262).

The literature of counterexile, on the other hand, finds its prototype in the Cynic-Stoic view of exile as cosmic freedom. Plutarch, among others, indicates that this view originates in the philosophical contemplation of the sun, the stars and the other heavenly bodies, which allows individual gazers to detach themselves from their immediate historical and political circumstances and become at one with the cosmos, converted into a universal, all-embracing home. In a literature of counterexile, according to Guillén,

> the poet learns and writes from his experience, moves away from it as situation or motif, while reacting to the social or political or, generally speaking, semiotic conditions of exile, through the very thrust of the linguistic and ideological exploration that enables him to transcend the original condition.
>
> (Guillén, 1990, 265)

From my perspective, what Guillén calls a 'literature of counterexile' is often enough a form of utopian literature that starts from a profound understanding of the exilic condition as a ludic-liminal space or *atopia*, where the emergence of alternative realities becomes possible. Instead of brooding over his exilic condition, yearning for the lost centre, or conversely engaging in the power game of replacing the centre with the margin, the exiled person becomes aware of his radical freedom.

Disentangling himself from the logic of war and the power contest, the exiled individual is now free to move from the marginal to the liminal – indeed to the 'cunicular', to employ Victor Turner's term – and unleash his creativity. He may thus imagine alternative worlds that are not governed by power, but by other grounding principles, such as universal love, human brotherhood, and a planetary, or even a cosmic, home. Although such principles are certainly utopian, they are nevertheless potentially real, because whatever arises in the human imagination may be actualized at some juncture in human history. Understood in this manner, the exilic condition may become a form of creative play, because the exiled individual can now perceive it as both free and joyful.

Utopia as exilic liminality

Guillén's observations about exile implicitly highlight its close correlation to utopia. In most Western literary traditions, utopia has often been conceived as a form of exile, in the sense that it is invariably placed away from the author's homeland, in a remote or imaginary location, or in a distant past or future, that is, in a *liminal* time-space.

The literary framing of a traditional utopian society contains, as a rule, a departure of the narrator and/or the hero of the narrative from his own land or soil on a sea voyage to distant, unfamiliar parts of the world. Incidentally, the word 'exile' comes from the Latin *exilium* or *exsilium*, being most likely formed by Latin folk etymology from *ex*, away, and *solum*, soil, land. The voyage often ends in a shipwreck, with the narrator or hero stranded on an unknown island or some other, hereto unheard of place, i.e. literally nowhere. In English, this meaning is underlined not only by Butler's *Erewhon*, but also, before him, by Samuel Hartlib's *Noland* or William Morris's *Nowhere*, while many French authors of literary utopias send their narrators to *pays de nulle part* (countries from nowhere).

Furthermore, the land where the utopian society is allegedly located is very hard to reach. Before the narrator or hero can gain access to it, in both a geographical and an intellectual-emotional sense, he has to undergo a veritable rite of passage, or liminal experience, such as a devastating storm at sea, shipwreck, pirate attack, crossing of almost inaccessible rivers, mountains and deserts or, in modern times, a plane or a spaceship crash, or a traumatic ride in a timemachine. The utopian world is also carefully circumscribed in terms of its architectural and socio-cultural landscape. It is set apart from the everyday reality of the narrator and his audience, having its own time, space and set of rules, just as any other ludic structure.

At the same time, the utopian world is not so far removed from everyday reality as to be unrecognizable by the narrator's audience. Rather, like other ludic spaces, it is an alternative world in which elements of everyday reality are reorganized and transformed into a new reality. In other words, although utopias are deliberately removed from the actual world, they nevertheless maintain subtle and complex links with this world, being ultimately designed to effect substantial changes on it.

One may finally note that the etymology of the term 'utopia' and its semantic cluster in general is as ambivalent as the ludic-liminal place it designates – an ambivalence that it shares again with exile. The term itself is a playful coinage of Thomas More (1516), who derived it from the Greek *ou* (no, not) and *topos* (place), that is, 'no-place'. Through another pun, More also created *eutopia*, derived from the Greek *eu* (good), that is, 'good place'. In his spirit, modern literati and philosophers created *dystopia*, bad place, and *uchronia* or *euchronia* (from the Greek *chronos*, time), denoting either a good (fictive) past, or a good, or bad, distant future, i.e. a *not-yet* place. Various golden age fictions from Homer and Hesiod to Virgil to Horace to Ovid can also be placed in the category of euchronias. Many futuristic worlds, predicated largely on scenarios often to be encountered in science fiction, belong to the category of uchronias. If these scenarios are nightmarish, one may call them *dyschronias*, to coin a new term ('new' at least in the context of cultural studies; it exists in the medical literature). Like exile, then, utopia may have both negative and positive intellectual-emotional connotations.

Play, liminality and the exilic-utopian imagination

I have come to the last section of my essay, in which I would like to propose the notion of the 'exilic-utopian imagination' to underline the fact that exile and utopia as ludic-liminal phenomena go well beyond any specific cognitive field and/or sphere of human activity. In this respect, the common distinctions drawn by contemporary scholars between religious, political and literary utopias become less significant, because they are all engendered by the same exilic-utopian imagination. This imagination may also go beyond the Western world and operate, albeit in different and specific ways, within other worlds as well. Indeed, one may venture to say that the exilic-utopian imagination is a common feature of all the power-oriented mentalities that have built large human civilizations on Earth.

At the same time, I would like to suggest that, even though the exilic-utopian imagination operates in most cultures and historical periods, across many different fields such as politics, psychology, philosophy, religion and literature, it can be said to reach its climax in the twentieth century. Indeed, exile and utopia have become so ubiquitous in our time that it would not be implausible to characterize the modern Western world itself as a product of an acute exilic consciousness, which often seeks to generate utopian schemes in an attempt to compensate for its exacerbated sense of ontological loss.

On the other hand, the exilic-utopian imagination does have a privileged place in literary discourse. Literature itself is a form of ludic liminality in relation to other forms of discourse, such as philosophical and scientific ones, ever since Socrates, in Plato's *Republic*, undermined literature's claims to knowledge and truth and banished it from his ideal state in order to install philosophy as the central cultural authority. In this sense, literary discourse can be seen as *atopia* or 'placelessness', because it always situates itself in a no-man's-land, in between fiction and truth, or in between other forms of discourse, including political ones. Thus, literature does not 'imitate' various realities (as traditional theories of literature as mimesis would have it), but stages or 'simulates' them in order to open them up to reflection and, possibly, reform.

Ironically, Plato's *Republic* is the first *literary* work to explore, in a dialogic form, the interplay between literature and politics in terms of exile and utopia in the modern state. I discuss this topic in some detail elsewhere (Spariosu, 2014, 67–80). Here I would simply like to note that the modern state itself is the result of large-scale utopian experiments in social engineering, such as the United States of America, which began as a Puritan religious utopia and was refashioned, in the eighteenth century, as the European Enlightenment's conscious social experiment; or the first French republic, which began with the utopian call to 'liberty, equality and fraternity', and ended up in a bloodbath and a return to monarchy. More recent examples include the various European communist and fascist states of the twentieth century. Another such recent example of a utopian actualization is the state of Israel, based on an interesting blend of secular and religious utopia that creates its own tensions and contradictions.

Many of these experiments were first proposed in a number of literary or quasi-literary works that largely claimed a fictional status in order to make their challenge to the sociopolitical *status quo* less threatening. In turn, once these projects became actualized, their unintended, disastrous consequences were first and foremost highlighted in literature. In fact, the ambitious utopian experiments in social engineering of the twentieth century have resulted in a considerable expansion of the literary genre of *dystopia*, from Zamyatin's *We* to Huxley's *Brave New World* to George Orwell's *1984*, to mention just three of the best known dystopian novels of the past century.

Paradoxically, the literary dystopias themselves, not unlike exile, often confront their readers with the experience of the void or emptiness, by relentlessly denying the possibility of any equitable social solution within a world centred on the will to power. This experience need not be felt as nihilistic despair (as it often is by Western readers) but, on the contrary, as liberation and complete detachment from such power-centred worlds. In this regard, I would like to invoke the words of a twelfth-century Saxon monk, Hugo de St. Victor:

> The man who finds his homeland sweet is still a tender beginner, he to whom every soil is as his native one is already strong; but he is perfect to whom the entire world is as a foreign land.
>
> (cited in Said, 1985, 259)

Here St. Victor refers to the ultimate level of atopia opened up by exile, which is now experienced as radical liminality. At this level, 'the perfect man' has 'extinguished' all of his attachments and is able to contemplate, serenely, the infinite ocean of stillness, out of which everything emerges and into which everything dissolves. Adopting the perspective of radical atopia would spell the end of the exilic-utopian imagination in its power-oriented guises. This imagination would consequently undergo an essential transformation in the way in which it experiences the void. Instead of perceiving it as negative and threatening, it would see it as a joyful exploration of the unknown, characteristic of much ludic activity, opening up liminal interstices through which alternative value systems can emerge.

In turn, these alternative values would belong to irenic worlds, outside a mentality of power, being the most appropriate to adopt within a global reference frame. Within that larger frame, one could then envisage the end of exile and the transcendence of the exilic-utopian imagination through the emergence of fully free and blossoming human communities that do not operate on a power mechanism of inclusion and exclusion, but on the irenic principle of symbiotic cooperation. Diogenes of Oinoanda, a Hellenistic philosopher from late Antiquity (c. AD 200), already anticipates the emergence of such an irenic, global world, when he inscribes the wall of an entire public Stoa with his Epicurean teachings and concludes:

> And not least we did this [inscription] for those who are called 'foreigners', though they are not really so. For, while the various segments of the earth give different people a different country, the whole compass of this world gives all people a single country, the entire earth, and a single home, the world.
>
> (Smith, 1992, Diogenes, Fragment 32)

Note

1 Parts of this chapter have been published previously (Spariosu, 2014).

References

Gennep, A. van (1909), *Rites de passage*, Paris: Emile Nourry.
Guillén, C. (1990) 'The sun and the self', in Jost, F. and Friedman, M. J. (eds) *Aesthetics and the Literature of Ideas*, Newark: University of Delaware Press.
Guthrie, K. S. (1987) *The Pythagorean Sourcebook and Library*, Grand Rapids, MI: Phanes Press.
Huizinga, J. (1950) *Homo Ludens: A Study of the Play Element in Culture*, Boston: Beacon.
Lubetzki, M. (1979) 'The early Bronze Age origin of Greek and Hebrew Limen, "Harbor"', *The Jewish Quarterly Review*, New Series, 69(3).
Said, E. (1985) *Orientalism*, London: Peregrine Books.
Smith, M. F. (ed. and transl.) (1992) *Diogenes of Oinoanda, The Epicurean Inscriptions*, Naples: Bibliopolis.
Spariosu, M. I. (1991) *God of Many Names: Play, Poetry and Power in Hellenic Thought from Homer to Aristotle*, Durham, NC: Duke University Press.
Spariosu, M. I. (1997) *The Wreath of Wild Olive: Play, Liminality and the Study of Literature*, Albany, NY: SUNY Press.
Spariosu, M. I. (2014) *Modernism and Exile: Liminality and the Utopian Imagination*, Basingstoke: Palgrave Macmillan.
Sutton-Smith, B. (1972) 'Games of order and disorder', paper presented to symposium on 'Forms of symbolic inversion', American Anthropological Association, Toronto, 1 December.
Turner, V. (1982) *From Ritual to Theater: The Human Seriousness of Play*, Cambridge, MA: MIT Press.
Trungpa, C. R. (1987) Commentary to *The Tibetan Book of the Dead: The Great Liberation through Hearing in the Bardo*, Boston: Shambala.
Wittgenstein, L. (1953) *Philosophical Investigations*, transl. (1986) Anscombe, G. E. M., Oxford: Blackwell.

2 Playing war – playing with fire
About dark games

Henning Eichberg

Play is normally regarded as a matter of pleasure and leisure, as being just free and friendly fun, as creative and harmless activity mainly related to children and their positive development and innocent laughter. This has been criticized as an idealization and romanticization of play (Hjelm, 2012). Empirically and analytically, the harmless fun aspect of play is only one part of the story. Hazard games may produce ludomania, a dependency on destructive power. In sport, anorexia as part of sport dependency is a well-known phenomenon, and risk games endanger the player's life. Here, however, attention shall be directed towards the larger field in the history of play and game, which unfolds between children's soldier play and military training.

Civilians and children playing war

An early modern narrative about the civil play of war was delivered by Laurence Sterne (1773) in his novel *The Life and Opinions of Tristram Shandy, Gentleman*. In a satirical way, Sterne portrayed Uncle Toby as playing war in his garden, building fortifications and using his servant for military actions of attack (as shown in the cartoon in Figure 2.1).

In a grotesque way, this narrative described – and at the same time took distance from – what was usual in Baroque time when the geometrical type of fortifications by bastions appealed to playful 'inventions' in civil society. Plans of real and ideal fortifications became, in the seventeenth and eighteenth centuries, widespread objects of collection, publication and even card play (Eichberg, 1989a).

At the turn of the eighteenth to the nineteenth century, the image of war changed fundamentally and lost its geometrical character. Martial play changed its character, too. Now soldier games became a standard role-play for young boys (Figure 2.2). Among the children of the industrial culture, the helmet, sabre, wooden rifle, drum, flag and hobby horse became popular play toys – and typical Christmas gifts (Lukasch, 2007).

Tin soldiers also became popular toys, as described by Hans Christian Andersen in his famous fairy tale. Later during the twentieth century, toy soldiers were produced in plastic and followed by fantasy warriors. These were

Figure 2.1 'Uncle Toby playing war'. Engraving by Henry Bunbury British cartoon collection in the Library of Congress, http://tomclarkblog.blogspot.dk/2010/08/tristram-shandy-siege-of-namur-by.html.

Figure 2.2 Playing soldiers. German children's book, nineteenth century, https://lood.wordpress.com/2007/02/26/kolme-soja-teerist/.

followed up by computer games, where war actions and shooting became a main genre, too. Also role-plays, spreading in young people's popular culture, have often taken their material from martial and military actions.

Among young people, parkour developed from the 1990s as a new movement activity. It has its roots in military parkour. As a form of running and jumping through the urban landscape, originally a military exercise this entered – surprisingly – into urban youth subculture and spread from there worldwide (Angel, 2011).

Among adults, reenactment became a way of playing military history. In the United States, the battle of Gettysburg from the Civil War played an especially important role. In Denmark, the soldier game 'Fredericia Battle 1848' was promoted in a similar way, reenacting war between Danish troops on the one side and German insurgents and Prussian troops on the other (Konzak, L. in Vestergaard, 2012).

In a very different way, military costume and exercise was adopted by the Funkenmariechen in the German Rhine Carnival. Women dressed in military guard uniform in the eighteenth-century style and performed exercise-like scene dances with erotic appeal. Originally, these carnivalistic dances had been danced by men.

In the case of Funkenmariechen, the agonistic element of war had disappeared. This was also true for those forms of exercise which transferred the geometrical order of military body training to gymnastics. This tradition spans from Turner gymnastics around 1810 and Slavic Sokol gymnastics to, on one hand, the twentieth century's communist Spartakiad (Roubal, 2007; Valk, n.d.) – with certain spin-offs to countries of the developing world – and on the other hand competitive marching in New Zealand (Macdonald, 2004) and cheerleading in the USA.

Thus very different elements have been adopted from military culture and transferred to civil play, game and dance. Costumes, weapons, forms of exercise, shooting and battle forms could be converted into activities of popular culture. This has happened sometimes with ironic undertones, sometimes in sporting competition and sometimes with elements of theatre and role-play.

Between civil society and the military

Play-like activities of half-military character have also given birth to phenomena of social organization placed between civil society and the military. At the end of the nineteenth century, Boys' Brigades in Britain began to organize soldier games and exercises with wooden rifles for young boys. These paramilitary activities aimed at integrating and socializing workers' youth, which was regarded as potentially dangerous, under the spirit of patriotism, imperialism and Christianity (Springhall, 1977). In Denmark, a similar boys' organization was set up under the name of Frivilligt Drengeforbund (Voluntary Boys' Association, FDF). And in Wilhelminian Germany, a so-called Spielbewegung (Play Movement) was set up in competition with the established Turner gymnastics and with Lingian Swedish gymnastics – and was at the same time connected with initiatives to strengthen Wehrkraft (military force) by playful paramilitary means (Hartmann, 2011).

This type of youth play took on new dimensions after 1900, when scouting appeared. The Boy Scout youth movement developed new patterns of soldier games and camping in the open air, continuing or renewing the military-like outfit with uniforms and badges as well as marching and parades. The scouting movement was the result of a fusion between the ideas of the British Lord Baden-Powell, who had (mis-) used boys as military scouts during the Boer War in South Africa, and the American Woodcraft movement, which built on elements from Native American (Indian) culture. Later on, Woodcraft separated again from scouting because of the militaristic character of the Boy Scouts (Eichberg and Jespersen, 1985).

Scouting-like activities and military games developed a special dynamic in a political context when paramilitary corps were formed in the time between the two World Wars. An early form of combining military sport with politically demonstrative exercise was developed by the Italian fascists. The poet Gabriele d'Annunzio designed for them a set of military-like rituals, exercises and uniforms (Blackshirts). They became a prototype spreading to rightwing corps formations in other countries – such as the German Stahlhelm organization and the Sturmabteilungen (SA) of the Nazi party, and the Austrian Fascist Heimwehr – but also to other and opposing political denominations such as the social democratic Reichsbanner and communist Roter Frontkämpferbund in Germany. They all combined marches, parades, exercises, mass displays and mass theatre productions with military games to demonstrate their political discipline and energy.

These paramilitary phenomena remained more or less restricted to the period between the World Wars, making up an important part of the public sphere at that time, notably the Fascist public sphere, which more broadly can be called *formierte Öffentlichkeit*: public sphere of formations (Eichberg, 1989b). After 1945, they mostly disappeared. However, some elements reappeared for shorter periods in right-wing formations such as the German Wehrsportgruppen during the 1970s and the Hungarian Guard in the 2000s. And in South Africa, white racist Afrikaner camps were organized for teenagers, combining play and military preparation. Their leader Franz Jooste characterized this combination: 'We train them playfully, but while they play we train them for war' (Njiokiktjien, 2012).

These formations and their military play were different from those historical remnants which transformed military exercise into folkloric display or shooting sport. These are characteristics of certain rifle associations, for instance in Denmark, Flanders and Germany (for South Tyrol: Koenig, 1989).

Silly walks – military service as play and game?

The soldier play of children and civilians as well as scouting and paramilitary games transformed elements of military practice into play and game. From here, questions arise of the degree to which the connection also works in the opposite direction, i.e. such that military practice in itself may contain elements of play and game. Is military service in itself perhaps a way of 'playing' war?

Military service consists to some relevant degree of bodily exercise: human beings move under command in certain geometrical formations. Body postures, steps and other bodily movements are trained in an atmosphere of collective discipline and precision. Parades and guards of honour, used for impressing foreign high-ranking visitors, are top phenomena of this puppet-like body drill. Historically, these patterns of exercise have their roots in the social geometrical warfare of the seventeenth and eighteenth century. Though this chess-like warfare became technically obsolete in the late eighteenth century, the practices of drill were not abolished, but during the nineteenth century reinterpreted and reinstitutionalized as pedagogical means for teaching manliness. The playful forms of body habit and bodily movement were now ascribed important disciplinary and 'educational values'.

The comedy group Monty Python has made the grotesque and playful dimension of 'Silly Walks' visible. The sketch from 1970 has mostly been understood as a satire of ministerial work. Yet silly walks and silly stands are fundamental for the basic formation of military worldwide. In this respect, (nearly) all states of the world have their Ministries of Silly Walks.

Marching in formation and singing are relics from social geometrical warfare, too. Nowadays, they are used for aesthetic and psychological purposes: internally, they encourage the soldier, giving him (or her) energy for his (or her) job of killing. And outwardly, they represent the army and deliver an attractive theatre-like display, impressing the public especially at parades. Marching and singing appeal to a certain human fondness for rhythmic play.

Furthermore, the military worldwide is characterized by uniforms. Uniforms with their specific decorations are far from the 'military need' of training for violence and killing people (Koenig, 1968). They are rather connected with the mask of play, which has been analysed by Caillois (1958). Through mask and uniform, the human being changes identity and plays a game of 'Who am I?' A uniform transforms the previously civil human being into the soldier, masking him as 'another' being. Furthermore, the military system has developed a complex pattern of ranking signs, medals and decorations, which deliver a colourful and theatrical picture of hierarchical character.

Aside from this world of presentation and representation, the word 'play' (German *Spiel*) appears directly in military training in the form of plan exercises, which in German are called *Planspiel* or *Sandkastenspiel*. By means of sand-tables and rock drills, warfare is taught in miniature form, especially in officers' schools. The miniature warfare appeals to the sense of play, which is not so far from children's play with soldier figures. A connection between sand-table play and children's play is the representation of military events in miniature form, as it is used by some museums. The Wehrgeschichtliches Museum, the German museum of military history in Rastatt, for instance, presents thousands of tin soldiers in numerous dioramas illustrating historical battles ('Wehrgeschichtliches Museum Rastatt', n.d.).

Through technological development, the traditional sand-table exercise has increasingly been replaced by computer simulation. The military game of shooting, tactics and strategy thus meets with computer games in civil youth culture.

Outside this world of simulation by media, military manoeuvres transfer the miniature play into the open terrain. Soldiers play war in the open air. Manoeuvres were also the roots for the outdoor games of scouting, in German called *Geländespiel*.

Especially during the Cold War, similar games were practised as emergency exercises. They simulated emergency situations such as war and civil defence events, terror, and natural catastrophes (Anderson, 2012). A transitional phenomenon between military preparation and civil play was the secret mobilization under the title of 'Stay behind' or 'Gladio'. The American secret services recruited young people for exercises and games of emergency. As the mobilized youngsters often were linked to violently anti-communist and extreme right-wing milieus, they sometimes used their training and weapons for neo-Fascist political violence, terror plots and paramilitary complots (Ganser, 2005). The pleasure of play and political mobilization were thus connected in this special focus group of young men.

Body exercise, march and song, uniform, sand-table play, computer simulation game, and manoeuvre – all these forms of play and game are practised either as an anticipatory war training or as disciplinary exercises aiming at psychologically making the soldier fit for obedience and killing.

These observations have a personal background lying in my own biography. As soldier in the German *Bundeswehr* during 1962–4 and subsequently as officer of reserve, I experienced the military play culture on my own body and by my own – voluntary – subjective engagement. This started with the game 'Atomschlag', which was practised during the first weeks of basic training. As a game of obedience or punishment, the corporal would shout: 'Nuclear strike!' in order to make us soldiers hastily lie down and protect our heads. I adopted this disciplinary play as my own measure as soon as I ascended in rank. Later, at Heeresoffizierschule, the cadet school in Hamburg, one of our jobs was to plan – with the help of maps – the tactics and strategies of military actions in our region, Lüneburger Heide. Hypothetically, a superior Russian tank attack from the East was assumed, compelling us to plan a nuclear strike in our country and to demand this from the nuclear artillery, which was placed behind our lines. We played this on paper, on our maps – and yet also in our imagination, in our brains. It took many years for me to understand what I had been doing. It took decades to penetrate the logic of this play of war, which demanded my own engagement for the nuclear destruction of my own home region – just 'as play', and yet as preparation for real emergency, too.

Military service can thus be seen as a dangerous game, anticipating hypothetical war situations through game-like scenarios. Military service shows a gliding transition between play and game – via exercise and training – towards real war and killing. Personally, I was lucky enough never to enter into war. But I remember the Cuban crisis of 1962, when we participated in threatening manoeuvre marches with tanks near the German–German frontier, and many of us – including myself – were eager to put our play into martial reality.

Later, I met the connection between play and war the other way round, from war to play. I knew from my Danish village a young man, Kim, who was sent to Afghanistan as a soldier. After some months, he returned home in a coffin – only his head was left. He was one of the first three Danish soldiers to lose their lives in this war – but this happened in a situation of play. Danish and German soldiers tried to disarm a rusty Soviet earth-to-air missile in Kabul – in order to obtain some souvenir. I attended Kim's funeral and heard the pathetic speeches of high-ranking military officers praising patriotism and glorifying the sacrifice of one's life for democracy and father-country. There was no word about play.

It is thus not only in military service and in exercises of preparation that one 'plays' war. There may also be deeper connections between play and war itself.

War and killing as play and game?

Connections between play and war have previously been discovered and reflected upon. They have been observed from very different perspectives: those of philosophy, cultural history and military history.

Friedrich Nietzsche (1883/5) exalted war as play and the warrior as player in the framework of a poetical phenomenology of play and power. In his aphoristic work *Thus Spoke Zarathustra* (author translation), Nietzsche evoked play in many lively images: the child's rolling wheel, the ball, dices, table games, musical play, dance, jumping and laughter:

> A foreplay I am for better players, oh my brothers! An example ['sample play']! Do it after my example!

> Innocence is the child and the oblivion, a restart, a play, a wheel rolling by itself, a first movement, a holy affirmation.

> Truly, Zarathustra had an aim, he threw his ball: now you, friends, are heirs of my aim, it is to you that I throw the golden ball.

> [About the will to power] This is the devotion of the greatest, that it is dare and a play of dice for the death. The human being, however, is the most courageous animal.... With sounding play it overcame any pain.

> Oh heaven above me, you pure! You high! ... – you should be a dance-floor for me for divine hazards, a table of gods for divine dice and dice players!

> And the day should be lost for us, when we have not danced at least once! And as wrong we should regard every truth, which is not connected with at least one burst of laughter!
>
> Uplift your hearts, my brothers, high! higher! And don't forget the legs! Raise your legs, too, you good dancers, and still better: stand on your head!
>
> Zarathustra the dancer, Zarathustra the light one, who waves by his wings … Zarathustra the soothsayer, Zarathustra the truth-laugher, … one who loves leaps and side leaps.

In Nietzsche's view, however, play was not just fun and harmless enjoyment:

> The human being … is the cruelest animal. It had the greatest pleasures on earth with tragedies, bullfights, and crucifixions; and as it invented hell, look, so this was its heaven on earth.
>
> My brothers in war! I love you from the ground up, I am and was of your kind. And I am your best enemy, too.... You say that it is the good cause, which even sanctifies war? I tell you that it is the good war, which sanctifies any cause.

Words like these could be understood – and indeed they were understood – as a praise of war and violence, and thus as prefiguring Fascism. However, this interpretation – not least by the Fascists themselves – ignored the playful character of Nietzsche's philosophy. Playing with contradictions and paradoxes, Nietzsche practised philosophy as provocative poetical play – as punk. Thus, his Zarathustra did not just evoke the coming great warrior, but also and not at least quite an opposite figure:

> Once one must come – one who can make you laugh again, a good merry Hanswurst, a dancer and wind and tomboy, any old fool: – what do you think about this?

The warrior and the fool – Nietzsche's philosophy cannot be classified unambiguously. In contrast to Friedrich Schiller's idealistic philosophy of play (and art) as contribution to human harmony, Nietzsche pointed towards disharmony, contradiction and split (Karoff, 2014).

Following a different logic, the Dutch cultural historian Johan Huizinga (1938) came across the play–war connection. In his classic *Homo Ludens*, where Huizinga claimed the root of any culture to be in play, he described medieval and Renaissance warfare as a sort of playful activity. In particular, knightly tournaments mediated between weapon exercise and play event. Huizinga's description could sound like an idealized picture, and indeed, he was criticized for confusing the ancient Greek term of *agon* with 'play' (Lämmer, 1996). But on the other hand, Huizinga's study may also be read as directed against the German Nazi philosophy of Carl Schmitt, who had evoked the state of emergency, the decision (of the Führer) and the definition of 'the enemy' as fundamentals for the political. In this respect, Huizinga's study of war as play had an anti-Fascist agenda.

Again in a different way, the Israeli historian Martin van Creveld (2013) presents a rich panorama of war games from prehistoric ritual warfare through Roman gladiator games and medieval tournaments to current computer games. However, Creveld is more interested in the playful elements of war and, thus, in the phenomenology of war (with generalizing and slightly naturalizing undertones) than in the phenomenology of play and its differentiation.

In recent times the connections between war and play have become visible on a new level in high-tech warfare. The American strikes against Iraq in 1991 and again in 2003, with their precision bombing, were presented in the mass media as a sort of computer game. This motivated the French philosopher Jean Baudrillard (1995) to a philosophical discussion about war as play under the title *The Gulf War Did Not Take Place*. Originally published in 1991 as essays in the French newspaper *Libération*, Baudrillard reflected 'Operation Desert Storm' in a counterfactual way, in the style of a science fiction novel – neither pure sociology nor pure poetry. With black humour, he concluded nonsense – contradicted by the facts and contradicting the facts. He described the event as a hyper-real simulacrum produced by and via the media. The mediated pictures showed 'clean war' – with nose cameras on 'smart bombs' – and few images of human causalities, which, in fact, were more than 100,000 in all. A new image of war was created, including disinformation, media hype and computer viruses. War unfolded in an 'abstract, electronic, informational space' – with some parallels to wealth unfolding in 'secret circulation of speculative capital'. The Gulf War was, thus,

- neither real (as it would be in a positivistic perspective)
- nor unreal (manipulation, mass propaganda, fraud – as in a moralistic perspective)
- but hyper-real, virtual war, informational events.

Baudrillard was criticized for this discourse as antirealist, following postmodern irrationalism. However, one can read this philosophical attempt as a differential phenomenology of war 'reality'. While classical war in one or another way had happened between two balanced sides, one could now observe high-tech warfare as slaughter and police operation, characterized by disparity of the two sides: a New World Order reflected in martial domestication and reduction of 'the other'.

This analysis, though controversial, touched the relation between war and play in a new way: war as computer game, as theatre play, as simulacrum. Furthermore and as a form of discourse, Baudrillard's study of the hyper-real non-war was not only *about* play, it was play itself – not unlike Nietzsche's *Zarathustra* – philosophy as play.

The 'hyper-real' connection between war and play was soon confirmed by phenomena on very different levels. The one is the level of high-tech development. Pictures of precision bomber squads show human beings in puppet-like geometrical order arrayed decoratively before their Star-Wars-like machine. This picture of the martial human being combines the seventeenth century's geometrical discipline of marionette-like order with high-tech. Against this background of practical martial anthropology, the weapons industry is highly interested in play and especially in computer games as means to develop their high-tech offer on the market. This is play without laughter.

On another level of military practice, the human body is treated quite differently – and now there is also laughter. In connection with the second Iraq war, in 2003, pictures came to the public showing 'funny' torture in the prison of Abu Ghraib. The naked bodies of Iraqi prisoners of war were piled up on each other in strange arrangements, with shrouded heads, and placed in painful positions. Over, around and behind the detainees, American soldiers posed with triumphant laughter.

Together with sexual abuse, rape, religious violation and torture in Abu Ghraib, these events evoked international protest and finally led to some military reprimands and criminal trials. However, the guilty torturers – as well as the military system as a whole – had difficulty recognizing their responsibility. This was similar to what had happened in cases of war massacres as in Vietnam – subjectively, the actors had just acted 'for fun'. The artificial arrangements as well as the laughter of the torturers witnessed the playful character of the event. Similar expressions of 'playful' war-connected violations also happened in Afghanistan.

Further connections between play and current processes in warfare can be seen in the phenomenon of child soldiers. More and more armies – often insurgents in Africa, but also militia such as Hezbollah in Lebanon – recruit children and train them for war and killing. On the faces of the children, one sees the pride of marching and parade, and the pleasure of weapon exercise. The phenomenon of child soldiers appeals, indeed, to the enjoyment of play and games. It thus meets with the traditions of nineteenth-century boys' play and of Baden-Powell's boy scouts from the Boer War.

This exploitation contrasts with the fact that children are some of the foremost victims of wars. In war, children have little reason to be proud or to laugh. In this respect, the 'hyper-real' connection between war and play also has real consequences.

Towards a phenomenology of war games and dark play

The historical – and historically changing – relation between war and play as well as the philosophical approaches to this relation lead to questions about the deeper connection between war and play. That play is not just harmless and joyful for all participants has already earlier been observed:

- In risk games, such as metro surfing or façade climbing under the influence of alcohol, the player may play hazard with his or her own life.
- Games may include cruel behaviour against – and killing of – animals.
- Bullying is also a playful activity – for the bullying person, though not for the bullied.
- Human beings are fascinated by horror movies. Horror is an element of play.
- There is an old tradition of playing with fire.
- Aggressive and anti-social children's play has, from a pedagogical perspective, been characterized as advantageous for development (Schousboe, 2003).

Dangerous old popular games could for instance consist of pulling each other into an uncomfortable situation: into the water (which is fun), against a pole (which will hurt) – or into a fire. A Danish woodcut from the sixteenth century shows one of these versions, the game 'Græsse ko', 'pulling the cow to the grass' (Figure 2.3).

Play research has labelled these forms as 'dark play' (Sutton-Smith 1983; Schechner 1988). The discovery of dark play was an important step in deepening the philosophical understanding of play. However, this classification can also tempt the philosopher into a trap of moralist dualism: what is 'dark' and what is 'light', what is good and what is evil? If one wants to avoid this dualism, a differential phenomenology has to be tried out.

For a comparative typology of the configurations of military play, the play types established by Roger Caillois (1958) can be useful. War games touch different categories:

- *Agon*: in wars as well as in war games, a 'blue' team may stand against a 'red' team. There is fight and competition.

Figure 2.3 Playing 'pulling the cow to the grass' (Møller, 1990–1, 4: 19).

- Mimicry: uniform makes the soldier 'another' being, which points into the direction of role-play, play with mask and identity.
- *Ilinx*: there is a lot of frenzy play involved in war and war games. Intoxicant effects follow with imitation play such as exercise, marching, song – and with killing?

Besides these classical differences established by the philosophy of play, one can also try other typologies. For instance, there are different dynamics leading from play to war or vice versa:

- Imitation: children imitate war and the life of soldiers in their games. They play 'as if'. First there is war, and then follows simulation.
- Play can also – in a different direction – lead away from war and killing, from antagonism to *agon*. A typical dynamic goes from war to sporting competition. Other developments led – in old popular games – to jousting (Danish *dyst*; see Møller, 1990/1, 4: 65–78), to gymnastic exercise, to dance (the Funkenmariechen) or – in current youth culture – to parkour.
- Play can furthermore, the other way round, be used for training for war and killing. This is the case with military plan games and manoeuvres as well as with the training of child soldiers. Here, the way leads from *agon*-play to antagonism, where the adversary becomes the enemy.

These dynamics depend also on the relations that are formed in play and games. People do not play only in symmetrical relations. Asymmetrical relations can for instance be found in play involving the killing of animals, in bullying comrades, and in the torture play of Abu Ghraib: the player plays with victims of play. But relations are more complex than just being symmetrical or asymmetrical. The Danish painter and anarchist philosopher Asger Jorn (1962: 38) showed this by designing triolectical football between three goals. Football between two goals promotes attack and aggression, he observed, while football between three goals will direct the players' focus towards defence. Three-goal football would take suspense from the game – would it make the game boring? Jorn's triolectic pattern had a political connotation, as it was developed amid the dualist tensions of the Cold War.

In any case, the attention to the war–play relation contrasts with the naive idealization of play, which is widespread in play research, and contradicts its optimistic tone of self-congratulation and naive pedagogical idealism. Nevertheless, the critical turn does not minimize the subversive element, which play also represents in the face of war and military violence. Here, inspirations can be found in the Chinese philosophy of life and play, which was developed by Lin Yutang (1944). Lin Yutang described human life as characterized by playful curiosity. The human player was prefigured by the fumbling and playfully delousing monkey, personalized by the ape king Sun Wukong of Taoist mythology. The human being is fundamentally a scamp and tramp, a fumbler and player – 'Mary, Mary, quite contrary'. This is a contrast to the figure of the disciplined and obedient soldier, which at Lin Yutang's time represented the ideal of the bourgeois normal individual – Lin Yutang wrote in the period of Fascism. The soldier is not only a player, but the player and the soldier are also in contradiction.

And yet the study of war–play leads to an 'evil' philosophy, questioning the beauty, harmony and friendliness of the human being. Play is neither just for fun and friendly pleasure nor just for harmless leisure. Play contributes in a shocking way to the anthropological understanding of war. From out of dark play, philosophy may have to rethink the question of what play is – and what war is. The critique of war and the military receives a new anthropological depth.

The study of dark play and war play can furthermore enrich phenomenological method by taking a distance from the monolithic phenomenology of play as good play. Instead, we have to consider a differential phenomenology of play – taking inner differentiations and contradictions seriously.

Moreover, an additional philosophical point concerns the 'definition' of play. It is a widespread assumption that play is defined by a limit between play and non-play. Gregory Bateson (1972) defined play in a classical way through the limit between 'This is play' and 'This is not play'. Children express this by challenging each other: 'Let's play!' This is useful on some analytical levels, and yet it may fail for important cases of dark play. In military contexts, the play-like forms of exercise, song, uniform and manoeuvre are not at all regarded as play, but as serious work and need. I myself as a young officer of the 1960s would have strongly denied that I was 'playing' war. I vividly remember my own deep indignation when I visited the museum of military history in Rastatt, presenting war using dioramas of thousands of tin soldiers. For me, this was deeply unserious – it reduced war to being 'just play'.

Certainly, war is not 'just play' – but also play is not 'just' play. The academic habit of definition has to be reflected (self-) critically: 'definition' assumes that there is a limit – Latin: *finis* – where there is no limit. As Nietzsche (1887, 2: 13) expressed it: 'Only something which has no history can be defined'. Historical change is one of the existential elements that fundamentally blurs the limits of human life and makes definition impossible. The definition of play, as of any human phenomenon, is a fundamental problem. In academic humanist studies, definition is naive.

A vivid picture of play can be currently seen in TV transmissions of state visits. Military guards of honour consist of people playing marionettes for the purpose of political-military representation.

Part of this role-play of 'silly walks' and 'silly stands' (Monty Python) are the serious grimaces shown by both the disciplined play-toy soldiers and the honoured politician. Though all participants are mature adult human beings, they put mimic masks on and play puppets with grotesque, bizarre bodily postures. In this case, there is no fun and laughter of play. The players do not express that 'this is play'. And yet, they play their role. They demonstrate the – shocking – closeness between play and war.

References

Anderson, B. (2012) 'Atmospheres of emergency: Speculation and the reality of atmospheres', paper presented at conference 'Understanding atmospheres', University of Aarhus, 2012, http://conferences.au.dk/fileadmin/conferences/Understanding_Atmospheres/abstracts.pdf (accessed 9 November 2014).
Angel, J. (2011) *Ciné Parkour: A Cinematic and Theoretical Contribution to the Understanding of the Practice of Parkour* [no place of publication].
Bateson, G. (1972) *Steps to an Ecology of Mind: Collected Essays in Anthropology, Psychiatry, Evolution and Epistemology*, San Francisco: Chandler.
Baudrillard, J. (1995) *The Gulf War Did Not Take Place*. Bloomington and Indianapolis: Indiana University Press, 1st edn (French) 1991.
Caillois, R. (1958) *Les jeux et les hommes. Le masque et le vertige*, Paris: Gallimard; English transl. (1962) as *Man, Play and Games*, London: Thames and Hudson.
Creveld, M. van (2013) *Wargames: From Gladiators to Gigabytes*, Cambridge: Cambridge University Press.
Eichberg, H. (1989a) *Festung, Zentralmacht und Sozialgeometrie* [Fortification, central power, and social geometry], Cologne and Vienna: Böhlau.
Eichberg, H. (1989b) 'Lebenswelten und Alltagswissen' [Life-worlds and everyday-knowledge], in Langewiesche, D. and Tenorth, H.-E. (eds) *Handbuch der deutschen Bildungsgeschichte* [Handbook of German History of Education], volume 5: *1918–1945*, Munich: Beck, 25–64.
Eichberg, H. and Jespersen, E. (1985) *De grønne bølger. Træk af natur- og friluftslivets historie* [The Green Waves: From the History of Outdoor Activities], Copenhagen: Fredningsstyrelsen; 2nd edn (1986) Gerlev: Bavnebanke; 3rd edn (2001) Vejle: DGI.
Ganser, D. (2005) *NATO's Secret Armies: Gladio and Terrorism in Western Europe*, London: Frank Cass.
Hartmann, H. (2011) *Der Volkskörper bei der Musterung. Militärstatistik und Demographie in Europa vor dem Ersten Weltkrieg* [The People's Body under Muster: Military Statistics and Demography Before World War I], Göttingen: Wallstein.
Hjelm, J. (2012) 'Tävlandet inom idrotten' [Competition in sport], *Forum for idræt* [Forum of Sports], 65–76.
Huizinga, J. (1938) *Homo ludens*, Haarlem: Tjeenk Willink; English transl. (1970) London: Paladin.
Jorn, A. (1962) *Naturens orden* [The Order of Nature], Copenhagen: Borgen.
Karoff, H. (2014) 'Om Friedrich Nietzsches legefilosofi' [On Friedrich Nietzsche's philosophy of play], in Karoff, H. and Jessen, C. (eds) *Tekster om leg* [Texts about Play], Copenhagen: Akademisk Forlag, 50–7.
Koenig, O. (1968) *Biologie der Uniform* [Biology of Uniform], Mannheim: Boehringer.
Koenig, O. (1989) *Tiroler Tracht und Wehr. Schützenkompanien aus dem Blickwinkel der Vergleichenden Verhaltensforschung* [Tyrol Costume and Defence: Rifle Companies in the Perspective of Comparative Ethology], Vienna and Munich: Jugend and Volk.
Lämmer, M. (1996) 'Hier irrte Huizinga. Zum Begriff des Spiels in der griechischen Antike' [Here Huizinga was mistaken: About the term of play in Ancient Greece], in Pfister, G., Niewerth, T. and Steins, G. (eds) *Spiele der Welt im Spannungsfeld von Tradition und Moderne* [Games of the World between Tradition and Modernity], Sankt Augustin: Academia, 34–9.
Lin, Y. (1944) *The Importance of Living*, Stockholm: Continental Book Company.
Lukasch, P. (2007) *Kinder- und Jugendliteratur zwischen 1900 und 1960* [Children and

Youth Literature between 1900 and 1960], www.zeitlupe.co.at/index.html (accessed 9 November 2014).

Macdonald, C. (2004) 'Putting bodies on the line: Marching spaces in Cold War culture', in Vertinsky, P. and Bale, J. (eds) *Sites of Sport: Space, Place, Experience*, London and New York: Routledge.

Møller, J. (1990–91/1997) *Gamle idrætslege i Danmark* [Old Sportive Games in Denmark], Gerlev: Idrætshistorisk Værksted.

Nietzsche, F. (1883/85) *Also sprach Zarathustra* [Thus Spoke Zarathustra], Chemnitz: Schmeitzner.

Nietzsche, F. (1887) *Zur Genealogie der Moral* [The Genealogy of Morals], Leipzig: Neumann.

Njiokiktjien, I. (2012) *Afrikaner Blood* [video], http://politiken.dk/kultur/kultur620px/ECE1768966/drengene-skal-laere-at-fjenden-er-sort/.

Roubal, P. (2007) *Embodying Communism: Politics of Mass Gymnastics in Post-War Eastern Europe*, PhD thesis, Budapest: Central European University.

Schechner, R. (1988) 'Playing', *Play and Culture*, 1, 3–19.

Schousboe, I. (2003) 'Leg og udvikling af antisociale kompetencer' [Play and development of antisocial competences], *Psyke and Logos*, 24, 228–56.

Springhall (1977) *Youth, Empire and Society: British Youth Movements, 1883–1940*, London: Croom; Hamden, CT: Archon.

Sterne, L. (1773/2003) *The Life and Opinions of Tristram Shandy, Gentleman*, London, Penguin.

Sutton-Smith, B. (1983) 'Die Idealisierung des Spiels' [The idealization of play], in Grupe, O., Gabler, H. and Gohner, U. (eds) *Spiel – Spiele – Spielen* [Play – games – playing], Schorndorf: Hofmann, 60–75.

Sutton-Smith, B. (1997) *The Ambiguity of Play*, Cambridge, MA and London: Harvard University Press, 2nd edn (2001).

Valk, E. (n.d.) *The Square: Bodies in Grid Formation*, www.adarotterdam.nl/media/uploaded_files/eventreportfiles/thesquare_bodiesingridformation.pdf (accessed 9 November 2014).

Vestergaard, V. (ed.) (2012) *Kommunikation med børn. Leg, læring og medier i et produktperspektiv* [Communication with Children: Play, Learning and Media in a Product Perspective], Vejle: Kids n'Tweens.

'Wehrgeschichtliches Museum Rastatt' (n.d.) in *Wikipedia*, http://de.wikipedia.org/wiki/Wehrgeschichtliches_Museum_Rastatt (accessed 9 November 2014).

3 Games and evil

Carl David Mildenberger

Many of the activities we engage in are morally undetermined. What I mean by this is that performing these activities might turn out to be either a good thing or a bad thing. Take giving advice as an example. Normally, it seems to be a good thing if we help somebody by giving her some (hopefully well grounded) advice. However, it is also possible to give advice to a mass murderer as to how to kill even more people. This is a very bad thing to do. Thus, giving advice is morally undetermined in the sense that performing this activity we might either be doing a good thing or a bad thing.

In this essay, I will put forward the claim that playing a game is an activity which is not entirely morally undetermined. Notably, I shall argue that when we are playing a rule-bound game, we cannot commit evil. Playing a game is an activity that is partly morally determined, as it is impossible to adopt an evil course of action and still be playing the game. The most extreme form of negative behaviour in the moral sphere, namely evil behaviour, is excluded from rule-bound games. This conclusion follows from what it is to play a rule-bound game. It is because of the defining properties of such games that playing a rule-bound game is a special activity from a moral point of view.

I will proceed in three steps in order to argue for this claim. First, I will briefly outline two classic accounts about what constitutes an evil action. I present both a Kantian account of evil – with a focus on the corrupted rules we follow when acting evilly – and Arendt's account of evil. She holds that even when we are abiding by the right rules, we might still be acting evilly. The second part of the argument then reconsiders two influential definitions of what it is to play a game: the classical contribution from Caillois (1961) as well as the contemporary approach of Juul (2003). In the third part, I will combine the theoretical findings on evil and on games. Notably, I will highlight how the examined definitions of playing a game seem to coincide in that they exclude evil from the sphere of games. The result of the discussion is the finding that, given the characteristic properties of rule-bound games, we can commit no evil while we are playing such a game.

Two accounts of evil

According to Kant (1998a) the moral law is a fact known to everybody. Whenever we are facing a morally challenging situation, upon reflection it is actually clear to us what ought to be done. For Kant, what we ought to do is to autonomously choose maxims, i.e. the rules that we use to guide our actions, that are in line with the moral law and act on them. To see if the maxims we are using to guide our actions truly meet the criterion of complying with the moral law, one has to check them using the categorical imperative. The most well-known formulation of the categorical imperative is the *universal law formula*, namely to 'act only in accordance with that maxim through which you can at the same time will that it become a universal law' (1998a, 4: 421). The imperative is a compass that facilitates distinguishing right and wrong.

Even with everybody knowing the moral law and having the categorical imperative to check their maxims, we still sometimes behave in evil ways. In *Religion within the Boundaries of Mere Reason* (1998b), Kant explains that this is because we have the predisposition to act in a good way, but also the propensity to act evilly. He distinguishes between the two concepts saying that a predisposition is something original, i.e. a constituting part of human nature, whereas a propensity is contingent in the sense that human beings, in principle, are thinkable without this propensity (1998b, 6: 29). Yet, it is this propensity which may induce us to adopt maxims for our actions which are not purely informed by the moral law.

For Kant, whenever our maxims are not in line with the moral law, they are corrupted. And whenever we act on corrupted maxims, we commit evil actions. Two of the forms of corruption Kant mentions are of particular interest to us (1998b, 6: 29–30). First, the maxims we follow may be corrupted because of *frailty*. If one respects the moral law when setting maxims, but succumbs to one's inclinations in the situations in which one should act according to them, frailty is the reason of acting on corrupted maxims. Roughly speaking, the idea is that we often choose the right rules to govern our actions, but that we also sometimes break them for our own benefit in situations in which we ought to respect them. Although we identified the right rule and intended to follow it, we do not actually do so when put to the test.

The second form of corruption is *impureness*. People may do something evil because the maxim that guides their behaviour is not purely motivated by the moral law, but rather is a mixture between respect of the law and self-love. For Kant, the intent with which we adopt a certain maxim plays a crucial role for determining its moral worth. Actions guided by impure maxims may seem good at first glance (e.g. a merchant using correctly adjusted scales) but should not be judged as being good (because some merchants may only do so out of the fear of losing customers). The maxim of the merchant always to use correctly adjusted scales is impure in this case, because it is not his only goal to abide by the moral law, but also to retain customers and make profit. Roughly speaking, the idea is that we might act evilly in some situations, because we simply chose the wrong rules to follow.

Frailty and impureness are reasons for the corruptions of our maxims, and thus precursors of evil actions. Still, Kant is convinced of man's fundamental goodness. This conviction is so strong that he deems us worthy of practising an *imitatio Dei* in the sphere of morality. This is precisely what one does when testing maxims with the categorical imperative: reasoning how a world featuring the self-chosen universal laws would look like.

Whereas Kant firmly believes that humans are not capable of being truly diabolical, i.e. of committing evil by acting on maxims that reject outright the guidance of the moral law, Arendt seems to be empirically confronted with precisely this situation when writing on the Second World War. She discovers a new kind of evil that Kant had not thought about. Arendt's main interest is to find out how seemingly ordinary people can act in morally outrageous ways. And what she finds is that rule-following might be one of the biggest causes of such behaviour.

According to Arendt, it is characteristic of evil that it creates a state of speechless horror that mutes all arguments. The biggest evil is such that has been committed by *nobody*, by human beings that decline to be persons, and that consequently can neither be *punished* nor *forgiven* (2005: 111–12). Such evil is committed by ordinary men – not by sadists – who turned into perpetrators only because they did what they had been told to do. These ordinary men can be said to be nobody, because they are not persons according to Arendt's definition. The perpetrators refuse to be persons, because they refuse to think for themselves and are not able to remember what they did. 'The greatest evil-doers are those who don't remember because they have never given thought to the matter, and, without remembrance, nothing can hold them back' (2005: 95). It is difficult to punish such evil. It seems as if it is rather the anonymous system of rules these men served that is blameworthy. It is impossible to forgive such acts of evil, because you can only forgive a person but never a certain act or a set of institutions that led to a crime. Arendt concludes that it is not necessarily narcissists or sadists who are dangerous, but ordinary people who execute orders according to rules. 'Therein lies the horror and, at the same time, the banality of evil' (2005: 146).

With the notion of the banality of evil, Arendt strongly contradicts the idea that abidance by generally accepted social rules is enough to do no evil. In contrast, we are confronted with the paradox that social rules can actually foster evil behaviour. Whereas *not following* social rules might be bad, people who *unconsciously followed* rules have done more and bigger evil. Put differently, the problem does not seem to be one of choosing the right rules or of always abiding by them. Rather, evil actions may arise where people blindly follow rules commonly perceived to be acceptable.

A further complication is the following one. The exact same activity – the individual, conscious critique of established rules – makes good people better and evil people worse (2005: 104). In a constant state of critique, good people might be able to prevent a lot of banal evil from happening, because many everyday rules may prove to be imperfect on closer inspection. In that same state, however, bad people might be inclined to throw overboard even the last remaining decency and morality. This is especially true as Arendt does not share Kant's conviction that everybody has a well-functioning moral compass that reliably teaches right from wrong (2005: 61).

Still, a constant state of critique is the best way to prevent banal evil from happening, according to Arendt. If we are reflecting on our actions instead of blindly following rules, banal evil of the kind committed by Adolf Eichmann is very unlikely to occur. In addition, such a constant reflection ensures that we become persons as regards our actions. If we think for ourselves, we are not nobodies, and thus we become unable of doing unutterable evil without even remembering it.

Note that both Kant's and Arendt's accounts of evil presented here are *formal* rather than material accounts. That is, rather than specifying that murder, rape, genocide and so on are evil actions, they tell us which formal conditions an evil action has to fulfil. Namely, in order to be evil, an action has to be an instance of acting on corrupted maxims or of blind rule-following with severe negative consequences. What I am arguing is that when we are playing games our actions do not meet these formal conditions and thus are not evil.

Playing games

Roger Caillois's *Man, Play and Games* (1961) is a classic locus for a definition of what it is to play a game. Caillois defines playing a game as an activity which is free (in the sense of voluntarily engaged in), separate (in time and space), uncertain (with respect to the outcome), unproductive, rule-governed and make-believe (1961: 9–10). For our purpose, the three most important characteristics Caillois highlights are a game's separateness, unproductiveness and rule-boundedness.

The first one of these criteria is very intuitive. Games are 'circumscribed within limits of space and time, defined and fixed in advance' (1961: 9). There is a place for playing a game, e.g. a chess board, and a time for playing a game, which is often fixed in advance.

In order to justify the criterion of unproductiveness, Caillois highlights that a characteristic of playing a game is that it 'is an occasion of pure waste: waste of time, energy, ingenuity, skill, and often money' (1961: 5–6). Games are unproductive in that they do not produce new value, like for example a work of art, but only exchange goods and value which already exists. That is, whereas gambling might surely lead to a redistribution of money, we end up 'in a situation identical to that prevailing at the beginning of the game' (1961: 10) with respect to the absolute amount of value present. The games we play, according to Caillois, characteristically are zero-sum games.

Note that this also implies that games are not destructive with respect to value. While it certainly is possible that within games the players are harmed financially, one player's loss always is another player's gain. This is not the case for players incurring non-compensable harms (such as bodily harms). This is why such harms have to be excluded from games. Certainly, when playing football, one might end up with bruises and maybe even a broken leg. But the more severe these harms become, the more contrary to the nature of games they are. For in the case of very severe non-compensable harms (e.g. a mutilation of some kind), it is not the case that '[a]t the end of the game, all can and must start over again at the same point' (1961: 5). With respect to these kinds of harms, games must be harmless.

Concerning the aspect of rule-boundedness, Caillois states that games take place 'under conventions that suspend ordinary laws, and for the moment establish new legislation, which alone counts' (1961: 10). Not all games imply rules (1961: 8). However, there certainly is a specific kind of game for which rules are essential. In Caillois's terminology, the component of *ludus* is very prominent in these kinds of games (1961: 13). Caillois coins the concept of *ludus* in order to express the thought one can classify games along the dimension of whether they stress free improvisation and carefree gaiety, or instead emphasize the aspects of arbitrary, imperative and purposely tedious conventions. The most paradigmatic kinds of games with a pronounced element of *ludus* are games which are designed in order to experience the pleasure of solving a problem – whose solution might in itself by pointless. Golf seems to be a good example. Although not all games feature rules, I shall restrict my argument against the possibility of evil in games to rule-bound games.

A more recent yet widely acknowledged definition of games comes from Juul (2003). Like Caillois, Juul provides us with a list of criteria that games have to fulfil.

> A game is a rule-based formal system with a variable and quantifiable outcome, where different outcomes are assigned different values, the player exerts effort in order to influence the outcome, the player feels attached to the outcome, and the consequences of the activity are optional and negotiable.
>
> (Juul, 2003: 35)

The ideas of rule-boundedness and separateness are just as central for Juul as they are for Caillois. Concerning the latter, Juul stresses that games are separate from real life in that they always have to be playable without real-life consequences. That is, although some games do feature real-life consequences, it is essential that they could also be played without these consequences.

> A specific playing of a game may have assigned consequences, but a game is a game because the consequences are optionally assignable on a per-play basis. That games carry a degree of separation from the rest of the world follows from their consequences being negotiable.
>
> (Juul, 2003: 35)

For Juul, a consequence of games being separate by having negotiable consequences is that games must also be harmless. '[T]he only way for a game to have negotiable consequences is to have the operations and moves needed to play the game [be] predominantly harmless' (2003: 39). He gives the example of games involving weapons as games with strong non-negotiable consequences. This criterion of harmlessness echoes Caillois's condition of unproductiveness in a very focused way.

Besides the ideas of rule-boundedness, separateness and harmlessness, Juul's definition integrates many points familiar from earlier attempts at defining games. This continuity in defining games is just as central for my argument as the orthodoxy of the definitions given.[1] The definitions echo each other in that certain crucial elements appear in them. As already stated, for my argument, the three properties of games as being rule-bound, detached from the proceedings of the real world, and harmless are of particular importance. It is not my goal here to accurately distinguish between different definitions, let alone to argue which one is best. All I want to show is that the definitions agree on some defining properties of games.

Evil in games

So how are the characteristic properties of games responsible for the impossibility of doing evil when playing a game? I will address evil arising from abiding by the wrong rules ('impureness'), evil arising from choosing the right rules but breaking them occasionally ('frailty'), and evil arising from choosing the right rules yet blindly acting in accordance with them ('banal' evil) in turn.

With respect to evil arising from abiding by the wrong rules, it is the rule-boundedness of games in conjunction with their detachment from the real world which is decisive in making games immune to evil. Although it seems reasonable to agree with Kant that human beings in general are prone to choosing the wrong maxims to guide their actions, this propensity does not impact on people agreeing on the rules of games in particular. Put differently, every rule of a game passes the test of the categorical imperative that one should only act in accordance with that maxim through which one can at the same time will that it become a universal law. Interpreting the categorical imperative as outlining a decision procedure for determining morally permissible maxims can most easily support this claim.

Consider for example the invention of a new game. First, the players autonomously formulate the rules of the game.[2] Second, for every rule, the players agree that it shall henceforth be a universal law for the game space and the time the play lasts and that everybody must act as the rule proposes. Finally, by setting out to play the game by the rules they agreed upon, the players demonstrate that they will to act on their chosen maxims.

In other words, the testing of maxims using the categorical imperative – usually a pure thought experiment – comes to life when determining the rules of a game. Creating a game world, the players actually practise the *imitatio Dei* that Kant deems them theoretically worthy of. In the detached game world, players are able to install their own universal laws. Of course, this newly erected world is not real and exists for a only limited amount of time. So we are talking of a form of limited universality here. But this should not hide the fact that games can be said to create worlds of their own. The social and interactive complexity of games can be so substantial that the predicate of 'creating a world' is well merited. It is a property common to many games to erect a *magic circle* around them and to feature a second, free unreality in which the game's rules are the only laws there are and universally valid (Huizinga 1955: 10).

The players lose themselves in the detached worlds of games. All that matters is where they are located with respect to the game space ('My figure is on this or that field of the board') and the timing of the game (using time specifications as for example 'being in the mid-game'). When playing a game, players are in a different reality which possesses its own unconditional laws: the rules of that particular game.

Thus, if one form of acting evilly according to Kant is to act on maxims which are impure, i.e. to act on maxims which would not pass the test of the categorical imperative, then games cannot exhibit this form of doing evil. The rules of games uniformly pass this test. The chosen rules of games are the universal laws for governing the game world; not only theoretically, but also practically speaking. And they are autonomously chosen and freely agreed to.

So let us turn to frailty next. Recall that evil due to frailty occurs when one initially chooses good rules to follow, but then breaks these rules in situations in which one should have stuck to them. With respect to evil due to frailty, it is again a game's rule-boundedness which is decisive. More particularly, it is the fact that games are governed by *constitutive* rules which makes them immune.

Following Searle (1979: 33–42), we can say that a certain activity is governed by constitutive rules if the behaviour that constitutes the activity only arises because a certain set of rules is followed. Games are a classic example, Searle argues. Consider golf. The characteristic behaviour that golf features, i.e. hitting a golf ball with a golf club in order to pot it in a hole in the ground, does not pre-exist the rules of golf (or the predecessors of this game). People only started to hit balls using clubs with the intention to pot them once they invented the game of golf. It is the rules of golf which prescribe that the ball must be hit with a club rather than being kicked or thrown, that it must be played as it lies, and so on. And without taking into account these rules, there is no meaning in performing the activities associated to golfing. Put differently, there simply is no behaviour that corresponds to golfing prior to the rules of golf being established.

In contrast, for activities governed by *regulative* rules, there is such behaviour (Searle, 1979: 33). A good example are interactions in the public sphere. There certainly are such interactions before the rules of etiquette, which govern these kinds of situations, come into being. The rules of etiquette regulate a behaviour which is, so to speak, already there before they are adopted in a second step.

Suits (1978) nicely captures the idea of constitutive rules with his example of rules deliberately complicating the achievement of the central goal of a game. In rugby, for example, forward passing is not allowed. Yet it is the central goal of the game to advance the ball. The situation, therefore, is the following.

In rugby, and in many other games, there are rules which prevent the achievement of the game's goals using the most efficient means. It is this practice of requiring less than efficient means for achieving the ends of the game which makes up the game in the first place. '[S]uch rules are accepted just because they make possible such activity' (Suits, 1978: 34).

Precisely because a game is governed by constitutive rules, it is not possible to break the rules of a game and still be playing the same game. In contrast to everyday life where violations of social rules happen rather frequently without causing major upheaval, in games, you cannot simply break a rule and go on playing. 'The rules of a game are absolutely binding and allow no doubt.... Indeed, as soon as the rules are transgressed the whole play-world collapses. The game is over' (Huizinga, 1955: 11). You cannot simply break a rule, e.g. by changing the way a rook moves in chess, without making it another game, causing the game as it took place until then to end immediately. When a player realizes that an incorrect move was made, his attention shifts from the experience of play to making sense of the rules; the game is halted for a moment, leaving only two possibilities. Either the incorrect move is undone or the game ends. Imagine the situation in which a chess player moves the rook diagonally for one time only. There is no way in which the game could simply go on after this incident. If the players continued to move pieces in ways contrary to the rules of chess, they would be playing a game other than chess. Thus breaking a game's rules, generally speaking, is never a minor problem but is an existential one. If one intentionally breaks or alters the rules of a game, the game one was playing ceases to exist. One cannot break the chosen rule of a game and thereby fulfil the condition of evil due to frailty, since the game falls apart in that very second. One can, so to speak, only do evil ending a game, but not playing it.

Two special cases merit attention. First, the case in which the game comprises a rule for how to punish a certain violation of another rule of the game. Think of fouls and yellow cards in football. In this case, a player might violate a certain rule of the game, e.g. the rule to play fair when tackling a player of the opposing team in too harsh a way, and yet the game does not end. In such cases, it is important to realize that what the punishment rule does precisely is to yield a guide as to what needs to be done in cases of rule-violation. The punishment rule states that if a player does X, then she has to be punished in way Y. By defining the appropriate course of action in the case of rule-violation, the behaviour which violates the first rule (i.e. the rule of fair play) is accounted for within the context of the game. What would be a violation ending play if there were no punishment rule in place becomes a foreseen special case. Thus, a harsh foul strictly speaking is not a rule violation within the context of football. Behaviour for which there is a clear rule of what has to be done should it occur in the context of the game can hardly be a violation of the game's rules in the strict sense. The real violation of the rules of football would take case in situations in which brutal tacklings were *not* punished. It is not the initial 'breach' of the rule that is the problem in such cases, but the failure to react to it in an appropriate way as prescribed by the game's punishment rules.

The second special case is that of undetected violation of rules by a cheat. A cheat does not explicitly break the rules. Rather, the cheat's non-compliance comes down to creating an exception of the universal rule. Unlike spoilsports, cheats want to go on playing 'on the face of it' (Huizinga, 1955: 11). Cheats neither perfectly comply with the game's rules nor totally ignore them: they create a permanent state of exception for themselves.

Cheating may go undetected for a very long time, and it might leave the game intact for all those who are not cheating. Still, the game ends at least for the cheat himself the second he cheats. Again, take the example of golf. Following Caillois, we can say that golf is 'a game in which a player at any time has the opportunity to cheat at will, but in which the game loses all interest from that point on' (1961: 83). Golf is very much about the idea to play against oneself and to let chance play its role. If one breaks the rules of golf, e.g. by secretly dropping a new ball in the rough when the original ball cannot be found, one does not simply continue to play golf in a slightly altered fashion. Rather, one is not any longer playing golf.

This fact seems to be most easily accounted for with respect to the playing experience of the cheat. At least the cheat knows that he is cheating. So he also knows that he is significantly influencing the extent to which chance determines the outcome of the round of golf he is playing. It is partly determined by chance whether somebody is able to find his ball in the rough when looking for it. And letting chance play a role in determining a game's outcome is essential to the experience of many games.[3] In particular, a meddling with chance in the way the cheat does is destructive with respect to the game of golf.

To summarize, breaking a game's rules is not just a usual rule transgression: it destroys the game or at least immediately pauses the regular course of play. Thus, if evil because of frailty is equivalent to breaking self-chosen rules, then those many forms of play featuring rules are not prone to satisfy this condition of evil.

With Arendt's findings on the banality of evil, the problem of the potential of evil in games becomes that, if we are blindly following rules, evil things might happen even if the rules are the right rules generally speaking. What helps to prevent evil of the banal kind from arising in games, however, is that play is inherently harmless. As Caillois and Juul agree, games are incompatible with the idea of players incurring serious bodily harm in the course of playing. Rather, as soon as enduring bodily consequences appear, the game is either interrupted or ends. However, if no serious harm can be done within the context of a game, then this prevents evil of the kind Arendt describes from taking place in games. Note that unlike Kant, Arendt also focuses on the consequences of an agent's actions rather than purely on the kinds of maxims he follows in order to define evil. For her, even those people who do not follow corrupted maxims or who are not malignant in any way can cause serious evil. But if a certain activity excludes the possibility that harmful consequences might arise in its course, this activity does not seem to be prone to the banality of evil.

To be sure, one might doubt to what extent this alleged harmlessness of games holds true in extremely competitive games. Sports, for instance, often carry a lot of injuries. But, as Juul rightfully emphasizes, 'it is part of how we treat these [more dangerous] games that injuries should be avoided' (2003: 39). Even in a state of competition, players try not to cause harm to their opponent. Play does not aim at inducing harm that transcends the boundaries of play but only at inducing 'harm' that minimizes your opponent's chances of winning, e.g. by capturing one of his pieces in chess. Although the goal of boxing is to knock out the opponent so that he cannot return to his feet before the referee counts to 10, it is not the goal to harm the opponent to the extent that he can *never* stand up again. The inherent harmlessness of games is the reason behind the existence of the technical knockout rule in boxing and what distinguishes it from plain fighting.[4]

The fact that we are aware that we are playing keeps us alert with respect to not causing serious harm to our opponents. This general attitude towards what playing a game is supports all players in keeping up that constant state of critique called for by Arendt, which presents the best way to prevent banal evil from happening. Because we know that we are playing a game, we are especially cautious not to cause harm. Thus, when we act as players, we act as persons in Arendt's sense. We reflect on our actions, particularly with respect to their potential harmfulness. On the occasion of a player intentionally harming his opponent everybody halts in awe.

A potential criticism might be that the focus on an abstract and idealizing definition of games excludes evil actions from concrete playing by what seems to be definitional prestidigitation. If games are defined as necessarily being harmless, and if evil is defined as involving harm, then of course evil cannot take place in games. But, one might ask, what can we really learn from such a conclusion based on conceptual grounds? However, one should notice that the property of harmlessness as ascribed to games is not the arbitrary result of personal intuition but of what anthropologists and sociologists find to be the actual use of this concept across different cultures. People only experience activities as playing games that are predominantly harmless.

If harm is being done in the context of the game, the game often does not just halt. Rather, the game world is abruptly shattered. In the very second that serious harm enters the scene, the game ends. Again, this is why there can be no evil in games, only evil ending games. The most notorious example in this respect might be the lethal fastball thrown by Carl Mays that fractured Ray Chapman's skull during a baseball game in August 1920. As soon as people realized what had happened, the substitutes ran on the pitch, ambulances arrived, and the game was disrupted. The game world was shattered so thoroughly that a trial for manslaughter against Mays was initiated. One can hardly imagine a more thoroughgoing destruction of the game world than a lawsuit asking questions about what a game is and what may legitimately happen in it from a theoretical point of view, with the looming threat of one of the players being convicted for what he has done.

It is because of the utter incompatibility of games and harmfulness, and because the players of games constantly uphold this spirit, that playing a game does not easily fall prey to threats of evil being caused by blind rule-following. As serious bodily harm is done in games, the game immediately pauses or ends for the very reason that such harm has been done. Thus, as with the other forms of evil, we find that given the inherent properties of the activity of playing a game, no evil can be committed while playing a game. Overall, we can therefore conclude that playing a game is not an activity which is entirely morally undetermined.

Notes

1 Notably, one could extend the continuity to Huizinga's (1955) original effort to define play.
2 The choices of the players are not less autonomous even when playing established games, since nobody is forced to play, say, chess by the traditional rules, as hundreds of chess variants reveal.
3 Concerning this point, see Caillois on the role of *alea* in games (1961: 10–19).
4 Although historically speaking 'plain fighting' might have been considered a sport or even a game, I think that Caillois and Juul provide us with convincing arguments as to why this opinion is misguided.

References

Arendt, H. (2005) *Responsibility and Judgment*, ed. Kohn, J., Berlin: Schocken.
Caillois, R. (1961) *Man, Play and Games*, transl. Barash, M., Urbana, IL and Chicago: University of Illinois Press.
Huizinga, J. (1955) *Homo Ludens: A Study of the Play-element in Culture*, Boston: Beacon Press.
Juul, J. (2003) 'The game, the player, the world: Looking for a heart of gameness', in Copier, M. and Raessens, C. (eds) *Level Up: Digital Games Research Conference Proceedings*, Utrecht: Utrecht University.
Juul, J. (2004) 'Introduction to game time', in Wardrip-Fruin, N. and Harrigan, P. (eds) *First Person: New Media as Story, Performance, and Game*, Cambridge, MA: MIT Press.
Kant, I. (1998a) *Groundwork of the Metaphysics of Morals*, ed. Gregor, M., Cambridge: Cambridge University Press.
Kant, I. (1998b) *Religion within the Boundaries of Mere Reason*, ed. Wood, A. and di Giovanni, G., Cambridge: Cambridge University Press.
Searle, J. R. (1979) *Expression and Meaning: Studies in the Theory of Speech Acts*, Cambridge: Cambridge University Press.
Suits, B. (1978) *The Grasshopper*, Toronto: University of Toronto Press.

4 Posthuman nature
Life beyond the natural playground

Stuart Lester

Introduction

> Our nation's children are ... missing out on the pure joy of connection with the natural world; and as a result, as adults they lack an understanding of the importance of nature to human society. If we do not reverse this trend towards a sedentary, indoor childhood – and soon – we risk storing up social, medical and environmental problems for the future.
>
> (Moss, 2012: 2)

> Despite successive attempts by intellectual critics to expose the dangerous politics of naturalisation, and to thereby challenge naturalist assumptions, idealised notions of nature and its associated key collateral terms, like childhood, still exert a seductive hold on us. Singularly deployed nature still sets the standards for what we think about as 'the good, the beautiful, the just and the valuable'.
>
> (Taylor, 2013: 15)

These opening extracts present the territory to be explored in this piece. On the one hand, there are numerous popular concerns, particularly in minority world contexts, that children are being deprived of nature and that untold misfortunes will result unless this is reversed. On the other, there is a growing disquiet that the idea(l) of nature presented through the 'childhood in crisis' rhetoric and beyond is in itself damaging. For a long time nature has been employed as a philosophical concept, an 'ideological node and a cultural repository of norms and moralism against women, people of colour, indigenous people, queers, and the lower classes' (Alaimo, 2010: 4). This chapter will add another exclusive dimension to this list, with particular focus on the potent use of nature in the contemporary composition of childhood and play and its distillation and manifestation in the concrete production of a 'natural playground'. This specific formation is taken as a representation of the ways in which constituents of nature, play, space and childhood assemble to form a seductive common-sense view of this relationship, an unquestioned orthodoxy of thought with its accompanying clichés and material effects (Deleuze, 1994).

The argument presented here asserts that this indiscriminate application of nature perpetuates the separation of childhood as a distinctive irrational, immature and needy life-period requiring nurture, protection and special places set apart from the everyday environments in which children get on and go on with their lives. It proposes that this particular relationship between adults, children and the environment is inequitable and does violence to all: 'attempts to buttress romantic perceptions of children's [natural] innocence, naivety and lack of discipline are really impositions of adult, dessicated ways of knowing ... the hypocritical and potentially destructive basis of adult domination' (Aitken, 2001: 184).

The aim here is to challenge and transform such separations. In developing this the chapter will not seek to unravel, verify or falsify the deep history of philosophical thought on nature. Following Deleuze and Guattari (1994), the intention is to investigate what concepts do rather than what they mean. This argument will also look for ways out of the well-worn route that draws a categorical distinction between objective realism and relativist/constructivist approaches (Castree, 2005; Braidotti, 2013). By doing so it rejects the ontological schism of the existence of a separate nature and associated nature–culture dualism. However the aim is not simply to dismiss nature out of hand but rather to pose the question 'how else might we think of this relationship?' and to examine what this might offer for reconfiguring not only childhood and play but ultimately human/non-human relationships, provoking an ethics that is not human-centred but accountable to the material world that is never merely an external place 'but always the very substance of ourselves and others' (Alaimo, 2010: 158).

The idea of 'nature'

For the most part the use of the term 'nature' is rarely explored in any depth; the very idea that something is 'natural', in contrast to society, assumes an unquestionable position (Castree and MacMillan, 2001) as an inert background against which humans construct their lives. Yet while seemingly self-evident and transparent, 'nature' is an elusive term; indeed following Williams (1983: 219) it is possibly 'the most complex word in the [English] language' and operates at multiple levels with wide-ranging consequences. Specific meanings of nature gain currency or acceptance because it is congenial to prevalent beliefs or the tastes of a certain age (Harvey, 2009). Tracing the genealogy of the term, Williams (1983) identifies three distinctive applications:

1 The essence or essential quality and character of something;
2 The inherent and intangible forces which direct the world;
3 The observable material world or the products and objects of nature – trees, mountains, animals etc.

The above general meanings have become entangled in complex and ambiguous ways with powerful discursive and material effects; the ways in which humans come to 'know' nature determines what it does (Taylor, 2013). The dominant idea, in minority world contexts, that nature exists as something apart from human is founded on philosophical arguments that promote the mastery or control over nature and natural forces (Harvey, 1996) while at the same time relying on an unchanging, impersonal and mute nature to offer universal laws and norms. Nature becomes the arbiter of truth and it falls to the natural sciences to reveal these immutable laws. It separates human agency from the world, delineating one from the other in a definitive way and forming the 'metaphysical cornerstone of modernity's self-understanding' (Anderson, 2009: 120). For the purposes of this chapter, this foundational division of powers between human and nature will be briefly introduced by examining two key strands of Enlightenment thought, namely ideals of self-realization (the aesthetic and creative powers of humans) and freedom and emancipation (from material wants and needs, insecurity, ignorance and so on). In doing so it is inevitably taking considerable liberties with philosophical ideas that have profoundly shaped human thought and practices over centuries.

Rousseau's (1762/1979) *Emile* is generally recognized as the most influential philosophical study of childhood in the Age of Enlightenment (Wolff, 2013) and his treatise still finds purchase in contemporary accounts of childhood and education (Taylor, 2013). It draws on Rousseau's wider concerns on the nature of human freedom and a basic premise that man was born equal and self-sufficient but through history is in chains (Rousseau, 1762/1979), 'defined by relations of inequality (rich or poor, noble or commoner, master or slave), dependent, full of false opinions or superstitions, and divided between his inclinations and his duties' (Bloom, 1979: 3). When read in this wider context, Rousseau's innovation in *Emile* is to switch focus from the man the child will become to what the child is before becoming man (Ryan, 2011) and thereby laying the foundations for the idea of the separate state of childhood and the promise it holds for improving the human condition. In *Emile*, Rousseau presents the period of childhood as the closest state to nature, a condition to be carefully nurtured by ensuring the child learns directly from nature and all that is good rather than the unnatural teachings of adults. Adult society is portrayed as contaminating (Aitken 2001); nature is an antidote to the evils of society and at the same time holds the promise of society's ultimate salvation.

A different reading of this relationship can be traced from Kant, notably in the formation of the *Metaphysics of Morals* (Paton, 1991). Again recognizing the gross oversimplification and reduction here,[1] the bare bones of this philosophical line suggests that the human condition has transcended nature and is no longer deceived by its basic perceptions and bodily sensations but guided by the one true proposition of existence proposed by Descartes, 'I think, therefore I am'; this is an indisputable truth that places rational thought and logic as the infallible bedrock of being. The Cartesian act of separation between mind and body has had profound effects on Western thought for centuries (Aitken, 2001). Kant's *Critiques* develop a further hierarchical and transcendental move by proposing that in order for human beings to interpret the world they must first impose certain structures on the in-flow of sensations; thus the mind can only make sense by ontological separations that classify and categorize the world into discrete entities so as to subdue often random and misleading perceptions. Kant proposes that the final end of nature must be human beings; only human beings use reason to set and pursue ends, using the rest of nature as means to their ends (Rohlf, 2014). Central to Kant's philosophy is the autonomy of man as a rational, self-legislating and -regulating individual. From this Kant concludes that we can have *a priori* knowledge that the entire sensible world – not just individual experience, but any possible human experience – necessarily conforms to certain universal natural laws (Rohlf, 2014). Therefore, to be human is to transcend the confines of nature to which the lives of all other creatures are bound (Hinchliffe, 2007); human knowledge is isolated from the world and imposes on the world ideally generated blueprints (Jones, 2009).

These philosophical traditions combine to present a view that 'man' has transcended nature while at the same time there is a longing to be closer to nature. Both of these act to present nature as external and eternal, a force that preceded but is now either tamed or ruined. But it poses a fundamental question 'How can humans be both of nature and beyond it'? If nature is understood as an open and dynamic system, 'how did the violation of nature in the form of Cartesian man manage to emerge as a being that forgets its own emergence?' (Colebrook, 2010: 31).

And this is the existential dilemma: humans are creatures that can know themselves and the world of which they are a part only by first taking themselves out of the world. As human reason becomes supreme, the earth becomes external and subordinate to man, the stage upon which skills are enacted. Humans are 'no longer inhabitants but exhabitants' (Ingold, 2011a: 111), occupying a privileged position by the freedom to rule themselves and to make their own world; everyone and everything that lacks this capacity can be viewed as heteronomous, that is operating to incontrovertible, external laws and forces, governed from without by 'nature' (Hinchliffe, 2007). This assumes great political significance: humans evoke natural laws to make judgements, classify and distinguish the order of things while at the same time absolving themselves of any responsibility for this state of affairs; some humans are defined as more human than others (Castree, 2006).

Natural childhood, natural play

The previous section crudely illustrates the ways in which nature and culture have become ontologically discrete categories in the minority world, a separation that still retains powerful and ubiquitous influence over the foundation of modern knowledge, filtering into everyday practices, habits and common sense (Jones, 2009). The distinction between autonomous 'self-rule' and being caught up in nature's strictures establishes a clear divide between the rational and reasonable man – the 'gold standard of human value' (Lee, 2005: 33) – and the heteronomous unenlightened child who must overcome their natural tendencies to become reasonable. This separation between adult and child is pervasive, as Lee (2005: ibid.) notes, 'ranking low on the scale of development [children] were to be distinguished from primitives and savages only by their status as treasured possessions, and if they were male, as future, civilised, reasoning individuals'.

The ideal of the natural child has a powerful effect on the Western adult imaginary of childhood (James et al., 1998); children are valued for their intrinsic properties of being pure and innocent and in need of protection from the violence and ugliness of contemporary society. Childhood is portrayed through an absence, or what it is not, 'extracted from social life' (Prout, 2005: 11) and caught in a strange time-warp; the child as a primitive creature is 'in harmony with nature, set free from the ravages of the time driven modern world [casting] children into a mythic past or a magical present' (James and Prout 1997: 242). At the same time, children's natural innocence is projected into the future as a form of redemption from the ills of the modern world. A natural childhood is a powerful utopian vision of adult hopes, enacted through multiple practices designed to both protect the child and propel them forward.

The performative effects of the natural childhood idea (1) are highly visible in the growing movement to restore children's contact with natural environments by supporting development 'in surroundings that instil a pure, unblemished, almost perfect way of life that is free from the polluting presence of dangerous others' (Matthews et al., 2000: 142). There are a number of complex and entangled forces associated with this movement, notably the continued affirmation of children's innate affiliation with nature that needs to be nurtured and protected, a legacy of Rousseau's romantic intrinsic child/nature relationship updated to align with contemporary environmental concerns (see for example Chawla, 1992, 2002, 2009; Pyle, 2002). The benefits from this immersion are children who will grow to have greater environmental awareness as adults (Ward Thompson et al., 2008; Wells and Lekies, 2006; Dillon and Dickie, 2012); nature cultivates habits, sensitivities, capacities and subjects who will be the future guardians of the planet. Given the importance of children's special relationship with nature, there is increasing concern that children are cut off from the natural world (see for example Moss, 2012; Faber Taylor and Kuo, 2011), a position highlighted and influenced by a number of prominent authors, most notably Louv's (2005) *Last Child in the Woods*. Louv draws together a range of diverse research studies (see Children and Nature Network, 2012), popular accounts and adult anecdotes to present a claim that modern childhood is in crisis. Thus not only is nature threatened by humans but childhood is itself an endangered species. While science has historically been employed to reveal the laws of nature, it is now increasingly used to 'validate nature's impeccable credentials to do its own thing … it is science that decrees that we must return these endangered children to nature and trust that nature alone will restore, heal, guide and teach them' (Taylor, 2013: 57). The idea of nature deficiency has now become a dominant cliché of childhood, evident in media reports and slogans from various 'child-saving' campaigns. It has also contributed to a burgeoning natural education movement, evident in the rise of such institutions as Forest Schools and natural nurseries/kindergarten that seek to keep the child away from the impedance and distortion of formal education (Rousseau, 1762/1979; Bertram, 2012).

Given that children's play is held to be a defining feature of childhood and central to an understanding of this life period (Wyness, 2006), the natural childhood discourse reinforces common-sense attribution of play's value as an expression of children's innocence and sense of wonder and their (and the planet's) salvation. Rousseau's Romantic philosophy, further advanced by, for example, Froebel's (1896) kindergarten movement and Montessori's (1989) pedagogy, suggest that the logic of nature can be revealed through meaningful play and playthings (Provenzo, 2009). Play, as an instrument for progress, combines with other modern rhetorics of self-expression, identity formation, self-actualization and creativity (Sutton-Smith, 1997) to produce idealized and 'organic' play forms, i.e. valued behaviours that sit comfortably with the long-established tradition of the child coming to emotional, social and cognitive maturity and independence through playful contact with nature. This is further reinforced by the romantic presentation of characteristics of play as natural, instinctive and free, which when coupled with the non-literality and irrationality of play perpetuates childhood as heteronomous. The conflation of nature, childhood and play generates and maintains the fabrication of their unitary stability (Ailwood, 2003), finding expression in contemporary spatial productions and practices, most notably in the context of this chapter, the natural playground. The following is a typical illustration of this production (White, 2004):

> [N]aturalized play environments do not depend on manufactured equipment. Rather than being built, they are planted – they use the landscape and its vegetation and materials as both the play setting and the play materials. Instead of being designed like a well-manicured adult environment, naturalized playgrounds are designed from a child's perspective as informal, even wild, and as a place that responds to children's development tasks and their sense of place, time and need to interact with the nature. They are designed to stimulate children's natural curiosity, imagination, wonder and discovery learning as well as nurture children's connectiveness with nature.

The outcome is a child that needs to be removed from their everyday worlds to negate the contemporary conditions of childhood; 'carried to its extreme children should be in childhood, and childhood has no place in modern society' (Gullov, 2003: 28). Moral and aesthetic naturalism, i.e. an unquestioned assumption that 'nature knows best', presents the final word (Demeritt, 2001).

De-naturalizing nature

Countering the idea of the existence of a 'real' nature, many scholars have highlighted that without humans there would be no nature, defining nature as a societal/human construct (Allen, 2011; Harvey, 1996). Rather than being the antithesis of culture, nature is social through and through (Castree and MacMillan, 2001). It is an ideology, a set of assumptions which gain acceptance as real and whose power and bias are concealed because they are thought to be beyond social contamination (Castree, 2005). A constructivist account maintains there is no unitary pre-given foundational nature but many natures that are active and entangled outcomes of cultural, economic, social, historical, material and political relations and forces. Ginn and Demeritt's (2009) analysis of the use of the term 'natural' in food processing and labelling illustrates the ways in which these forces combine to pass judgement. According to the UK's Food Standards Agency (2008: 15):

> 'Natural' means essentially that the product is comprised of natural ingredients, e.g. ingredients produced by nature, *not the work of man or interfered with by man* [italics added]. It is misleading to use the term to describe foods or ingredients that employ chemicals to change their composition or comprise the products of new technologies, including additives and flavourings that are the product of the chemical industry or extracted by chemical processes.

The idea of food production excluding any trace of human action is an impossible standard, a point not lost on the Food Standards Agency (2008: 16) who qualify the use of the term to 'foods of a traditional nature, to which nothing has been added and which have been subjected only to such processing as to render them suitable for human consumption'. By definition, this attempt to categorize what is natural positions humans outside of nature with their contaminations of culture and technology. As Ginn and Demeritt (2009) observe, the conflation of traditional with natural strengthens this relationship; change is impossible without alienation from these forces. Applying this line of argument to the production and accompanying rhetoric of a natural playground suggests that these spatial arrangements are somehow free from human artifice and therefore more valuable sites for childhood. By doing so it glosses over the chequered political and economic history of the playground movement as sites of containment of children's bodies and desires (for further discussion see Ward, 1979; Kozlovsky, 2008; Lester, 2014). It promotes an idea of a fixed, pure, unsullied space that can be classified and labelled by a range of variables, ascribing certain relations within and between spaces (Harvey, 2009). A natural playground has distinctive qualitative features relative to other spaces while at the same time contributes to the increasing segmentation of life through binary arrangements of nature/culture, adult/child, work/play and so on that institute and enact a blueprint of ideal child development. Each segment works in concert with adjacent territories to regulate the movement of life to prescribed temporal/spatial patterns, collectively forming a 'plane of organisation' (Deleuze and Guattari, 1988). Adult desire for children to be located in nature marks the search for a utopian other time (lost childhoods) that can be reclaimed through a utopic other place (pure nature). The primary value across this relationship is children's potentiality (Castañeda, 2002). Nature is 'out there' waiting to fill children's deficits and lack, protect their state of innocence and produce future guardians of a threatened planet; it is a negative and reactive bond of shared vulnerability to common threats between the human and non-human world (Braidotti, 2013).

However, while contesting a pure nature and childhood, the de-naturalizing nature discourse itself may merely serve to reverse power in the nature/culture binary (Ryan, 2011; Castree and MacMillan, 2001) by privileging epistemological over ontological issues (Barad, 2007), making matter mute and closing down all kinds of promiscuous possibilities 'from human wonder at the world to experimenting with ways of living that are of benefit to a range of earthly inhabitants' (Hinchliffe, 2007: 46). The dilemma here is to overcome the ways in which nature and culture, the given and the constructed, are constantly separated. How might we think differently and why does this matter? These two interwoven questions form the basis for the remainder of this chapter.

How does nature matter?

While the wide-ranging natural childhood/play movements outlined to date are well-meaning and generally benign, they perpetuate categorical boundaries between the human and non-human world to the detriment of both and unwittingly add to the ways in which they devalue, exclude and silence certain forms of human and non-human life (Alaimo, 2010). As may be seen from the above brief analysis, the logic that holds nature in place is quite perverse (Barad, 2011) yet pervasive and persuasive. The constant dilemma is that once the boundaries between nature and culture have been established, then it becomes impossible to think differently within this framework. What is needed is an analysis that does not 'presume that the terms on either side of equivalence relations are given' (Barad, 2011: 123).

It is here that the discussion introduces the foundations for such an analysis, rooted in Deleuze and Guattari's (1994) passive vitalist philosophy and extended through a range of what might be tentatively referred to as post-human/new materialist thinkers. The foundational principles of Deleuze's ontology of immanence is a commitment to perceiving life, so often treated as immaterial, emerging through continuous and discontinuous self-organizing connections and relations whose outcomes are not determined in advance by intrinsic properties of already formed matter (Colebrook, 2005a). There is no form or principle which guides life; 'all we have is the potential for difference and variation' (Colebrook, 2005b: 293). Mind and matter are attributes of one substance from which possibilities of difference can be actualized. As may be apparent, Deleuze counters the dominant strain of a philosophy of transcendence that would have a difference of being between some beings, replacing it with a view that the earth is an indivisible generative entity, 'a pulsing body of productive forces' (Clark, 2011: 19). Such a perspective relegates cognition in favour of relations that are always determined by different flows and forces (physical, organic, cultural and so on) and their specific affects (Colebrook, 2010). Rather than subsuming life into a pre-existing framework of knowledge and thereby reducing it to more of the same (Massumi, 2002), posthumanism overturns the idea of the stable human being, the Cartesian *cogito* and the reasoning/reasonable figure of Kantian thought (Braidotti, 2013), to replace it with a de-centred non-dualistic understanding of nature–culture intra-action that disputes the privilege afforded to discursive practices and their representations to determine what is 'real'. It stretches beyond the human/non-human binary to present a more-than-organic world in constant flux and flow. This is obviously a cursory introduction to a movement that cannot be reduced to one coherent narrative that finds divergent expressions in a number of theoretical developments including Deleuze and Guattari's (1988) rhizomatics and assemblages, Actor Network Theory (Latour, 2005) and feminist new materialisms (Braidotti, 2013; Alaimo and Hekman, 2007; Barad, 2007; Haraway, 1991, 2007). Ideas of the posthuman also influence transdisciplinary accounts of childhood (Prout, 2005), nature (Hinchliffe, 2007; Whatmore, 2002) and space (Massey, 2005; Ingold, 2011a).

These diverse lines of enquiry have collective value in getting out of the nature–culture bind, and this chapter pays particular attention to Barad's (2007)[2] compelling concept of 'agential realism' which proposes that all matter *performs* and has agency, nothing exists in isolation and everything affects; 'agency is a matter of intra-acting, it is an enactment not something that someone or something has' (Barad, 2007: 178). The world exists and goes on through continuous change, a dynamic process of becoming different. Life emerges through these movements not as a connection between pre-existing entities that form a temporary alliance before returning to a self-contained state; individuals are composed from their ongoing intra-action or entangled acts of intra-relating, always caught up and produced through relationships with other bodies and materials in non-linear and indeterminate ways. But these entanglements are 'real', not in the sense of representation of something that already exists but in that each moment of intra-activity has real effects and these effects become components and forces for further intra-activity. This presents a different perspective on the narrow attribution of agency to humans: all kinds of organisms and matter are performative agents caught up in acts of co-creation. From this, there can be no division between bodies, discourses, things and matter since they are always in a relationship of intra-action, mutually shaping in all sorts of iterative and prospective patterns (Barad, 2007). Materials do not present themselves as objects with a common essence that bestows a fixed objectness/objectivity; rather, they actively partake in the very processes of the world's ongoing generation and regeneration (Ingold, 2011b). They affect discursive understanding just as much as discursive understandings affect materials: they are material-discursive practices (Barad, 2007). Pursuing this theme, the following observation is introduced here (Noren-Bjorn, 1982: 29):

> A girl throws a stone in the water. She listens to the plop and watches the rings forming. Another girl comes up and tries to hit a 'target' in the water. The girls begin to keep score of how many times they get a hit and to discuss what 'counts'.

An exclusionary nature–culture perspective and the privileging of individual human agency allow the possibility of inscribing an identity to play (a classifiable behaviour that is set apart from other behaviours), players (exercising individual freedom/agency, personal choice and control) and the environment (an immutable and inert background that only comes to life through human activity). A posthuman perspective refuses to reduce this to the presumed individual foundational origins and imposition of meanings. The event is emergent and situated; time, space, bodies, materials and meanings come into co-existence and are iteratively reconfigured through each intra-action, thereby making it impossible to 'differentiate in any absolute sense between creation and renewal, beginning and returning, continuity and discontinuity, here and there, past and future' (Barad, 2007: ix). The intra-active event produces a diffractive pattern of relationships, a 'dance of relating' (Haraway, 2007: 25) with overlapping ripples of encounters and actions, exemplified by the stones hitting the water to create waves that interfere and cancel each other out; 'all the dancers are redone through the patterns they enact' (Haraway, ibid.). Space, time, bodies, matter are de-naturalized in the constitutive dynamics of playing, a line of flight that differently differentiates the plane of organization. There is no organizing centre here, no pre-existing form and no reality outside of their continued production; they are overlappings of the same world, 'stones, too, have histories, forged in ongoing relations with surroundings that may or may not include human beings and much else besides' (Ingold, 2011a: 31).

Playing, as a classification and representation given to a certain style of performative entanglement of inseparable bodies, materials, elements and affects, emerges as a meshwork 'woven from the countless threads spun by beings of all sorts, both human and non-human, as they find their ways through the tangle of relationships in which they are enmeshed' (Ingold, 2007: 3). This entanglement of bodies and materials is not best accounted for in terms of causality and independently existing identities. It is not a matter of choice in a liberal–humanist sense (Dolphijn and van der Tuin, 2012). There are only entanglements and intra-actions; an environment, as the space which surrounds at any given moment, is not prefigured but enacted through encounters between organic/inorganic materials and as long as life goes on, environments are continually being made and remade (Ingold, 2011b; Massey, 2005). The idea that there is an external nature, accompanied by cultural interpretation of this real nature, no longer works (Law, 2004); 'we inhabit a corporeality that is never disconnected from our environment' (Alaimo, 2010: 156). From this perspective, environment should not be confused with nature: the world can only exist as 'nature' for those beings that do not belong there, who are set apart and can look upon it with a sense of detachment, 'from such a safe distance that it is easy to connive in the illusion that it is unaffected by his presence' (Ingold 2011b: 20). The nature–culture division, along with the promotion of natural childhood and play, is not a given but is just one way in which intra-actions are 'cut' to produce discursive–material distinctions between human and non-human, and by doing so produce powerful effects. The challenge is to account for the contribution they make to their differential constitution, their inclusions and exclusions (Barad, 2011). The concern is with the processes in which specific realities are produced and reproduced and how sometimes, as in the nature–culture divide, they appear embedded, immovable and real (Law, 2004).

So why does nature matter?

The ways in which nature is currently produced in relation to childhood and its material-discursive effects has assumed a degree of common sense such that to suggest reconfiguring this relationship would itself seem to be an 'unnatural' move (Taylor, 2013). Nature, and by inference humans, are fixed: positivism constitutes nature as a passive object that can be fully known and used to meet human ends, while constructivism attributes agency purely to human activity. The consequences of this are profound in establishing idealized and nostalgic figurations which position both children and nature as vulnerable and in need of rescuing. Playing is commandeered to the child- and nature-saving movement and becomes embroiled in sentimental and romantic spatial productions.

A posthuman position produces a radical alternative image of life as an assemblage of forces and flows, intensities, passions and desires that produce and solidify in space and consolidate in time. An intra-active reading of play unties it from conventional understandings; a manoeuvre that rather than cutting playing into some presumed foundational, situated and discrete cause–effect relationship reconfigures playing intransitively, that is, as a fluid, discontinuous and indeterminate process. Playing is quintessentially the process of life going on in an affirmative manner. The rhythms and patterns of the co-creation of playful moments configure spacetimes of intimacy and affectivity when/where life is more vital. Such moments matter: they are meshworks that make more liveable worlds and as such are of important ethical consideration. As Barad (2007) suggests, ethics is paying attention to the entangled intra-actions in which we are always enmeshed and the possibilities they present for creating the world differently. Pursuing this, Braidotti's (2012) reading of Deleuze's ethics stresses an active relational ontology; the ethical instance is not located within a subject with individual moral agency but is caught up in a set of intra-actions with both human and inhuman forces intent on co-creating ethical sustainability. The seemingly casual comment from one child to another about 'what counts' is a moment in which intra-actions begin to cohere; a collective desire to maintain affirmative relations by producing sufficient stability to sustain further possibilities for joyful action. These moments are embodied and embedded entangled lines of responsibility and accountability, always experimental; nothing is certain in where it is going. Subjectivity is not a matter of individuality but a relation of response-ability to all the components (the 'others') that constitute the environment in a 'world that is always already an ethical matter' (Dolphijn and van der Tuin, 2012: 69).

Accountability implies taking account of the ways in which discursive-material practices effect cuts and what is excluded from mattering (Barad, 2007); it is not a given that nature exists out there, that playing is classifiable, development is teleological and so on. A messy, multiple and material posthuman environmental ethics is concerned with movement across time, space, matter and bodies and 'reconfigures the human as a site of emergent material intra-actions inseparable from the very stuff of the rest of the world' (Alaimo, 2010: 156). As such, an ethics of mattering is to take account for our part in the meshworks of life in which we are entangled, an awareness of one's condition of interaction and the capacity to affect and be affected to enable life to flourish (Braidotti, 2006). It reconfigures ethics from a universal moral code that positions nature as out there to be protected and cared for to take account of the local, contingent, relational and collective everyday practices that constitute affirmative environmental intra-connections. Rather than seeking to separate childhood in nature to address perceived deficiencies and vulnerabilities, far greater attention is given to ways in which the heterogeneous and messy components of life can get on and go on together. What is presented here overturns segmented life-spaces and offers a promising approach to how they might be differently enacted to produce a more just and equitable account. It is an opening attempt to find a way out of worn-out binary productions and to rethink causality, agency, power and ethics in such a way that the understanding of the world, and what it is to be human, is drastically changed (Barad, 2007); a move to 'invent forms of ethical relations, norms and values worthy of the complexity of our times' (Braidotti, 2013: 86).

Notes

1 For a more nuanced appreciation of Kant's and post-Kantian contributions to materialism, see for example Bennett, 2010; Dixon *et al.*, 2012.
2 Barad's exposition of agential realism has been developed over time, with particular reference to the work of quantum physicist Niels Bohr – it is, as would be expected, a complex entanglement and it is impossible to do justice to the range of ideas and their possibilities in such a short chapter. Hopefully what is presented here retains a fidelity to some of the central themes without reducing them. It may also inspire the reader to pursue these lines of enquiry further.

References

Ailwood, J. (2003) 'Governing early childhood education through play', *Contemporary Issues in Early Childhood*, 4(3), 286–98.
Aitken, S. (2001) *Geographies of Young People*, London: Routledge.
Alaimo, S. (2010) *Bodily Natures*, Bloomington: Indiana University Press.
Alaimo, S. and Hekman, S. (eds) (2007) *Material Feminisms*, Bloomington: Indiana University Press.

Allen, C. (2011) 'On actor-network theory and landscape', *Area*, 43(3), 274–80.
Anderson, J. (2009) 'Transient convergence and relational sensibility: Beyond the modern constitution of nature', *Emotion, Space and Society*, 2, 120–7.
Barad, K. (2007) *Meeting the Universe Halfway*, Durham, NC: Duke University Press.
Barad, K. (2011) 'Natures queer performativity', *Qui Parle*, 19(2), 121–58.
Bennett, J. (2001) *The Enchantment of Modern Life*, Princeton: Princeton University Press.
Bennett, J. (2010) *Vibrant Matter*, London: Duke University Press.
Bertram, C. (2012) 'Jean Jacques Rousseau', in Zalta, E., Nodelman, U. and Allen, C. (eds) *Stanford Encyclopedia of Philosophy*, Stanford, CA: Stanford University.
Bloom, A. (1979) 'Introduction', in Rousseau, J.-J. (1762/1979) *Emile*, New York: Basic Books.
Braidotti, R. (2006) *Transpositions: On Nomadic Ethics*, Cambridge: Polity Press.
Braidotti, R. (2012) 'Nomadic ethics', in Smith, D. and Somers-Hall, H. (eds) *The Cambridge Companion to Deleuze*, Cambridge: Cambridge University Press.
Braidotti, R. (2013) *Posthuman*, Cambridge: Polity Press.
Castañeda, C. (2002) *Figurations: Child, Bodies, Worlds*, Durham, NC: Duke University Press.
Castree, N. (2005) *Nature*, London: Routledge.
Castree, N. (2006) 'Posthuman geographies', *Social and Cultural Geography*, 7(4), 501–4.
Castree, N. and MacMillan, T. (2001) 'Dissolving dualisms: Actor-networks and the reimagination of nature', in Castree, N. and Braun, B. (eds) *Social Nature Theory, Practice, and Politics*, Oxford: Blackwell.
Clark, N. (2011) *Inhuman Nature: Sociable Life on a Dynamic Planet*, London: Sage.
Chawla, L. (1992) 'Childhood place attachments', in Altman, I. and Low, S. (eds) *Place Attachment*, New York: Plenum Press.
Chawla, L. (2002) 'Spots of time: Manifold ways of being in nature in childhood', in Kahn, P. and Kellert, S. (eds) *Children and Nature*, Cambridge, MA: MIT.
Chawla, L. (2009) 'Growing up green: Becoming an agent of care for the natural world', *Journal of Developmental Processes*, 4(1), 6–23.
Children and Nature Network (2012) *Children and Nature Worldwide: An Exploration of Children's Experiences of the Outdoors and Nature with Associated Risks and Benefits*, available at: www.childrenandnature.org/documents/C149/ (accessed 14 August 2014).
Colebrook, C. (2005a) 'Introduction', in Parr, A. (ed.) *The Deleuze Dictionary*, Edinburgh: Edinburgh University Press.
Colebrook, C. (2005b) 'Univocal', in Parr, A. (ed.) *The Deleuze Dictionary*, Edinburgh: Edinburgh University Press.
Colebrook, C. (2010) *Deleuze and the Meaning of Life*, London: Continuum.
Deleuze, G. (1994) *Difference and Repetition*, London: Athlone Press.
Deleuze, G. and Guattari, F. (1988) *A Thousand Plateaus*, Continuum: London.
Deleuze, G. and Guattari, F. (1994) *What is Philosophy?* London: Verso.
Demeritt, D. (2001) 'Being constructive about nature', in Castree, N. and Braun, B. (eds) *Social Nature Theory, Practice, and Politics*, Oxford: Blackwell.
Dillon, J. and Dickie, I. (2012) *Learning in the Natural Environment: Review of Social and Economic Benefits and Barriers*, Natural England Commissioned Reports, Number 092.
Dixon, D., Hawkins, H. and Straughan, E. (2012) 'Of human birds and living rocks: Remaking aesthetics for post-human worlds', *Dialogues in Human Geography*, 2(3), 249–70.

Dolphijn, R. and van der Tuin, I. (2012) *New Materialism: Interviews and Cartographies*, Ann Arbor, MI: Open Humanities Press.

Faber Taylor, A. and Kuo, F. (2011) 'Could exposure to everyday green spaces help treat ADHD? Evidence from children's play settings', *Applied Psychology, Health and Well-Being*, 3(2), 282–303.

Food Standards Agency (2008) *Criteria for the Use of the Terms Fresh, Pure, Natural etc. in Food Labelling*, London: Food Standards Agency, available at: www.food.gov.uk/sites/default/files/multimedia/pdfs/markcritguidance.pdf (accessed 14 August 2014).

Froebel, E. (1896) *The Education of Man*, New York: Appleton.

Ginn, F. and Demeritt D. (2009) 'Nature: A contested concept', in Clifford, N., Holloway, S., Rice, S. and Valentine, G. (eds) *Key Concepts in Geography*, London: Sage, 300–11.

Gullov, E. (2003) 'Creating a natural space for children: An ethnographic study of Danish kindergarten', in Olwig, K. and Gullov, E. (eds) *Children's Places*, London: Routledge.

Haraway, D. (1991) *Simians, Cyborgs and Women: The Reinvention of Nature*, London: Free Association Books.

Haraway, D. (2007) *When Species Meet*, Minneapolis: Minneapolis University Press.

Harvey, D. (1996) *Justice, Nature and the Geography of Difference*, Oxford: Blackwell.

Harvey, D. (2009) *Cosmopolitanism and the Geographies of Freedom*, New York: Columbia University Press.

Hinchliffe, S. (2007) *Geographies of Nature*, London: Sage.

Hinchliffe, S. and Whatmore, S. (2006) 'Living cities: Towards a politics of conviviality', *Science as Culture*, 15(2), 123–38.

Ingold, T. (2007) *Lines: A Brief History*, London: Routledge.

Ingold, T. (2011a) *Being Alive: Essays on Movement, Knowledge and Description*, London: Routledge.

Ingold, T. (2011b) *The Perception of the Environment*, London: Routledge.

James, A. and Prout, A. (eds) (1997) *Constructing and Reconstructing Childhood*, London: Falmer Press.

James, A., Jenks, C. and Prout, A. (1998) *Theorising Childhood*, Cambridge: Blackwell.

Jones, O. (2009) 'Nature–culture', in Kitchen, R. and Thrift, N. (eds) *International Encyclopedia of Human Geography*, Oxford: Elsevier.

Kozlovsky, R. (2008) 'Adventure playgrounds and postwar reconstruction', in Gutman, M. and De Coninck-Smith, N. (eds) *History, Space and the Material Culture of Children*, New Brunswick: Rutgers University Press.

Latour, B. (2005) *Reassembling the Social: An Introduction to Actor-Network-Theory*, Oxford: Oxford University Press.

Law, J. (2004) *Enacting Naturecultures: A Note from STS*, Lancaster: Lancaster University, available at: www.comp.lancs.ac.uk/sociology/papers/law-enacting-naturecultures.pdf (accessed 19 August 2014).

Lee, N. (2005) *Childhood and Human Value*, Maidenhead: Open University Press.

Lester, S. (2014) 'Play as protest: Clandestine moments of disturbance and hope', in Burke, C. and Jones, K. (eds) *Education, Childhood and Anarchism*, London: Routledge.

Louv, R. (2005) *Last Child in the Woods: Saving our Children from Nature-deficit Disorder*, New York: Algonquin Books of Chapel Hill.

Massey, D. (2005) *For Space*, London: Sage.

Massumi, B. (2002) *Parables for the Virtual*, Durham, NC: Duke University Press.
Matthews, H., Limb, M. and Taylor, M. (2000) 'The "street" as thirdspace', in Holloway, S. and Valentine, G. (eds) *Children's Geographies*, London: Routledge.
Montessori, M. (1989) *Education for a New World*, Oxford: Clio Press.
Moss, S. (2012) *Natural Childhood*, National Trust, available at: www.nationaltrust.org.uk/document-1355766991839/ (accessed 2 September 2014).
Noren-Bjorn, E. (1982) *The Impossible Playground*, New York: Leisure Press.
Paton, H. (1991) *Immanuel Kant: The Moral Law*, Abingdon: Routledge.
Prout, A. (2005) *The Future of Childhood*, Abingdon: RoutledgeFarmer.
Provenzo, E. (2009) 'Friedrich Froebel's gifts: Connecting the spiritual and aesthetic to the real world of play and learning', *American Journal of Play*, 2(1), 85–99.
Pyle, R. (2002) 'Eden as a vacant lot', in Kahn, P. and Kellert, S. (eds) *Children and Nature*, Cambridge, MA: MIT Press.
Rohlf, M. (2014) 'Immanuel Kant', in Zalta, E., Nodelman, U. and Allen, C. (eds) *Stanford Encyclopedia of Philosophy*, Stanford, CA: Stanford University.
Rousseau, J.-J. (1762/1979) *Emile*, transl. Bloom, A., New York: Basic Books.
Ryan, K. (2011) 'The new wave of childhood studies: Breaking the grip of bio-social dualism?' *Childhood*, 19(4), 439–52.
Sutton-Smith, B. (1997) *The Ambiguity of Play*, Cambridge, MA: Harvard University Press.
Taylor, A. (2013) *Reconfiguring the Natures of Childhood*, London: Routledge.
Ward, C. (1979) *The Child in the City*, Harmondsworth: Penguin.
Ward Thompson, C., Aspinall, P. and Montarzino, A. (2008) 'The childhood factor – Adult visits to green places and the significance of childhood experience', *Environment and Behaviour*, 40(1),111–43.
Wells, N. and Lekies, K. (2006) 'Nature and the life course', *Children, Youth and Environments*, 16(1), 1–24.
Whatmore, S. (2002) *Hybrid Geographies*, London: Sage.
White, R. (2004) *Young Children's Relationship with Nature: Its Importance to Children's Development and the Earth's Future*, available at: www.whitehutchinson.com/children/articles/childrennature.shtml (accessed 18 August 2014).
Williams, R. (1983) *Keywords*, New York: Oxford University Press.
Wolff, L. (2013) 'Childhood and the Enlightenment', in Fass, P. (ed.) *The Routledge History of Childhood in the Western World*, Abingdon: Routledge.
Wyness, M. (2006) *Children and Society: An Introduction to the Sociology of Childhood*, Basingstoke: Palgrave Macmillan.

Part II
Play, aesthetics and performance

5 A disavowal of games

Chris Bateman

Defining 'game'

What constitutes a 'game'? This is not as straightforward a question as it first seems, although there have been plenty of people who have valiantly thrown themselves into the fray in its pursuit. As I have discussed in depth elsewhere (Bateman, 2011), the topic has been a central battleground within game studies as a field, with many different competing perspectives – as well as garnering considerable attention within philosophy. The stepping-off point for this debate within the latter field is Wittgenstein's *Philosophical Investigations* (1958), in which it is observed that 'game' is a fuzzy concept that resists any simple definition – the literal point of definition for Wittgenstein's term 'family resemblance'. This has led in turn to an extensive exploration of the term 'game' by philosophers, prompting Mary Midgley (1974) to question whether the meaningfulness of the term had been lost.

However, Midgley still defends the idea of 'game' as a viable concept by recognizing that both it and art meet specific human needs. Since those needs clearly do have a structure, we must have a legitimate basis for presuming a unity to these concepts – and this parallel with art is an interesting tangent that can help to illuminate the nature of the problem. Philosopher of art Kendall Walton has suggested that the question 'what is art?' is 'troubled and seriously contested' (2007: 148). He concludes that it is the very concept of 'art' that has proved a barrier to understanding art, suggesting that if we instead understand representational art in terms of *fiction* – using, for instance, his own make-believe theory of representation (Walton, 1990) – many of the problems disappear. He quips: 'It's that darn concept of art that has made it so hard to understand art' (2007: 160). In what follows, I extend Walton's methods in respect of the intractable dispute over 'what is art?' to the equally intractable discussion 'what is a game?' and suggest, in a direct parallel, that it's that darn concept of 'game' that has made it so hard to understand games.

My method here is both observational and philosophical, drawing from empirical work only briefly to help orient the path of the discussion once the scope of the problem has been sketched. Primary to my method, however, is a kind of Wittgensteinian challenge *not* to think but to *look* (1958: §66), and – following his suggestion that the meaning of a word is how it is used – the core explananda I wish to philosophically examine are specific definitions of 'game' that have been used. These are taken from game studies, game designers and philosophers with an interest in play, with the definitions explored having been chosen for the interesting aspects of the claims made, rather than any assumption of authoritative expertise in each case. The point of each example definition of 'game' is that the word is being used in a specific way, making different epistemological, ontological and instrumental claims, and that the way it is used in each case includes certain activities and artefacts and excludes others. My claim is that specific aesthetic values are being valorized in the choice of what is included – and thus what is excluded is implicitly denigrated in some ill-defined way.

By means of this Wittgensteinian investigation I thus hope to uncover the aesthetic values that are deployed in connection with games – and hence reveal a variegated landscape of play, within which all games (whatever this term is intended to mean) find their place. To do this, we must first disavow the concept of 'game', to set it aside entirely so that we can 'look rather than think' – for if we come to this table armed with our own specified concept of 'game' it will skew our understanding of other perspectives. This abandonment of a clear definition for 'game' is the necessary first step to get to a deeper understanding of games and play, and thus to uncover the conceptual unity that Midgley attests (contra to Wittgenstein, in her reading) can be found in the concepts of 'game' and of 'art'. It is my claim, however, that the upholding of conceptual unity against a backdrop of diverse individual cases is not contra-Wittgenstein at all, but rather an application of his methods. To understand the boundary conditions of play and games we have to step away from the battlefield where these disputes have occurred – and only a disavowal of games can get us there.

Foregrounding fiction

Since a more usual method of enquiry is to define terms and then explore, the disavowal of games is not in itself enough to begin our investigation. Following Walton, who effectively disavowed 'art' in order to understand art, I shall begin by providing a specific understanding of *fiction*, namely Walton's make-believe theory of representation, which I have dubbed *prop theory* in its general application (Bateman, 2011). Fiction, according to Walton (1990), denotes what is to be imagined, and Walton's methods are based upon identifying specific props (such as paintings, movies, toys or games) that prescribe specific imaginings. Each prop has associated with it a fictional world, and imaginative participation with this world (via a game of make-believe) is the means by which we participate with artworks – including games.

For instance, when we look at Van Gogh's *Wheatfield with Crows* (1890) as it hangs in the Van Gogh Museum in Amsterdam, it is prescribed that we imagine that we are looking at a cloudy sky – even though the brushwork does not in any strict sense resemble any sky that sober people have ever seen above them. In the fictional world of this painting, the sky is constructed from apparent brush marks (in marked contradistinction to the work of the 'Old Masters', who worked to conceal their brushwork and present a more, shall we say, photorealistic painting style). The prop (the painting) prescribes the fictional world (the wheat field, sky and crows), which we access via the imaginary game we play when we look at it.

Similarly, when we watch Akira Kurasawa's *Dreams* (1990) there is a segment in which an art student encounters Van Gogh in a field, before later finding himself lost among Van Gogh paintings. The prop (the movie) prescribes that we imagine a fictional world where a man is dreaming of Van Gogh, and within the dream enters the Van Gogh paintings. We, the viewer of the movie, engage with this fictional world (or rather fictional *worlds*, in this case, representing several of Kurasawa's own dreams) via the imaginary games we play as we are watching the movie.

To give one final example, when we play the level 'Painted Swampland' in *New Super Mario Bros. U.* (Nintendo EAD, 2012) the prop (the game) prescribes that we imagine a fictional world where a swamp is constructed out of Van Gogh-like brushwork that nonetheless contains all the familiar Mario game frippery of pipes and mushrooms. We participate with this fictional world either by playing the game or by watching it played. We could even participate with this fictional world just by watching a screenshot of this level, although of course the nature of our participation would be different in each case.

Regardless of the nature of the prop in question, the basic situation remains the same. The qualities of the prop prescribe specific imaginings, and what it is that we are expected to make-believe is the fiction that can be associated with that prop. The fiction forms an imagined world, and we participate with that world via a game of make-believe that we play with the prop. Walton says 'what is true is to be believed; what is fictional is to be imagined' (1990: 41). This is the essence of prop theory: representational works (including games) prescribe specific imaginings, and we participate with those artworks by playing imaginary games with them. This is clear and unproblematic in the case of the Mario example given above, but Walton's methods apply just as equally to the film or painting example. Indeed, his interest is in the latter kind of artworks – it is only with my own work that his theory has been applied to games (Bateman, 2011).

Detailed descriptions of prop theory can be found elsewhere (Walton, 1990 in respect of representational art; Bateman, 2011 in respect of games) – the important point for the current investigation is that prop theory gives us a foundational understanding for play as essentially entailing fiction-prescribed imaginings. These prescribed imaginings *include* the rules of games – such that, for instance, players of the playground game 'It' (or 'Tag') are prescribed to imagine that one player who is 'it' has the capacity to transfer the imagined status of 'it' to another player by touching them. In the fictional world of 'It', it is true that one and only one player is 'it' – or, as Walton might put this, it is fictional that one and only one player is 'it' in the game of 'It'.

A relationship between rules and fiction is not a new application to understanding games – Jesper Juul had previously suggested that videogames could be understood as 'half-real', consisting of 'real' rules and 'imaginary' fictions (Juul, 2005). However, I dispute Juul's ontological assumptions here: the rules are not 'more real' than the fiction. The claim that they are rests on presumptions as to what constitutes reality, assertions which are simply not necessary here. If the claim to reality rests in the immutability of the rules of videogames – a position defended by both Juul and Miguel Sicart (2009) – it is worth appreciating that the rules of a videogame can be changed (by hacking, to give just one instance) *more easily* than the fictional content. That the aforementioned 'Painted Swamp' is to be imagined *as a swamp* is not subject to any significant change. Furthermore, as the example of 'It' highlights, *the rules of a game are themselves imagined*. Nonetheless, Juul's division into fiction and rules is a useful one provided it is stripped of its ontological assumptions. Armed with Walton's prop theory and an acceptance of rules and fiction as essential components for play activities (whether or not they are to be understood as games), we are ready to begin examining specific definitions of 'game' and to uncover the implicit aesthetic value judgements therein.

The aesthetics of play

Crawford's taxonomy of creative expression

There is no better place to start this investigation than the definitions provided by game designer Chris Crawford (1984, 2003). Crawford sets out to organise all forms of creative expression into a taxonomy via a series of disjunctive questions, with the following structure:

- What is the motive of the creator? If 'beauty', it's *art*; if 'money', it's *entertainment*.
- For entertainment: is it interactive? If yes, it's a *plaything*.
- For playthings: is there a defined goal? If no, it's a *toy*; if yes, it's a *challenge*.
- For challenges: is there an agent to compete against? If no, it's a *puzzle*; if yes, it's a *conflict*.
- For conflicts: can you impede your opponents? If no, it's a *competition*; if yes, it's a *game*.

We can see here that Crawford has defined a set of gates that an activity or artefact must pass through to qualify as a game – which is something that was created for money, is interactive, has a defined goal, has one or more agents to compete against, and has the means to impede such opponents. This is, frankly, an extremely strange perspective as to what constitutes a game – for a start, software such as Tale of Tale's *The Endless Forest* (2006), in which players meet online and play at being deer together, falls at the first gate because it was not made with commercial motives. (Indeed, it fails *all* Crawford's tests except 'is it interactive?').

What strikes me most clearly about this taxonomy is the sense at which aesthetic values are being used here to strike off certain forms of play from qualifying as a game. A game, according to Crawford, is not just challenging, but competitive – and more than that, directly competitive. If you cannot actively *hurt* your opponents, it is not a game to Crawford. It is possible to object that Crawford does not mean to valorize this kind of play – for instance, he separates 'art' at the first gate but is clear that he does not intend to denigrate art by doing so. Nonetheless, it is difficult to avoid the implication here that for Crawford the apex of the play of games is in their directly competitive mode, and as such I shall call the aesthetic value on display here in the definition of game a *conflict aesthetic*.

This is not the only aesthetic value being applied here, however, and I will also identify Crawford as picking out an *agency aesthetic* that is characterized by the question 'is it interactive?' (i.e. can the player do something to it or with it?) and a *victory aesthetic* that is characterized by the presence of goals and challenges. For Crawford, the meaning of 'game' is an expression of these three aesthetic values – agency, victory and conflict. As we will see, he is far from alone in sharing these specific values, but they are by no means a complete set.

Costikyan's critical language

A decade after Crawford's original presentation of his taxonomy (1984), tabletop game designer Greg Costikyan (1994) offered a substantial rebuttal, suggesting instead:

> A game is a form of art in which participants, termed players, make decisions in order to manage resources through game tokens in the pursuit of a goal.... What's key here? Goals. Opposition. Resource management. Information.

Although Costikyan pushes back against Crawford's approach – most noticeably by rejecting the first 'gate' and defining games as 'a form of art' – he still shares at least two aesthetic values with Crawford, namely the victory (goals) and conflict (opposition) aesthetics. What has been added are 'resource management and information', which are presented in the specific context of player decisions. This corresponds to the oft-quoted aesthetic assertion of game designer Sid Meier, who claimed in conversation that 'a good game is a series of interesting choices'. This represents a *decision aesthetic* that valorizes the process of making choices, which might be understood as related to Crawford's wider *agency aesthetic*.

Costikyan goes further than this, however, in suggesting that 'almost every game has some degree of puzzle-solving', giving examples such as a strategy-making in a military game as solving the puzzle of optimal attack with specific units, or the use of terrain in a first person shooter game as solving the puzzle presented by the environment. His argument is intended to block Crawford's fourth gate, that segregates puzzles from conflicts (and thus from games) – but it represents another aesthetic value judgement, what I shall call the *problem aesthetic*, which views all play as a form of puzzle resolution.

Although his definition of 'game' in itself does not stray that far from Crawford's aesthetic values, Costikyan also shows a markedly wider perspective when he considers what can 'strengthen games', namely diplomacy, colour (that is, fiction beyond the game rules), simulation, variety of encounter, position identification, role-playing, socialization and narrative tension. These can be grouped into roughly three clusters of aesthetic values: a *social aesthetic* (diplomacy, socialization), an *imaginative aesthetic* (colour, position identification, role-playing) and an *uncertainty aesthetic* (variety of encounter and narrative tension). The social aesthetic is something not often brought into focus, while the imaginative aesthetic valorizes the fictional elements of play in a way quite contrary to the rules-focus of most game designers (such as the one we will look at next). As for the uncertainty aesthetic, we will return to this point later.

Koster's fun as learning

Another game designer, Raph Koster (2012), provided a definition of 'game' that focuses upon the player's activities, rather than the artefactual nature of the game as an object:

> Playing a game is the act of solving statistically varied challenge situations presented by an opponent who may or may not be algorithmic within a framework that is a defined systemic model.

Putting the player first in this way may seem to prioritize the play over the game, but this sentence conceals an opposite (although largely complementary) stance by suggesting that the framework within which the player's actions take place is 'a defined systemic model'. This allows this definition to be reversed such that a game is 'a defined systemic model with which players face opponents who present statistically varied challenge situations that the player solves'. Once again, we can see the victory ('challenge situations') and conflict ('presented by an opponent') aesthetics, but 'statistically varied' hints at something else interesting, discussed below. What is largely new here, however, is the elevation of the systemic elements above all else – and this *systems aesthetic* is something game designers seem to be drawn towards. Costikyan gestured in similar directions with his allusions to resource management, which in itself implies game systems.

However, Koster does not spend much time drawing out this side of his perspective because he is much more interested in espousing a *learning aesthetic*, which is at the centre of his book *A Theory of Fun for Game Design* (2005). This viewpoint effectively defines all kinds of fun that obviously do not entail learning (such as rollercoasters) as 'not fun' before concluding that fun can be understood as learning. As this sentence makes clear, this argument is based on a rather narrow perspective on games – and interestingly, upon a viewpoint we have already encountered. Consider this statement from Koster:

> Games are puzzles to solve, just like everything else we encounter in life [and] serve as very fundamental and powerful learning tools.
>
> (2005: 34)

We have already seen this value judgement in claims made by Meier and Costikyan: Koster's learning aesthetic is only a teleological gloss upon the more general problem aesthetic.

Malone's optional informational complexity

Another aesthetic value related to learning that can be applied to games and play is rather harder to reach via any stated definition of game, but it can be found in the work of the researcher Thomas W. Malone. Writing in 1980, Malone suggests:

> Curiosity is the motivation to learn, independent of any goal-seeking or fantasy-fulfillment. Computer games can evoke a learner's curiosity by providing environments that have an *optimal level of informational complexity*.... In other words, the environments should be neither too complicated nor too simple with respect to the learner's existing knowledge. They should be *novel* and *surprising*, but not completely incomprehensible.
>
> (1980: 66)

Malone recognizes the victory aesthetic here ('goal-seeking') as well as the imaginative aesthetic ('fantasy-fulfilment') and the learning aesthetic ('motivation to learn') – but he is drawing out a very different point here, noting that curiosity is *in itself* a motivation to play. This *curiosity aesthetic* has not, to my knowledge, ever been used in definitions of 'game', yet it could easily by deployed in this way; some game designers also make this kind of link between curiosity and learning, e.g. Dan Cook (2007). Alas, I do not have the space to explore this point further here, although I have done elsewhere (Bateman, 2014d).

McGonigal and Suits: victory without conflict

In most of the cases where the victory aesthetic is invoked, the conflict aesthetic goes with it. One rare exception is the game designer Jane McGonigal (2011), who suggests:

> when we're playing a game, we just know it. There's something essentially unique about the way games structure experience. When you strip away the

genre differences and the technological complexities, all games share four defining traits: a *goal*, *rules*, a *feedback system*, and *voluntary participation*.

The interesting point here is that McGonigal recognizes the victory aesthetic ('a goal') but she *does not* presume a conflict aesthetic. The same kind of aesthetic perspective on games can be found in the works of a philosopher she proudly cites in her own work: Bernard Suits. In his first paper on the subject (1966), Suits offers this definition:

> to play a game is to engage in activity directed towards bringing about a specific state of affairs, using only means permitted by specific rules, where the means permitted by the rules are more limited in scope than they would be in the absence of rules, and where the sole reason for accepting such limitation is to make possible such activity.

In his later work (1978), Suits refines this definition as well as offering the more succinct 'playing a game is the voluntary attempt to overcome unnecessary obstacles'. The echoes of this perspective are present in McGonigal's reference to 'voluntary participation'. Suits and McGonigal offer a view of games as rewarding activities, where the enjoyment comes in part by the accepting of limitations. This perspective, which I shall term the *reward aesthetic*, can be understood precisely as the victory aesthetic stripped of the assumptions of the conflict aesthetic – a very different set of aesthetic values than the presumption of direct competition in Crawford and Costikyan.

Caillois and Malaby: uncertainty

Lastly, it is worth considering one of the first individuals to study games and play: Roger Caillois. In his seminal work on the subject (1962), Caillois suggests that everything that constitutes play is free (non-obligatory), separated by limits specified in advance, uncertain, unproductive, governed by rules, and entails make-believe. The involvement of rules and make-believe is the foundation of our inquiry and must be set aside for now, but this still leaves three specific values quite different from those we have seen in the definitions of game designers: play (and hence games) must occur without obligation; play entails uncertainty; play must be non-productive.

The last of these represents a disputed claim: as Castronova (2005) notes, massively multiplayer games severely blur the lines as to what kinds of play can be considered 'productive', especially in the context of those 'gold farmers' who are employed to play the game for the purpose of raising money but continue to play for pleasure after work. It made sense to suggest non-productivity at the time Caillois was writing – now it is far less clear that this will hold. But in relation to Caillois's point that play must occur without obligation, we see a theme already foreshadowed in the discussion of McGonigal and Suits: Caillois is the first to recognize a *voluntary aesthetic* that marks out aesthetic values of a certain kind of freedom in the context of play. This point is also raised by Elliott Avedon and Brian Sutton-Smith (1971), who claim 'we can define a game as an exercise of voluntary control systems'.

Even more interesting here is Caillois's claim that play entails uncertainty – a point that is also alluded to by Costikyan when discussing those elements that strengthen games. Another clear expression of this uncertainty aesthetic occurs in the work of anthropologist Thomas Malaby (2007: 96), who in his attempts to disentangle 'play' from 'game' and 'work' from 'play' suggests:

> A game is a semibounded and socially legitimate domain of contrived contingency that generates interpretable outcomes.

The concept of 'contrived contingency' and 'interpretable outcomes' are core to Malaby's approach and dovetail with Caillois's uncertainty aesthetic. But under the aesthetic values implied here, we are a long way from the kinds of practices and artefacts covered by the definitions of 'game' provided above. The uncertainty aesthetic seems so broad as to reach out far beyond the space constrained by the conditions of aesthetic values such as victory, conflict and problems.

A landscape of play

The above has excavated a ragtag collection of aesthetic values, but without some form of organization it will be difficult to see how the disavowal of games will leave us with any clearer point of reference than when we began. One possible way of approaching this problem is to let empirical considerations suggest philosophical directions, and it is this method that I wish to invoke here. Specifically, I want to draw from my own empirical work observing the play styles that different players express through their play, as well as from my hypothetical connections between these play styles and neurobiological work reported by a variety of researchers. The complete exposition of these empirical and hypothetical roots can be found elsewhere, e.g. in the *IEEE Handbook of Digital Games* (Bateman, 2014a).

For our current discussion, the constraints of space require me to focus simply upon the basis of the patterns and how they connect to the aesthetic values discussed above. Although I have putatively related these to specific neurotransmitters in my work, for brevity I will focus instead upon the emotions that are the phenomenological face of the underpinning biological substrate. This also has the benefit of removing any risk that I might seem to be advocating some kind of positivistic or reductionistic ideology – such is never my intent, as I have made clear in both *The Mythology of Evolution* (2012) and *Chaos Ethics* (2014c). My view is rather that to get at anything close to the truth, in any situation, requires a consideration of multiple perspectives – precisely because there is no external vantage point from which to render a wholly objective description.

The victory and conflict aesthetics so clearly valorized by Crawford but also praised by the vocal majority of videogame players who write about the subject can be organised around the emotion that Paul Ekman (1992) terms *fiero* and which I have suggested can simply be called *triumph* (Bateman, 2011). As Nicole Lazzaro (2003, 2009) observes, this is frequently attained against a background of struggle – it tends to be 'triumph over adversity' – and this means players holding the aesthetic preference for triumph also tend to be capable of enduring frustration (Bateman, 2014a), an expression of anger (Ekman, 1992). This corner of the landscape of play matches what is described by Caillois's (1962) *agon*, or games of competition, and is epitomized by all kinds of sports. It represents an important aspect of play, but when individuals take their aesthetic preference for this kind of play and valorize it above all others (as Crawford arguably does) it results in a narrow understanding of what play can be. For a great deal of my time as a game designer, I have been arguing against this conflation of games with competition (e.g. Bateman and Boon, 2005).

However, triumph is not only achieved by enduring frustration; it can also be attained by enduring boredom or confusion – a situation which occurs most frequently when challenges are viewed *as a problem to be solved* – the problem aesthetic, discussed above. The decision, learning and systems aesthetic can to some extent be understood as expressions of this same tendency, in the latter case because formalizing a situation as a system invites the interpretation of ideal solutions to the problems thus schematized. The same emotional reward – triumph – is sought, but it is not sought through competition and challenges of skill, per se, but through the mental process of problem solving. As such, the problem and victory aesthetics are twins, separated only by the aesthetic preferences and attitudes of those preferring one side over the other.

McGonigal and Suit's reward aesthetic can be seen as the intersection between these paths, a more general statement of the pursuit of success (victory in challenge, or the overcoming of a puzzle), without any commitment to one approach over the other. We can connect this with the emotions of excitement and relief (Ekman, 1992), perhaps the most general experiences of play, in so much as any experience of *fiero* will inevitably also generate excitement, but many other kinds of play produce the excitement *without* ever producing triumph. An advantage of making this connection is that it shows that the emotional reward for play need not be the 'hot' payoff of the victory aesthetic: it can be the substantially 'cooler' release of relief. This could also be connected with Caillois's (1962) pattern of *ilinx* or vertigo.

Malone's curiosity aesthetic, on the other hand, marks out a very different approach to play, one where the motive is not success as such but simple exploration of the activity being pursued, whatever that might be. Of course, curiosity may also compel a player towards success in a manner similar to the problem aesthetic, and there is presumably an overlap here that would be difficult to eliminate. Nonetheless, in many kinds of play – and particularly in narrative play (including that of tabletop role-playing games and children adopting adult roles for play) – curiosity about how the situation will develop appears as a clearer motivation than victory or problem-solving. While not calling it an emotion as such, some researchers, including Lazzaro (2009) do count curiosity as an emotion-like experience, and certainly the experience of curiosity has associated emotions such as wonder (Ekman, 2003). The imaginative aesthetic foreshadowed in Costikyan seems to fit comfortably here, and the agency aesthetic might be seen as a crossover between curiosity and problem-solving: the decision aesthetic (grouped above under the problem aesthetic) seems to belong in some ill-defined manner with the desire for agency, which is understood by some players precisely as the power to make meaningful decisions (e.g. Wardrip-Fruin *et al.*, 2009).

The social aesthetic mentioned by Costikyan appears to serve a different role from those aesthetic values discussed above, since it does not seem to be a motivator of play, per se. Rather, certain players seem to prefer playing socially, while others seem to prefer playing alone, and many players are comfortable with both forms of play (Bateman, 2014a). In terms of emotions, amusement and *Schadenfreude* (pleasure in the misfortune of others) have been suggested as central to the social experience of play (Lazzaro, 2003, 2009), although much of the enjoyment of sociality lacks any specifically named emotional response. Here we seem to be dealing with an aesthetic value that affects the nature of the *practices* of play without placing any clear limitations on the *contents* of the play – although it should be noted that the conflict aesthetic (grouped above under the more general victory aesthetic) requires a social element, since it is not possible to compete without an opponent. This could be distinguished from those kinds of play mentioned under the curiosity aesthetic, such as tabletop role-playing and children's communal games of role-taking. A player who valorized social aesthetics might engage in both kinds of play, depending upon which other values they possessed.

Finally, the uncertainty aesthetic I have linked to Caillois and Malaby (although it is also hinted at by Costikyan) can be related to the voluntary aesthetic from Caillois, Suits and McGonigal. This, as I suggest above, is the most general aesthetic position on play, so much so that many things that would not normally be considered games – including, but not restricted to, stories (Bateman, 2014b) – would fall under its remit. Rather than seeing this broad scope as a flaw in this aesthetic conception, I want to suggest that uncertainty can be understood as the condition within which *all* play occurs – that the uncertainty aesthetic is the broadest of all possible values that could be held in connection to games and play. If there is no uncertainty, there can be no play. Ritual, as Malaby attests, is effectively the opposite pole to play.

This collection of aesthetic values, organised in this way, suggest a landscape of play that can be understood by a metaphor of a twin-peaked mountain upon a forested island. The two peaks of the mountain are the victory and problem aesthetics, with their two separate-but-related routes towards 'triumph over adversity' – indeed, this approach to play has been characterized in some cases as 'mountain climbing' (see Bateman and Boon, 2005). The foothills of these peaks represent the reward aesthetic, and here in these foothills lies a metaphorical village representing the social aesthetic. The rest of the island is a mysterious forest, representing the imaginative aesthetic. Finally, the island is situated in a vast ocean representing the uncertainty aesthetic, within which (I am suggesting) all play can be positioned.

Conclusion

The studying of games and play can be distorted by the prior aesthetic values that are brought into that activity. By disavowing 'game' as a concept, and thus stepping away from any given stance on the aesthetics of play, we can explore different definitions of 'game' as characterizing specific aesthetic values within a wider landscape of play. This metaphorical landscape has distinct features that can be characterized both by the emotions that are invoked and the kind of definitions that are deployed in support of one set of aesthetic values or another. It is as Mary Midgley suggested: there is a unity to play, since it depends upon human needs which do have a structure. But the structure of those needs is not in itself unitary: like Wittgenstein's concept of 'family resemblance', many different aesthetic values are expressed in the pursuit of play.

References

Avedon, E. M. and Sutton-Smith, B. (1971) *The Study of Games*, New York: John Wiley and Sons.
Bateman, C. (2011) *Imaginary Games*, Winchester and Chicago: Zero Books.
Bateman, C. (2012) *The Mythology of Evolution*, Winchester and Chicago: Zero Books.
Bateman, C. (2014a) 'Empirical game aesthetics', in Angelides, M. C. and Agius, H. (eds) *IEEE Handbook of Digital Games*, Hoboken, NJ: Wiley-IEEE Press, 411–43.
Bateman, C. (2014b) 'What are we playing with? Role-taking, role-play, and story-play with Tolkien's legendarium', *International Journal of Play*, 3(2), 107–18.
Bateman, C. (2014c) *Chaos Ethics*, Winchester and Chicago: Zero Books.
Bateman, C. (2014d) 'Implicit game aesthetics', *Games and Culture*, 14 December, doi:10.1177/1555412014560607.
Bateman, C. and Boon, R. (2005) *21st Century Game Design*, Boston: Charles River.
Caillois, R. (1962) *Man, Play and Games*, transl. Barash, M., London: Thames and Hudson.
Castronova, E. (2005) *Synthetic Worlds: The Business and Culture of Online Games*, Chicago: University of Chicago Press.
Cook, D. (2007) 'The chemistry of game design', *Gamasutra* [online], www.gamasutra.com/view/feature/129948/the_chemistry_of_game_design.php (accessed 11 August 2014).
Costikyan, G. (1994) 'I have no words and I must design', *Interactive Fantasy*, 2, available at: www.interactivedramas.info/papers/nowordscostikyan.pdf (accessed 11 August 2014).
Crawford, C. (1984) *The Art of Computer Game Design*, Berkeley, CA: Osborne/McGraw-Hill.
Crawford, C. (2003) *Chris Crawford on Game Design*, Indianapolis: New Riders.
Ekman, P. (1992) 'An argument for basic emotions', *Cognition and Emotion*, 6(3/4), 169–200.

Ekman, P. (2003) *Emotions Revealed: Recognizing Faces and Feelings to Improve Communication and Emotional Life*, New York: Times Books.
Juul, J. (2005) *Half-Real: Video Games between Real Rules and Fictional Worlds*, Cambridge, MA: MIT Press.
Koster, R. (2005). *A Theory of Fun for Game Design*, Scottsdale, AZ: Paraglyph Press.
Koster, R. (2012) '"X" isn't a game!' Raph Koster's website [online], www.raphkoster.com/2012/03/13/x-isnt-a-game/ (accessed 11 August 2014).
Kurasawa, A. (1990) *Dreams [Yume]* [film], Burbank, CA: Warner Bros. Pictures.
Lazzaro, N. (2003) 'Why we play: Affect and the fun of games', in *The Human-Computer Interaction Handbook: Fundamentals, Evolving Technologies, and Emerging Applications*, New York: Lawrence Erlbaum, 679–700.
Lazzaro, N. (2009) 'Understand emotions', in Bateman, C. (ed.) *Beyond Game Design: Nine Steps Towards Creating Better Videogames*, Boston: Charles River, 3–49.
Malaby, T. M. (2007) 'Beyond play: A new approach to games', *Games and Culture*, 2(2), 95–113.
Malone, T. W. (1980) 'What makes things fun to learn? Heuristics for designing instructional computer games', in Lehot, P., Loop, L. and Gorslinem, G. W. (eds) *Proceedings of the 1982 Conference on Human Factors in Computing Systems (CHI '82)*, New York: ACM Press, 63–8.
McGonigal, J. (2011) *Reality is Broken: Why Games Make Us Better and How They Can Change the World*, London: J. Cape.
Midgley, M. (1974) 'The Game Game', *Philosophy*, 49(189), 231–53.
Nintendo EAD (2013) *New Super Mario Bros. U* [videogame], Kyoto: Nintendo.
Sicart, M. (2009) *The Ethics of Computer Games*, Cambridge, MA: MIT Press.
Suits, B. (1966) 'What is a game?', *Philosophy of Science*, 34(2/June), 148–56.
Suits, B. (1978) *The Grasshopper: Games, Life and Utopia*, Edinburgh: Scottish Academic Press.
Tale of Tales (2006) *The Endless Forest* [videogame], Gent: Tale of Tales.
Van Gogh (1890) *Wheatfield with Crows* [painting, held at Van Gogh Museum, Amsterdam].
Walton, K. L. (1990) *Mimesis as Make-believe: On the Foundations of the Representational Arts*, Cambridge, MA: Harvard University Press.
Walton, K. L. (2007) 'Aesthetics – what? why? and wherefore?', *Journal of Aesthetics and Art Criticism*, 65(2/Spring), 147–61.
Wardrip-Fruin, N., Mateas, M., Dow, S. and Sali, S. (2009) 'Agency reconsidered', *Breaking New Ground: Innovation in Games, Play, Practice and Theory – Proceedings of DiGRA 2009*, available at: http://eis-blog.ucsc.edu/2009/08/agency-reconsidered-again/ (accessed 14 August 2014).
Wittgenstein, L. (1958) *Philosophical Investigations*, transl. Anscombe, G. E. M., Oxford: Blackwell.

6 Lessons in playing

Robert Morris's *Bodyspacemotionthings* 2009 as a biopolitical environment[1]

Tim Stott

Robert Morris's *Bodyspacemotionthings*, first exhibited in 1971 at the Tate Gallery and restaged in 2009 at Tate Modern, is a work of art that invites participants to engage physically with various movable objects and structures. At its first exhibition, as I discuss below, participants took this as an invitation to play but then played too much or incorrectly. As a result, after a catalogue of injuries and a great deal of institutional anxiety, the exhibition was closed. Its 2009 restaging, by contrast, allows for a more orderly play by reorganizing *Bodyspacemotionthings* as a playground of sorts, which produces and governs certain freedoms, principally, of course, the freedom to play. In this way, the catastrophe of 1971 is avoided in 2009. This essay will analyse just how *Bodyspacemotionthings* in 2009 accomplishes this and will consider what, in turn, this might show us about current correlations between play and governance in artistic playgrounds.

Three questions form the basis for what follows. The first identifies the inquiry most broadly, as it asks how we might think the correlation of play and governance in a way other than that of opposition. After all, governance of a playground cannot disallow play. Second, how, in particular, does *Bodyspacemotionthings* organise and govern play and thereby allow us to study this correlation? Third, what happens to our understanding of aesthetic play – that is, play that one associates often but not exclusively with the experience of art – when a work of art is organised and governed thus? In answer to these questions, I propose an analysis of *Bodyspacemotionthings* consistent with Michel Foucault's studies of methods of liberal, and especially advanced liberal, governance, because this is governance that seeks to allow players to be free to play. The operation of such methods of governance would make the playground constructed by *Bodyspacemotionthings* a biopolitical environment, by which is meant an environment that rationalizes certain 'problems posed to governmental practice by phenomena characteristic of a set of living beings forming a population' (Foucault, 2004a: 323). The phenomenon in the present case is, of course, play. If *Bodyspacemotionthings* is such an environment, then our understanding of aesthetic play must take into account the organizing function and modality of constraints and rules that are both governmental and ludigenic, i.e. productive of play.

Lessons in playing 85

Governance, or what Foucault calls the conduct of conduct (2004a: 192), faces a compelling problem in the organization of a playground, because play is, intuitively and by most if not all definitions, a volitional activity. It is something a player must choose to do, which fact distinguishes play from obligatory activities. Clearly this does not mean that, once accepted, the rules, commitments and entitlements of play are not binding, at least for the duration of play. The problem for governance is how to conduct those whose conduct is necessarily contingent, those who are and must remain capable of doing otherwise. Players can always, as Michel de Montaigne famously wrote of his cat at play, 'begin or refuse' (Montaigne, 1575–80/2003: 401). Faced with play, the problem is how to govern without governing too much, a problem at the heart of what Foucault has called 'the game of liberalism'. As Foucault writes:

> The game of liberalism – not interfering, allowing free movement, letting things follow their course; *laisser faire, passer et aller* – basically and fundamentally means acting so that reality develops, goes its way, and follows its own course according to the laws, principles, and mechanisms of reality itself.
>
> (2004b: 50)

The other aspect of this game involves knowing when to intervene in order both to secure against disorder or injury and to reproduce the freedoms that this game demands and consumes. Advanced liberal governance 'consumes freedom, which means that it must produce it. It must produce it, it must organize it' (2004a: 65). This is governance that, ideally, lets things happen within a secured or securable environment suited to the production and organisation of natural freedoms and 'in which there would be action not upon the players of the game but upon the rules of the game' (ibid.: 265). At an environmental level, interventions manage a horizon of possible conduct while, ultimately, letting players decide how they conduct themselves, in the knowledge that the free conduct of players will be variable, unpredictable to some degree, and even deviant (ibid.: 265–6). With his analysis of advanced liberal governance, Foucault moves from the critique of discipline in *Surveiller et punir* (1975) to a critique of the production and management of freedoms, where, as Rose and Miller (1992) argue, subjects can be governed by means of their freedom to choose. Foucault captures the peculiar rationale of this when he writes of the governance of subjects produced in such a way as 'to be free to be free' (2004b: 65).

The figure of the player is exemplary here, because she necessarily accepts and adapts to the reality of a given environment, a playground, in order to play freely. Arguably, a player experiences play '*when it is impossible for the actor* [the player] *to differentiate projects available by voluntary fiat from assessed situational possibilities*' (Csikszentmihalyi and Bennett, 1971: 46). In other words, there is play when there is a direct match between an actor's capacity to act and the possibilities and requirements for action within a certain environment. A primary function of the much-discussed 'magic circle', first described in Huizinga's seminal text *Homo Ludens* (1955: 10), is to maintain an environment of manageable and, so to speak, playable complexity, wherein situational possibilities do not exceed those projects available to a player by voluntary fiat. Where such excess does occur, the player is more likely to experience confusion and anxiety than play. One might suppose, then, that the ideal operation of a method of environmental governance would be to construct a playground that correlates directly with a player voluntarily pursuing certain ludic projects.

In manuscript notes (which were not used) to the lecture of 21 March 1979 at the Collège de France, Foucault himself describes the operations of this new governmental reason using the model of what sounds very much like a playground (2004a: 266). Its principal aspects are:

> The definition around the individual of a framework loose enough for him to be able to play; The possibility for the individual to regulate effects [in order] to define his own framework; The regulation of environmental effects [especially with regard to] non-injury [and] non-absorption [i.e. playing too seriously]; the autonomy of these environmental spaces.

This is governance that both invests through and through in the production of natural play and takes this latter to be that which limits and even amends governance. It would be a mistake, therefore, to think of play as a naturally occurring activity that is then governed in some way, a view still widespread in the play literature, especially that which defines play as natural insofar as it derives from an autonomous volition. An Irish paper by the National Children's Office states this view succinctly: 'play is what children do when no-one else is telling them what to do' (2004: 11). If this is the case, then naturally occurring play is quite rightly opposed to and precedes authoritarian or disciplinary methods that tell players what to do. A player who does not wish to obey this disciplinary command can legitimately appeal to her play as a naturally organised activity in need of no additional regulation. What the player must and ought to do are given by the game itself. Yet in view of Foucault's analysis, as already noted, such natural play would be both product of and limit to governance, so that what the player must want to do in order to play does not precede or stand in opposition to the governance of that playground in which this play occurs. In fact, the assertion of play as a naturally occurring activity independent of governance might function as a necessary correlate to a method of governance that measures its operations and interventions against the occurrence of natural freedoms. Nature is, for Foucault, something that 'runs under, through and within the exercise of governmentality. It is its indispensable skin, so to speak'. For those who govern, it is the invisible face to their own actions: 'Not a background, but a perpetual correlative' (2004a: 18). This correlation troubles any claim that there is a natural choreography or organization to playgrounds, or that play is a natural impulse to be protected and nurtured.

For this reason, I believe, we need to look at play as an unnatural freedom, something that correlates with governance and something constituted not by an autonomous volition but by rules and constraints that are internal to play. If this is so, then our next step would be to ask what type of rules and constraints these are and by what means they operate. Rules of play, in particular, must constitute play in the sense that they identify what the player 'must *want to* do to accomplish the practice constituted by the rule' (Chauvier, 2007: 35). This means that they are not necessarily imposed as something extrinsic and normative to a natural or already existing practice, as though rules merely summarize from particular cases that precede them (Rawls, 1955: 23), or as though they merely regulate what happens anyway. If rules are internal to play they can be either constitutive or optimizing, in the sense that they define play or determine best play, respectively. Clearly, any playground must align with the constitutive rules of the play that is to take place there, and even seek to optimize the opportunities for players to follow these rules. What a player must want to do and what she can do must be consistent with what the playground allows her to do. This returns us to the problem of governance outlined above, but now in the knowledge that an analysis of rules and constraints might show how governance correlates internally with play. I return to this discussion of rules and constraints in due course, after a more detailed account of *Bodyspacemotionthings*.

Bodyspacemotionthings helps us find out how the rules and constraints of play might be both governmental and ludigenic, but not without complicating matters further. This is because it consists of a governed environment in which play lacks constitutive rules, an example of what Morris will call, many years later, 'an interrogative space', a world of the question rather than the statement (1997: 298). What players must want to do in order to play is not entirely clear. If there are constitutive rules to play, they are still to be arrived at through an 'interrogation' of the materials and constraints at a player's disposal. I argue that it is here, in the guidance through environmental interventions of those engaged in this pursuit, that advanced liberal governance can be seen to operate.

A further complication is that we can describe as aesthetic the play of those in pursuit of these rules. By aesthetic is meant play in which, to borrow Podro's definition, '[the] objects and sensuous stuff of the world are ... actively felt for, celebrated and elaborated upon' (1982: 14). Although it is a matter of considerable debate just what, if any, might be the defining characteristics of aesthetic experience, Beardsley's definition still can be useful here. For him, aesthetic experience is one of fixed attention to sensuous features of objects, of intensity and concentration, one that 'hangs together' and has a unity and completion that distinguishes it from other experiences. Furthermore, aesthetic objects are 'objects *manqués*'. They are make-believe in the sense that they offer 'complexes of qualities, surfaces' which might command our admiration or other types of engagement but which do not commit us to any practical action (1958: 527–9). This description of aesthetic experience appears very like a description of play, an experience of intensity, closure and distinction, and of provisional commitments that often have little practical consequence, performed in the mode of the *as if*.... Indeed, Beardsley writes that some experiences of play have these characteristics and are therefore aesthetic (ibid.: 530). This certainly appears to be the case with *Bodyspacemotionthings*, where we find a particular alignment of governance and aesthetic play.

As already noted, the 2009 exhibition of *Bodyspacemotionthings* at Tate Modern restages part of a 1971 exhibition at the Tate Gallery. For both, Morris invited the public to engage with a number of movable structures (ledges, see-saws, tightropes, climbing chimneys, balance beams, a large wooden sphere, a hollow granite column, a steel ramp, and steel wedges tied to ropes) and to test their balance, strength, effort, luck and cooperation by clambering, wobbling, climbing, crawling, pushing, rolling, teetering, dragging and, no doubt, various tricky combinations of these. In 1971, in a way largely unprecedented at the time, these structures invited 'the physical participation of the public' in the pursuit of new perceptual experiences (Compton and Sylvester, 1971: unpaginated). In 2009, this invitation still held, of course, but participants had learnt how better to organise their play, as we shall see.

Prior to the 1971 exhibition, Morris had developed a principle of 'anti-form' in sculptural construction (see Morris, 1968, 1969). This principle engaged aleatory and indeterminate processes to undo conventions of sculptural form and allowed Morris to arrive at form unexpectedly through exploration of the constraints and consistencies of particular materials.

However, as David Sylvester writes, the felt pieces in which Morris began his explorations also denied anti-form (Compton and Sylvester 1971: 11):

> The felts impose firm restrictions on what one can do with them.... And it is as if the form were indeterminate in order to enhance awareness of the inevitability with which a given material determines what can be done with it. The felts are a lesson about making.

Art had become, for Morris (1970/1993), a form of making that sought order 'in the "tendencies" inherent in a materials/process interaction'. The structures of *Bodyspacemotionthings* were supposed to expand these 'lessons about making' to include unknown others. In a letter dated 19 January 1971 (quoted in Bird, 1999: 95–6), Morris wrote to the Tate curator Michael Compton that it was time

> to press up against things, squeeze around, crawl over – not so much out of a childish naïveté to return to the playground, but more to acknowledge that the world begins to exist at the limits of our skin and what goes on at that interface between the physical self and external conditions doesn't detach us like the detached glance.

There are two things of note here. First, *Bodyspacemotionthings* was not supposed to solicit a return to the playground, as Morris believed this would encourage puerile or frivolous engagement. Second, instead, Morris encouraged engagement that would be aesthetic in the sense outlined above. Participants were invited to feel for, that is, to press, squeeze and crawl their way to an understanding of the materials at their disposal. However, as critic Guy Brett (1971) described it, 'An orderly participation was expected, but pandemonium broke out'. After four days, the exhibition was closed 'by enthusiasm' (to be reopened days later as a more conventional retrospective, without the participatory works). Rayner Banham, writing for the *New York Times* (1971), found elements of the carnivalesque in this enthusiasm. Brett himself understood it more as a return of the repressed, which disrupted the regulatory and authoritarian institutions otherwise governing social life at that time. Although the invitation to participate was an invitation to sensory exploration, its implications, Brett argued, were that the work of art interacted directly with a social context that entered into the work in unexpected and sometimes destructive ways (see Bird, 1999: 104).

Morris had anticipated a more orderly and exploratory type of play, similar to that which he had experienced in the studio, in which the constraints of the structures would make specific demands on players and would provide clear lessons in playing, limiting arbitrariness or naivety in participation. As Morris wrote a year before the 1971 exhibition, 'Objects project possibilities for action as much as they project that they themselves are acted upon' (1970/93: 90). An ideal response to these demands and possibilities was shown in Morris's accompanying film *Neo Classic*, shot in one evening two days before the opening of the exhibition, which follows a naked woman and two clothed men, one of whom is Morris, as they soberly explore the structures. The specific demands were detailed, too, in the exhibition catalogue and in the layout of the exhibition itself, which grouped together three types of structures. The first were relatively passive objects to be acted upon by participants. The second could be moved by participants but could also affect or choreograph their behaviour in some way. The third consisted of fixed structures that would clearly determine and constrain participation. Having been felt for through play, these demands of the materials, structured as they were, might furnish constitutive rules, which in turn might institute new behavioural and perceptual possibilities. Or so Morris hoped. Again, evidently this did not occur as planned. Hilary Floe (2014) has spoken of similar 'over-participation' evident in a number of roughly contemporary exhibitions in England, including Mark Boyle and Joan Hills' happening *Oh What a Lovely Whore* at the Institute of Contemporary Arts, London, in 1965, and the private preview of *Pioneers of Part-Art* at the Museum of Modern Art, Oxford, in 1971. In all three cases, an exhibition that demanded ludic participation and interaction was brought to a halt because participants played up to and beyond the point of catastrophe.

The 2009 restaging of *Bodyspacemotionthings*, then, presented a governmental problem. How might one make sure that the aesthetic play anticipated by Morris could occur unimpeded but without catastrophic consequence? In other words, how could *Bodyspacemotionthings* in 2009 become what Tony Bennett (2005) has called a 'civic laboratory'? First, it is clear that in 2009 people had learnt how to behave in large public exhibitions.[2] They took turns and queued, of which some critics disapproved (Hudson, 2009), and were discrete and orderly in their play. Second, the playground was secured against catastrophe and was organised in such a way as to guide participants toward the specific demands of each structure, as Morris originally had intended. Precautionary measures were taken, including: (i) the provision of a greater number of sandbags to guide the movements of the sphere and the cylinder; (ii) the placement of either rubber mats or cushions under those structures from which a player might fall; (iii) the use of a mesh to close in the climbing ramps; (iv) the use of stop blocks to prevent either end of the see-saw from touching the ground; (v) the decommissioning of a rope for swinging – to be retained as a sculpture, but not as an object of play; (vi) the widespread use of plywood rather than the scrap metal and rough timber originally used by Morris; (vii) supervision by gallery assistants; and (viii) the disclaimer, which shifts responsibility on to the individual player. These measures, which we might describe as environmental interventions upon the constraints of play, allowed enough contingency and uncertainty for scrapes, bumps and fun, of course. Play was not disallowed, expect with those structures, such as the rope, that were deemed too risky. Through such precautions, *Bodyspacemotionthings* was governed in a way that still allowed for aesthetic play to occur. So, knowing this, and to return to my earlier questions, how did this governance operate through constraints and rules that were both governmental and ludigenic?

As noted, there are no constitutive rules for *Bodyspacemotionthings*. Initially, at least, there is no instituted play. There is no game. To return to our previous discussion, constitutive rules do not guide a practice such as play. They define it. If a player does not follow them, she does not play the game. Like Rawls, quoted above, John Searle distinguishes between regulatory and constitutive rules, adding that 'constitutive rules do not merely regulate, they create or define new forms of behaviour' (1969: 33–4). For example, one could not take a wicket if the rules of cricket did not exist. These rules define what counts as taking a wicket. As Searle puts it, 'X counts as Y in context C' (ibid.: 35), where X would be the activity of catching the ball without allowing it to bounce after the batsman has hit it, Y would be this catch counted as a wicket, and C would be the rules of cricket that allow for something like a wicket to be taken by a catch, something like a batsman to hit a ball that has been bowled to him, and so on. Again, these are rules not for something a player must do, but could do otherwise. They are for something she must want to do. In cases where they are constitutive, rules are not imposed upon an activity that would be otherwise unruled or ruled in a different manner. They are not external or additional to play. The activity Y is logically dependent upon the rules of the game and only has a specific consequence, e.g. taking a wicket, as an 'institutional fact' (ibid.: 51). It is for this reason that, Searle argues, constitutive rules create the possibility for new forms or new specifications (i.e. descriptions) of behaviour (ibid.: 35). Catching a ball after someone had hit it with a piece of wood no doubt existed as an activity before the rules of cricket were formulated, but taking a wicket in this way did not. In light of the above, we can see that at stake in the pursuit of constitutive rules in *Bodyspacemotionthings* is the institution of new forms, or at least new specifications, of behaviour. How, then, was this pursuit governed?

I have already suggested that we often expect governance to be disciplinary and to operate in a regulatory and authoritative manner that is external to a practice of play. Certainly, such governance is evident in *Bodyspacemotionthings* and would describe the disclaimer ('Sensible footwear must be worn', 'Please do not run inside the installation', and so on), any interventions made by the gallery assistants, and the delimitations made by the line dividers. We find here examples of the regulation of environmental effects described above by Foucault, especially with regard to 'non-injury' and 'non-absorption'. As noted, regulatory rules always can be resisted by appeal to supposedly natural play, which would require no such external intervention. In this view, players have no need for someone to tell them what to do, and can choose to dash from one structure to another, to climb in flip-flops, and so forth. This opposition of natural play and regulation was very much evident in the catastrophe of the 1971 Morris retrospective, with regulation having the final word. The question arises as to whether or not playing in flip-flops, for example, is to play better, or to better feel for constitutive rules. An answer to this question is beyond the scope of this essay. Here, I claim simply that in its correlation with advanced liberal governance, play is very much an unnatural freedom, which means that the relation to governance is different to that of regulation and refusal. To understand how this is so, we must consider how governance has an internal, not external, relation to play.

With *Bodyspacemotionthings*, as well as regulatory rules, which always might be transgressed or resisted, there are also optimizing constraints, which are not yet rules, and which have an internal relation to the play that follows from them. An example is the use of plywood and the increased provision of sandbags. These interventions seek to produce optimal or best play: play that is, again, discrete and contained, without serious injury, but also play in which the optimal function of each structure is guaranteed, so that the ball rolls evenly along a path, the chimneys are fit for climbing, and so forth. The player must ask himself, Given these constraints, how can I or we best play? As such, these constraints guide a player toward best play, which is to say, play that is secured, governable, and consistent with the intentions of Morris. As Chauvier writes, we can formulate on the basis of these constraints rules which suppose 'some kind of science of the materials of the practice, or even some kind of reflection upon the happy and unhappy experiences that occur in this domain of practice' (2007: 28–9). These would not be rigid, normative rules, but would remain open to further 'happy or unhappy experiences' and therefore to the variety and contingency of players' conduct. They would allow for adventure, one might say, and for stylizations, and could even provide the basis for appraisals of play. But, arguably, they would not allow for new forms or new specifications of play unless they became constitutive rules. As optimizing rules, they are simply a means to an end, namely, best play. Although internal to play they are not essential to it. In 1971, Morris assumed that the material constraints of each structure would guide participants toward the establishment of new specifications of play. Without optimizing rules, however, participants produced a seemingly ungoverned playground.

For this reason, we should pay close attention, as Morris intended, to the specific demands of these materials and to the sensuous features that constrain. As objects of aesthetic play, the climbing chimneys, ramps, see-saw and so on are complexes of surfaces and qualities that are governed at precisely the level at which they are felt for. Constitutive rules are, again, to be felt for, and this makes the amendments made to materials highly significant, for two reasons.

First, as this is aesthetic play, we would expect it to consist of an unusually concentrated and focused attention. If this is the case, then the fact that an object is made from plywood rather than timber has a consequence greater than the decreased likelihood of cuts and splinters. We might remember that the questions of what an object does and how it feels tend to precede the question of what a player can do with it. Second, it is on the basis of their experience of these materials that players might establish constitutive rules for their play. Only such rules could institute new perceptual and behavioural forms. In 2009, *Bodyspacemotionthings* was governed in such a way that these forms are, again, consistent with the intentions of Morris and secured against injury or disorderly play.

In conclusion, *Bodyspacemotionthings* encourages a player to pursue or play toward the discovery of constitutive rules, to take certain lessons in playing based upon the perceptual and behavioural capacities of movable structures and to institute new possibilities for these. Foucault's analysis of biopolitical governance allows us to study how in this case governance operates by securing the environment, through both regulations and optimizing constraints, in which this pursuit can occur and not by providing those constitutive rules that a player must follow in order to play. To some degree, players are free to feel for and institute their own forms of play. But, again, we must remember that through optimizing amendments to material constraints, in particular, and not necessarily through external regulations, governance has an internal relation to play in this environment. When a player accepts the constraints of a particular environment, a playground, as she must in order to play, she finds a match between her own ludic projects, even her aesthetic play voluntarily pursued, and a method of governance that seeks to let things happen. In this way, those rules and constraints that are ludigenic also can be governmental. In such a case, we can no longer think of the relation of play and governance as one of opposition, but should instead think of them as correlates. This means that the players of *Bodyspacemotionthings* are also players of the game of liberalism as it engages in the production and organization of freedoms. Their play is both governed and something they must want to do. The role of artistic playgrounds in securing this correlation, even as they also encourage aesthetic play, should not be underestimated, but, still, one wonders how the institutional facts of ruled play, should they have been established in the case of *Bodyspacemotionthings*, might have affected the operations of such governance.

Notes

1 Parts of this essay are taken from Chapter 6 of Stott (2015).
2 This observation was made by Tate curator Jessica Morgan during 'Fun and Games: The Gallery as Adult Play Centre', a panel discussion held on Friday 29 February 2008 at the Institute of Contemporary Arts, London (www.ica.org.uk/16819/60-Years-of-Curating-the-podcast/Fun-and-Games-The-Gallery-as-Adult-Play-Centre.html, accessed 18 September 2008).

References

Banham, R. (1971) 'It was SRO – and a disaster', *New York Times*, 23 May, 28.
Beardsley, M. (1958) *Aesthetics: Problems in the Philosophy of Criticism*, New York: Harcourt, Brace and World.
Bennett, T. (2005) 'Civic laboratories: Museums, cultural objecthood, and the governance of the social', *Cultural Studies*, 19(5/September), 521–47.
Bird, J. (1999) 'Minding the body: Robert Morris's 1971 Tate Gallery retrospective', in Bird, J. and Newman, M. (eds) *Rewriting Conceptual Art*, London: Reaktion Books.
Brett, G. (1971) 'Channelling energy', *The Times*, 11 May, 11.
Chauvier, S. (2007) *Qu'est-ce qu'un jeu?* Paris: Vrin.
Children's Play Council, PLAYLINK and National Playing Fields Association (2000) *Best Play: What Play Provision Should Do for Children*, London: NPFA.
Compton, M. and Sylvester, D. (1971) *Robert Morris*, London: Tate Gallery.
Csikszentmihalyi, M. and Bennett, S. (1971) 'An exploratory model of play', *American Anthropologist*, 73(1), 45–58.
Floe, H. (2014) 'Discover the rainbow in yourself? Three instances of play and pandemonium', 'Ludic Museum' conference, Tate Liverpool, 31 January–1 February 2014.
Foucault, M. (1975) *Surveiller et punir: Naissance de la prison*, Paris: Gallimard.
Foucault, M. (2004a) *Naissance de la biopolitique: Cours au Collège de France, 1978–1979*, Paris: Seuil/Gallimard.
Foucault, M. (2004b) *Sécurité, territoire, population: Cours au Collège de France, 1977–1978*, Paris: Seuil/Gallimard.
Hudson, M. (2009) 'Works of art you can get stuck into', *Daily Telegraph*, 26 May, 23.
Huizinga, J. (1955) *Homo Ludens: A Study of the Play Element in Culture*, Boston: Beacon Press.
Montaigne, M. de (1575–1580/2003) 'Apology for Raymond Sebond', *The Complete Works: Essays, Travel Journals, Letters*, transl. (2003) Frame, D. M., London: Everyman's Library.
Morris, R. (1968) 'Anti-form', *Artforum*, 6(8/April), 33–5.
Morris, R. (1969) 'Notes on Sculpture 4: Beyond objects', *Artforum*, 7(8/April), 50–54.
Morris, R. (1970/1993) 'Some notes on the phenomenology of making: The search for the motivated', *Artforum*, 8(8/April), 62–6, repr. in Morris, R. (1993) *Continuous Project Altered Daily: The Writings of Robert Morris*, Cambridge, MA: MIT Press.
Morris, R. (1997) 'Professional rules', *Critical Inquiry*, 23 (2), Winter: 298–321.
National Children's Office (2004) *Ready, Steady, Play! A National Play Policy*, Dublin: The Stationery Office.
Podro, M. (1982) *The Critical Historians of Art*, New Haven and London: Yale University Press.
Rawls, John (1955) 'Two concepts of rules', *The Philosophical Review*, 64(1/January), 3–32.

Rose, N. and Miller, P. (1992) 'Political power beyond the state: Problematics of government', *British Journal of Sociology*, 43(2/June), 173–205.

Searle, J. R. (1969) *Speech Acts: An Essay in the Philosophy of Language*, Cambridge: Cambridge University Press.

Stott, T. (2015) *Play and Participation in Contemporary Arts Practices*, London: Routledge.

7 Oasis of happiness – the play of the world and human existence
Eugen Fink's multidimensional concept of play

Núria Sara Miras Boronat

Eugen Fink and the phenomenological movement

'By playing, we celebrate our existence' (Fink, 1995: 414–15),[1] writes Eugen Fink in his last work on philosophical anthropology, *Grundphänomene des menschlichen Daseins* ('Fundamental phenomena of human existence', posthumous, first published in 1979).[2] In my view, this short sentence summarizes the multiple dimensions through which Fink approaches play in his thought: play as a symbol of the world; play as a phenomenon deeply rooted in human existence, understanding human existence as a particular form of being in the world that is celebrated by playing. On my way to reaching this conclusion, I will follow Fink's concept of play through different topics and at different points in time – i.e. by reconstructing the development of his thought and aiming to achieve the final synthesis of three different approaches: cosmology, philosophical anthropology and ontology, which build up a complex philosophical system (Fink 1995; Nielsen and Sepp 2006; Hilt 2011). The thesis defended here is that Fink's multidimensional concept of play is precisely what would allow a synthesis of these three philosophical fields of study.

Eugen Fink (born Konstanz, 1905; died Freiburg, 1975) was a German philosopher and pedagogue, one of the most complex and original thinkers of the phenomenological movement of the twentieth century. Though less well-known outside philosophical scholarship than other thinkers in this movement, such as Edmund Husserl and Martin Heidegger, his life and career were closely linked to theirs. To introduce him, I will briefly highlight some relevant aspects of Fink's biography which we know thanks to his daughter, Susanne (Fink 2006).

In 1929 Fink wrote his PhD thesis under the supervision of Husserl and Heidegger. His research topic was 'picture and the unreal'.[3] In normal circumstances, Fink would have had a brilliant career inside the German academy, but at an early stage of his academic development he was confronted with a very difficult decision. Husserl, his mentor, was a Jew who had retired from the University in 1930 as Professor Emeritus but continued to teach private seminars, in which Fink was very active. In 1933, the Nazi laws suspended Jews from all public service, and Fink was warned to distance himself from Husserl if he wanted to stay at the University. Out of friendship and loyalty, however, Fink continued to work for Husserl as his private assistant[4] until the latter's death in 1938. Together with Husserl's widow and the monk Leo van Breda, Fink saved Husserl's *Nachlass* from the Nazis and took his papers to Louvain, where he emigrated with his wife Martl. One of the photographs taken of Fink during this period depicts a handsome young man wearing a hat in the style of Humphrey Bogart;[5] the whole episode would have made a worthy 1940s *film noir*.

After World War II, Fink returned to Germany with his family. In 1948 he was appointed Professor of Philosophy and Educational Science at the University of Freiburg, where he founded the Husserl-Archive in 1950 and was in charge of several cultural institutions. Despite their opposite standpoints concerning the 'Husserl affair' and the vast differences in their political convictions, Fink maintained a lifelong friendship with Martin Heidegger, and in the winter term of 1966, they taught a joint seminar on Heraclitus in Freiburg which was considered 'legendary' among the philosophical scholarly community. Besides his philosophical mentors, Fink was also in close contact with other thinkers of the phenomenological movement, especially Jan Patočka,[6] Alfred Schütz,[7] Maurice Merleau-Ponty[8] and José Ortega y Gasset.[9] Fink's large philosophical work remained at the University of Freiburg.[10]

But what we do mean by the term 'phenomenology'? Phenomenology designates both a disciplinary field in philosophy and a philosophical school (of course, the first would have been impossible without the second). As a philosophical school, it was initiated by Brentano and Husserl and pursued to some extent by Heidegger, Sartre, Jaspers, Gadamer and Lévinas, among others (Gadamer, 1963/99; Spiegelberg, 1982; Sepp, 1988; Waldenfels, 1992; Lembeck, 2005; Zahavi, 2007). If Fink's work has not been as popular as that of the thinkers mentioned here, this may merely be due to the fact that his entire *oeuvre* is still to be published.[11] Other reasons may be Fink's rather peculiar style of writing and thinking and the complexity and variety of his interests, most of which went beyond phenomenology in the strict sense.

How do we justify putting all these philosophers together under the same heading, when at first sight they seem to be heterogeneous? Their common motto, as Gadamer (1963/99: 117) recalls, was: 'Back to the things in themselves!', meaning that philosophy has to be grounded in the primary sources of our perception. Thus, as a philosophical method, phenomenology is generally considered to be a method of description of phenomena, i.e. of things in the world as we experience them through the structures of our consciousness. The word 'phenomenon' presupposes a distinction between what things are in reality and how they appear to us. However, by focusing on phenomena as the basis of the science of being, phenomenology tries to avoid both the assumption that we can know things as they *really* are (naive realism) and the contrary assumption that the only access that we have to things is unavoidably the one guaranteed by our consciousness, and, therefore, we can only be certain about our ideas, not about their content (idealism). For phenomenology, these two extreme positions rely on an artificial separation between the subject (the entity who perceives) and the object (the entity perceived). Phenomenology considers that the two entities are indistinguishable in the act of perception.

This general assumption about knowledge can be considered the cornerstone for all phenomenologists. But as we have already seen, phenomenological scholarship includes a wide range of scholars with very different interests. Phenomenology has been described and defined in an infinity of ways by its practitioners.[12] Brentano, for instance, considered it as a sort of 'descriptive psychology'. One of the most concise and elegant definitions, in my view, is that of Lembeck, who describes phenomenology as 'work on facticity' (Lembeck, 2005: 5). In a recent introduction to phenomenology, Dan Zahavi (2007: 7–8) summarizes the main directions in which the philosophy is currently being pursued. Two of them appear to me to be particularly interesting for introducing Fink's work on phenomenology and play: the first is that phenomenology offers a model of human existence as a bodily, social and cultural being-in-the world, and the second is that it proposes the concrete analysis of phenomena which are relevant for other sciences, such as 'picture', 'encounter with foreign cultures', 'social structure', and so on.

These two general directions in phenomenology help us to understand why Fink's contribution to the concept of play should be named a 'phenomenology of play'. According to the first direction, the central assumption in Fink's thought, as we will see, is that human existence is conditioned by its natural, social and cultural character. His analyses of play as a human phenomenon take this into account. According to the second, Fink considers play as a crucial phenomenon which requires a structural and ontological analysis to elucidate its constitutive elements. In Fink's concept of play these two general phenomenological directions have, as we stated above, a threefold basis: cosmology, anthropology and ontology. Fink's approach to play is multidimensional: play as a metaphor or symbol of the world, as a core phenomenon of human existence, and as an ontologically distinct phenomenon.

The play of the world: cosmic play

The first dimension of play in Fink's thought is revealed by cosmology, the philosophical discipline that aims to give a philosophical explanation of the nature of the cosmos or universe. Thus, if play has a cosmological dimension, this means that the nature of play is related to the nature of the cosmos.

'Cosmic play' is a recurrent topic in Fink's thought, but I would like to pay special attention to his famous book on Nietzsche. For Fink, Nietzsche 'has the vision of the cosmos as a tragic play' (Fink, 2003: 13). Fink's references to play in his interpretation of Nietzsche are abundant and substantial, and they cover the majority of Nietzsche's works, from the *Birth of Tragedy* to *Zarathustra*. I will focus specifically on the passages in which Fink elucidates the Ancient Greek influences on Nietzsche's philosophy.

Cosmic play appears in one of Heraclitus's most famous and enigmatic fragments: '*Aion* is a child at play, playing draughts; the kingship is a child's'

(Heraclitus, 1962: xviii).[13] Nietzsche's explanation of this fragment in *The Birth of Tragedy* is that Heraclitus's metaphor likens the world's creative power 'to a playing child, who sets down stones here, there, and the next place, and who builds up piles of sand only to knock them down again'. (Nietzsche, 2007: 114). How is the metaphor to be interpreted? Is this innocent, free, purposeless play? Or is it capricious and arbitrary, with no sense of purpose? How can the image of a child playing be analogous to what intrinsically rules the world? For Nietzsche, only children and artists can play in the true spirit of the play of the world:

> In this world only play, play as artists and children engage in it, exhibits coming-to-be and passing away, structuring and destroying, without any moral additive, in forever equal innocence. And as children and artists play, so plays the ever-living fire. It constructs and destroys, all in innocence. Such is the game that the aeon plays with itself. Transforming itself into water and earth, it builds towers of sand like a child at the seashore, piles them up and tramples them. From time to time it starts the game anew. An instant of satiety – and again it is seized by its need, as the artist is seized by his need to create.
> (Nietzsche, 1988: 62)

This is the sense of the analogy: things in the world are in perpetual change: appearing, disappearing, transforming or evolving. Only play can represent this endless creativity of movement that is carried out only by means of its intrinsic force, as the artist creates her work.[14] This, for Fink, is 'Nietzsche's metaphysical intuition' (Fink, 2011: 37). The metaphor of the child playing finds a broader context within Zarathustra's doctrine of the eternal return. In Nietzsche's appropriation of the eternal return, Fink sees a whole new interpretation of life built upon a new cosmology (Fink, 2003: 160–1). Children's and artists' play is the key concept to express the very essence of the world:

> Nietzsche makes the human playing, the playing of the child and the artist into a key concept for the universe. It becomes a cosmic metaphor. This does not mean that the human ontological modality is uncritically applied to being in its entirety. Rather vice versa: the human essence can only be conceived and determined through play if man is conceived in its ecstatic openness towards the existing world and not simply as a thing among other things within the cosmos distinguished by the faculties of mind and reason.
> (Fink, 2003: 171)

The new cosmology that understands life in the universe as perpetual becoming (Fink sometimes calls it 'ontology of becoming') allows a new perspective on the human's place in the cosmos. Only when we understand the play of the world and the play of the being as a kind of artistic freedom, as a work of art that creates and recreates itself, can we be open to the great game that occurs in front of us and of which we are a part. This comprehension of cosmic play leads us to Nietzsche's formula of the *amor fati*, i.e. loving and embracing our own destiny. *Amor fati* is 'the will that does not resign itself to fate, but participates in the cosmic play' (Fink, 2003: 172). Participating means accepting play as a positive dimension of freedom, understanding 'the playful, risky dimension of human existence' (Fink, 2003: 62).[15] *Amor fati* is defined by the playful attitude of children and artists at play that can say 'yes' to the world:

> The child is innocence and forgetting, a new beginning, a game, a wheel rolling out of itself, a first movement, a sacred yes-saying.
> Yes, for the game of creation my brothers a sacred yes-saying is required.
> The spirit wants *its* will, the one lost to the world now wins *its own* world.
>
> (Nietzsche, 2006: 17)

Play as a fundamental phenomenon of human existence

Fink's reading of the Nietzschean *amor fati* may be a good example of his rich and suggestive philosophical style. As I stated above, cosmic play as a metaphor of the world's dynamic is just a preliminary step on the way towards a more comprehensive system. Grasping this ontology of becoming as play is accompanied by an attitude towards it as openness to an infinite movement of re-creation. It is interesting to note that the metaphor builds upon a representation of a very common human situation: a child just playing draughts (in Heraclitus's version) or making sandcastles (in the Nietzschean one). This image helps us to understand the intrinsic movement of the universe as a vast game with energies and materials. The anthropomorphic[16] vision of the world's play allows us a glimpse of how things go. But can this vision tell us something about human play? Why is play the only human activity that allows this understanding of the world? How is play related to other human activities?

Fink's approach to this question is a part of a system of philosophical anthropology. Philosophical anthropology, generally speaking, is a field within philosophy that tries to elucidate the specificity of the human being before other types of being. It is not, as Fink understands it, an effort to summarize all the contributions made by the positive sciences (such as medicine, psychology, ethnology, sociology, history, etc.) on the comprehension of man; neither is it a foundation programme for these sciences (Fink, 1995: 24–5). That was the justification of traditional philosophy, to serve as a foundation for any possible science. Another traditional assumption that Fink rejects is the one that sees the human being as a being between natural beings, and God as a medium between these two realms of being. Furthermore, Fink's approach tries to avoid the constant comparison with other forms of life (natural or transcendent) that we find in the tradition of Western metaphysics. Fink wants to ground a philosophical anthropology rooted in what distinguishes the human kind of being; therefore, he sometimes uses the term 'ontology of the human being' (Fink, 1995: 436).

For Fink, human existence is the only form of existence that searches for sense in living (animals cannot give sense to their existence, gods have no need to), and so he attempts a 'radical earthly anthropology based upon the self-interpretation of the human existence'. (Fink, 1995: 29). It is not only reason that characterizes the specificity of human existence, it is the fact that all human existence is open to the inescapable mystery of being, open to the world of objects and open to the interpretation of its own situation. Fink seeks to reveal the fundamental structure of human existence attending to the fact that this existence is specifically the one that refers to itself by interpreting itself (Fink, 1995: 85). To sum up: this approach is anthropological, because it focuses on the existence of human beings, and it is philosophical because it is an interpretation of existence by which existence transforms the self-evident in its existence into questionable.

The structure of human existence is equated to what Fink calls 'the fundamental phenomena of human existence'. These phenomena are: death, work, power, love and play. In other words: the human being is essentially a worker, a player, a lover, a fighter and a mortal (Fink, 1995: 106). Why are these phenomena 'fundamental' and 'fundamentally human'? By 'fundamental' Fink understands a phenomenon that occurs in any individual human existence by which this existence finds itself referring to objects, nature and other human existences. They are fundamental because they cannot be reduced to any other phenomenon, in spite of being intrinsically related to each other. And all of them share another important characteristic: they are all twofold, sometimes ambiguous; they are the expression of deep human contradictions. Death belongs to our condition; we are constantly confronted with our own finitude; work represents our struggle for survival against nature; power represents the struggle for or against domination; love or *eros* is the way we individuals transcend our individual finitude through the perpetuation of the species. And play stands for reference to our imagined, projected possibilities.

Unfortunately, the phenomenological and ontological argumentation for the fundamental phenomena cannot be reproduced in this space. One might be surprised by the list proposed by Fink. It is clear that work and power are exclusively social and historical phenomena and, as such, fundamentally human. In Fink's view, animals and gods do not present any equivalent form of organization to the state or to the world of work, being both the result of very complex historical and social processes. We can also accept that love or erotic behaviour has specifically human traits. But how can it be that, according to Fink's programme of philosophical anthropology, death and play are essentially human phenomena? He is not denying the undeniable fact that animal forms of life are also mortal. What Fink is saying is that human beings are the only beings in nature that relate consciously to this natural fact and can reflect on the whole sense of their existence in the knowledge of this fact. For this reason he asserts that only humans can *die*. And he gives the same reason for rejecting animal play;[17] Fink argues that only humans can play because play is the genuine production of symbolic meaning.

Play belongs to the realm of fantasy. It is 'the fundamental form of the human dealing with the possible and the unreal' (Fink, 1995: 360). This is for Fink a human paradox: that we spend our lives projecting possibilities 'in the future realization of our desires and expectations; that those expectations and desires are rarely fulfilled … but that we can always find an "oasis of happiness" when we forget our struggling, postpone our striving, and just play' (Fink, 1995: 362). In play we can be whatever we want, we can choose our companions, and we can decide when play starts and when it ends. Play is the *representative* human phenomenon *par excellence* because it can bring every human situation to life.[18] As Fink states in a later work: 'We play with the serious, the authentic, the real. We play with work and struggle, love and death. We even play with play'. (Fink, 1960: 101). Therefore play is not just one human activity among many; it is the most basic and fundamental phenomenon and its special status is due to its unique and extra-ordinary nature.

Oasis of happiness: ontology and the structural analysis of play

The ontology of play was addressed by Fink a couple of years later in a short essay called *Oase des Glücks. Gedanken zu einer Ontologie des Spiels* ('Oasis of Happiness: Thoughts on an Ontology of Play', 1957). 'Ontology' is, in Fink's terms, the study of play as a substantive reality, its elements and structure. Why does he use the metaphor of 'oasis of happiness' to elucidate the nature of play? The metaphor expresses that play is a 'secure point of evasion that allows us to stay (briefly) in the present' (Fink, 2010: 18). But Fink does not want to reduce play to the traditional view that identifies it with leisure or with time out from work or serious life. This view has been defended by a tradition of scholars of play who ascribed to it very important biological and social functions such as rest, experimentation, or aesthetic enjoyment of the arts.[19] For Fink the relevance of play goes beyond a functional analysis of it.

Play is an autonomous activity that we pursue with no reference to an external purpose because it has 'only internal finalities which do not transcend' (Fink, 1960: 100). Fink subscribes to a view that is widely held in the study of play, which sees play as autotelic. The absence of an external goal is a perspective of play from outside. What can be said about play's inner structure? The structural analysis pursued by Fink yields the following elements of play: delight, meaning, community, rules, equipment and play-world.

Fink's analysis of play tries to identify not only its constitutive elements but also its inherent ambivalence. For understanding this I suggest rephrasing Fink's structural elements in more general categories. The structure of play is thus explained through the following components: emotions, sociality, rules, objects and play-world. Play is necessarily bound to emotions; there is a 'passion of the soul' (Fink, 1960: 102). From the perspective of the player, the range of the emotions we can experience is quite broad. Take, for example, tragic play, where we may even cry or feel distress when we identify ourselves with the role we are playing. But deep inside we are always conscious of the double dimension of play: what must prevail is *delight* (*Spiellust*), the possibility of moving in the interplay of the freedom and opportunities that play creates.

Fink sees play essentially as a social phenomenon, as something rooted in every social existence. Play is playing together, playing *with* someone. Even in solitary play, the player 'is often playing with imaginary partners' (Fink, 1960: 102). Play institutes *community (Spielgemeinschaft)*, even when the community is not a real but a potential one (e.g. spectators, or future or imaginary players). As in any human community, there is an indeterminate space for creativity in accordance with the *rules* (*Spielregel*) that are freely accepted by the members of the community. There is no play without rules; rules create play. Fink says something very interesting here concerning the normative status of rules in the game: breaking the rules is not the same as breaking the law in ordinary life. The kind of sanctions and the consequences of contravening the agreed prescriptions are qualitatively different. Breaking the law in normal life can have unpleasant consequences; breaking the rules of play means stopping the game (or even starting a new one).

We use objects for play: play-equipment or *play-things* (*Spielzeug*). But play-things are not only artificial objects; we may use ordinary objects in an extraordinary way. What makes an object a play-thing is not its natural properties but how we interact with it. Therefore, play-things entail two types of properties that overlap with each other: the 'real' object, with its natural, intrinsic properties, and the 'magical' property we may ascribe to it in play. For example, within the realm of natural objects a wooden stick is just a piece of wood, but at the same time in a particular play-world it can be a magic wand which is able to cast spells, move things, and so on.

But above all, play is a creation of meaning (*Spielsinn*). The final and most important part of Fink's structural analysis is devoted to this crucial feature of play: its symbolic, magical aspect, the constitution of a play-world that blurs the lines between reality and fiction (Fink, 2010: 22). Here Fink introduces a new term in relation to play: the *speculative*. 'Speculative' here means a specific type of *reproducing or representing*. The 'speculative' is a mirroring of the world performed by something which is structurally equivalent to the world. In this sense, play is a *symbol of the world*. Fink reminds us that there have been other symbols of the world in the history of philosophy. Philosophers of the past have identified particular objects or entities with the essence of the world:[20] for instance, Thales said that 'everything is water'; for Plato 'everything is light' and for Hegel 'everything is spirit'. These symbols are more than a simple picture of the world: they structurally represent the world's inner and constitutive force.

How is it possible that human play can act as the *mirror of the world*, i.e. *reflect the world's inner essence*? This mirroring is not a simple *imitation*, but a revelation of world's deep structure, which is common with the structure of human play (ontology of play) and therefore with the structure of human existence (philosophical anthropology). Play is a kind of activity by which humans can create worlds of meaning (and destroy them) only through a creative force coming from the inside. Play is also pure movement; it presents phenomena in a constitutive order that reflects what it is and what it is not. Play reproduces the dialectic interplay of being and nothingness. Play is also representative, for it can represent any other human action (even play itself can be a part of larger play). Play is the relation to all the possible relations and references in human existence (Fink, 1995: 408).

The circle made up of cosmology, anthropology and ontology is closed by Fink's 'speculative concept of play'. I have tried to present this circle following a natural order, but in Fink we do not find any indication that there is a linear ranking among these three aspects of play. We can reach the core of the matter starting from any of them, as if we were following a Möbius strip. At the end of this journey, we can see why Fink places play not only at the basis of human existence but also at the heart of philosophy (Fink, 1960: 3). Philosophy, like play, stands for our openness to the world and for the possibility of interpreting our existence in its multiple dimensions.

Notes

1 The original says 'Der Mensch spielt, wo er das Dasein feiert'. I have tried to find a more suggestive translation than a literal one, which could be 'Human beings play where they celebrate their existence'.
2 Following San Martín (2006), his work on anthropology should be understood as a philosophical project in two stages, the first one corresponding to *Natur, Freiheit und Welt* (seminar lessons offered in 1951 and 1952); the second one to be developed in the aforementioned *Grundphänomene des menschlichen Daseins* (1955). In this chapter I am only referring to this second stage.
3 The title of his Dissertation is *Vergegenwärtigung und Bild. Beiträge zu einer Phänomenologie der Unwirklichkeit* ('Picture and Presence: Contribution to a Phenomenology of the Unreal'). It was reprinted shortly afterwards under the long title 'Contributions to a Phenomenological Analysis of the Psychological Phenomena Conceived under the Following Denominations: "Think as if", "Imagine Something" or "Fantasy"' (*Beiträge zu einer phänomenologischen Analyse der psychischen Phänomene, die unter den vieldeutigen Titel 'sich denken als ob' 'Sich etwas bloß vorstellen, 'Phantasie' befaßt werden*, 1930). This first work already shows Fink's lifelong interest in the phenomena of the imaginary and of the symbolic.
4 This collaboration with Husserl was intense and fruitful; see in Brunzina (2004).
5 Some pictures of Eugen Fink are available online at the website of the Philosophisches Seminar at the University of Mainz. See Fink (2006).
6 Patočka was one of the promoters of the Charta 77, a Czech human rights movement. He died after being interrogated by the police for 10 hours. One of his most influential works is *Heretical Essays in the Philosophy of History* (1975).
7 Like many other intellectuals, Schütz emigrated to the United States in 1939. His work was devoted to the phenomenological foundation of social science. *The Phenomenology of the Social World* (1932) is considered to be his major contribution to both phenomenology and social science.
8 Merleau-Ponty's major contribution to phenomenology was his work *Phenomenology of Perception* (1945), in which he developed an 'ontology of the flesh'.
9 Ortega y Gasset was a Spanish philosopher who introduced the phenomenological movement into the Spanish-speaking countries.

10 The critical edition of his work is currently being published by the Verlag Karl Alber under the auspices of the Eugen Fink Forschungsstelle of the Johannes Gutenberg Universität Mainz. The project started in 2005. I am grateful to Stephan Grätzel and Annette Hilt of the University of Mainz for their valuable advice concerning Fink's thought.

11 The complete critical edition of Fink's work will comprise 30 volumes (Nielsen and Sepp, 2006). My impression is that Fink's contribution to phenomenology and philosophy is already being acknowledged, but he is read far less than his mentors, Husserl and Heidegger, or than other contemporary phenomenologists such as Sartre and Lévinas. By the time Fink turned 60, some of his works had been translated into Spanish, French, English, Italian and Japanese, which means that he was beginning to reach a larger audience worldwide (see von Hermann, 1970). However, I find it significant that, for instance, Wall proposes a 'revised phenomenology of play' after considering the most influential phenomenologies of play, those of Heidegger, Gadamer and Derrida: Fink is not mentioned as a phenomenologist of play even though he paid much more attention to play as an ontologically distinctive phenomenon than the others and his view is closest to Richard Kerney's proposal, which Wall takes as an example of his own developmental perspective, that 'play is the endless imagination of life's unfolding possibilities' (Wall, 2013: 39). Nor is Fink mentioned in the compilation of definitions of play by Salen and Zimmermann (2004). This absence could be due to the fact that Fink's reception is still, so to speak, under construction.

12 See Smith (2013). It could be said that Husserl's project, his entire life and effort, was devoted to the definition of what phenomenology should be.

13 'Aion' could be translated as 'time', but there is no consensus within the scholarly community about the exact meaning of the term. More on this enigmatic fragment in Aichele (2000).

14 Homan (2013) develops the analogy between play and the metaphysics of the artist in Nietzsche in a very interesting direction.

15 Fink's 1946 text entitled 'Nietzsches Metaphysik des Spiels' is a very valuable condensation of other insights of his into play. It includes reflections that are developed further in other longer essays, but it is extraordinary complex. I consider Fink's later *Nietzsche's Philosophy* a more mature work that expands on the insights of this earlier attempt.

16 In Fink we find a strong thesis about play: only humans can play in a genuine way, therefore we can only speak metaphorically of the 'play of animals' or 'the play of gods' (Fink, 2010: 13). In this sense, he remains at a non-empirical level, quite distinct to other approaches prior to his work, such as those of Buytendijk (1933) or Gulick (2011). Fink justifies this decision by appealing to the announced program of a philosophical anthropology, seeking a grounding structure for all empirical manifestations of play. Another reason for rejecting the play of animals and gods is that play is a genuine production of meaning and therefore only a being whose entire life is self-interpretation has the imaginative resources to produce meaning.

17 See note 16.

18 This is true especially in tragic play, in theatre and in other human forms of representation such as ritual and festival. Fink plays here with the many meanings and derivates of the German word *Spiel*: *Schau-spiel* (theatrical performance) or *Schau-bühne des Lebens* (play and life as a drama, play as staging life. See Fink (1995: 384, 406).

19 For instance, Karl Groos (1922) uses three concepts to explain the benefits of play: *Erholung* (rest, amusement, relaxation, break), *Entspannung* (relaxation, recreation), *Ergänzung* (complement, addition).

20 A symbol is more than a mere imitation or mirroring in the sense of the ancient *mimesis*. In the case of play, we cannot take it as a 'picture of the world'. For Fink this is a crucial aspect of play as a symbol of the world: a picture is a product, a result of the representation whereas play is the act of *producing meaning*, an act of mediation (Fink, 1960: 111).

References

Aichele, A. (2000) *Philosophie als Spiel: Platon, Kant, Nietzsche*, Berlin: Akademie Verlag.
Brunzina, R. (2004) *Edmund Husserl and Eugen Fink. Beginnings and Ends in Phenomenology 1928–1938*, New Haven and London: Yale University Press.
Buytendijk, F. J. J. (1933) *Wesen und Sinn des Spiels. Das Spielen des Menschen und der Tiere als Erscheinungsform der Lebenstriebe*, Berlin: Kurt Wollf Verlag/Der Neue Geist Verlag.
Fink, E. (1957) *Oase des Glücks. Gedanken zu einer Ontologie des Spiels*, Freiburg: Alber.
Fink, E. (1960) 'The ontology of play', *Philosophy Today*, 4(2), 95–109.
Fink, E. (1995) *Grundphänomene des menschlichen Daseins*, Freiburg am Breisgau and Munich: Karl Alber.
Fink, E. (2003) *Nietzsche's Philosophy*, London: Continuum.
Fink, E. (2010) *Spiel als Weltsymbol*, Freiburg am Breisgau and Munich: Karl Alber.
Fink, E. (2011) 'Nietzsches Metaphysik des Spiels', in Nielsen, C. and Sepp, H. R. (eds) *Welt denken. Annäherungen an die Kosmologie Eugen Finks*, Freiburg am Breisgau: Karl Alber, 25–37.
Fink, S. (2006) 'Die Biographie Eugen Finks', in Böhmer, A. (ed.) *Eugen Fink. Sozialphilosophie, Anthropologie, Kosmologie, Pädagogik, Methodik*, Würzburg: Königshausen and Neumann, 267–77, available at: www.blogs.uni-mainz.de/fb05philosophie/forschungsstellen-und-weitere-einrichtungen/fs_eugenfink/biographie/ (accessed 31 August 2014).
Gadamer, H.-G. (1963/1999) 'Die phänomenologische Bewegung (1963)', in *Gesammelte Werke. Neuere Philosophie I*, Tübingen: Mohr Siebeck, 105–46.
Groos, K. (1922) *Das Spiel. Zwei Vorträge*, Jena: Verlag von Gustav Fischer.
Gulick, L. H. (2011) *A Philosophy of Play*, Charleston: BiblioLife.
Heraclitus (1962) *The Cosmic Fragments*, Cambridge: Cambridge University Press.
Hilt, A. (2011) 'Mimetische Ereignisse. Bildlichkeit und der Spielraum der Unwirklichkeit zwischen Sein, Mensch und Welt', in Fabris, A., Lossi, A. and Perone, U. (eds) *Bild als Prozess. Neue Perspektiven einer Phänomenologie des Sehens*, Würzburg: Königshausen and Neumann, 55–70.
Homan, C. (2013) 'Whoever cannot give, also receives nothing: Nietzsche's playful spectator', in Ryall, E., Russell, W. and MacLean, M. (eds) *Philosophy of Play*, London: Routledge, 98–108.
Lembeck, K.-H. (2005) *Einführung in die phänomenologisch Philosophie*, Darmstadt: WBG.
Nielsen, C. and Sepp, H. R. (2006) 'Das Projekt einer Gesamtausgabe der Werke Eugen Finks', in Böhmer, A. (ed.) *Eugen Fink. Sozialphilosophie, Anthropologie, Kosmologie, Pädagogik, Methodik*, Würzburg: Königshausen and Neumann, 286–93.
Nietzsche, F. (1988) *Philosophy in the Tragic Age of the Greeks*, Washington: Regnery Publishing.
Nietzsche, F. (2006) *Thus Spoke Zarathustra: A Book for All and None*, Cambridge: Cambridge University Press.
Nietzsche, F. (2007) *The Birth of Tragedy and other Writings*, Cambridge: Cambridge University Press.
Salen, K. and Zimmerman, E. (2004) *Rules of Play: Game Design Fundamentals*, Cambridge, MA: MIT Press.
San Martín, J. (2006) 'Natur und Verfassung des Menschen. Zur Anthropologie Eugen Finks', in Böhmer, A. (ed.) *Eugen Fink. Sozialphilosophie, Anthropologie, Kosmologie, Pädagogik, Methodik*, Würzburg: Königshausen and Neumann, 114–27.

Sepp, H. R. (1988) *Edmund Husserl und die phänomenologische Bewegung. Zeugnisse in Text und Bild*, Freiburg am Breisgau: Karl Alber.

Sepp, H. R. (2006) 'Totalhorizont – Zeitspielraum. Übergänge in Husserls und Finks Bestimmung von Welt', in Böhmer, A. (ed.) *Eugen Fink. Sozialphilosophie, Anthropologie, Kosmologie, Pädagogik, Methodik*, Würzburg: Königshausen and Neumann, 154–72.

Smith, D. W. (2013) 'Phenomenology', in Zalta, E. N. (ed.) *Stanford Encyclopedia of Philosophy*, available at: http://plato.stanford.edu/archives/win2013/entries/phenomenology/ (accessed 31 August 2014).

Spiegelberg, H. (1982) *The Phenomenological Movement*, Dordrecht: Kluwer.

Von Hermann, F. W. (1970) *Bibliographie Eugen Fink*, Den Haag: Martinus Nijhoff.

Waldenfels, B. (1992) *Einführung in die Phänomenologie*, Paderborn: W. Fink.

Wall, J. (2013) 'All the world's a stage: Childhood and the play of being', E. Ryall, Russell, W. and MacLean, M. (eds) *Philosophy of Play*, London: Routledge, 32–43.

Zahavi, D. (2007) *Phänomenologie für Einsteiger*, Paderborn: W. Fink.

8 Homer and competitive play

Daniel A. Dombrowski[1]

Introduction

What is sport? What ought it to be? In the present chapter I will try to make a contribution to the scholarly tradition that responds to questions such as these with the answer: competitive play. (See a longer version of the present chapter in Dombrowski, 2012.)

I have a twofold purpose. First, an understanding of sport's general character as competitive play can help us to read Homer more insightfully. Second, this reading will boomerang back to us to further illuminate the contemporary thesis of sport as competitive play as developed through the method of reflective equilibrium. Because present-day efforts to understand what sport is and ought to be are in many ways continuous with those of the ancient Greeks (indeed much contemporary thinking about sport is historical thinking that is often unknowingly taken over from the ancient Greeks), it will be fruitful to move from contemporary philosophy of sport to Homer and back again in a way that mutually illuminates these two concerns (see Miller, 2004a, 2004b).

Something like the questions mentioned above have been around for a long time. The first great works of literature in Western civilization, Homer's *Iliad* and *Odyssey* from the ancient Greek period about 3,000 years ago, depict sporting events at least three times. In each of these episodes we seem to get different responses to our questions. (References to Homer will be from the Rouse translations, Homer, 2007a and 2007b; for the Greek text I will use the Loeb editions, Homer, 1954 and 1960.) The first episode involves 'pickup' games which suggest that sport is a type of pure play and is nonserious. The second suggests that sport is competitive play, which involves a blend of seriousness and nonseriousness, strange as that sounds. William James had this approach in mind when he spoke of sport as the moral equivalent to (immoral) war or as a moral replacement for war. But the third episode suggests that sport is ultra-serious, even warlike. As George Orwell urged in opposition to James, sport *is* war by other means (see James, 1984; Orwell, 1968).

Their delight was in dancing

After the sack of Troy, Odysseus eventually washed ashore in Phaiacia and was tended by the princess of that land, Nausicaa. The king, Alcinoos, invited this stranger (who was not known to be the famous Odysseus) to some sport events so as to convince the stranger of the Phaiacians' prowess. After the Phaiacians had participated in a footrace, wrestling, the long jump, the discus and boxing, attention shifted to the stranger so as to determine if he had any ability. The fact that the stranger had endured hardships at sea led some of the Phaiacians to be sceptical, despite the fact that Athena had graced Odysseus with some additional size and strength for the occasion.

Here Odysseus faced a dilemma. On the one hand, the common assumption among the thousands who were assembled seemed to be that there was no greater glory for the living than that found in sport victory. On the other hand, Odysseus was weighed down with matters that were more serious than mere games in that his ship was being prepared for his renewed quest to make it home to Ithaca.

Odysseus submitted to the test because his initial reluctance to participate gave the (mistaken) impression that he was not interested in sport. Indeed, he wished to respond to the taunt that suggested that he had no sport ability. Specifically, he picked up a discus and hurled it far beyond the distance covered by the previous discus throwers. This feat was even more impressive given the fact that his discus was heavier than those used previously. In the ancient discus event, the weight would get progressively heavier with each throw, but Odysseus went immediately to the heaviest discus.

His success with the discus led him to challenge anyone present to a contest in other events: boxing, wrestling, running or archery (his boast regarding this last event presaged the deadly archery contest at the end of the *Odyssey*). His only fear concerned the footrace because his adventures at sea had debilitated his legs; but his upper body strength remained intact and hence gave him confidence regarding his ability to box and wrestle and shoot arrows.

There was no occasion, however, for Odysseus to prove himself in any events in addition to the discus due to the friendly intervention of Alcinoos. Herein lies the nonseriousness of the sport events of the Phaiacians. Despite the fact that the infinitive *athleuein* (to compete for a prize) and its cognates are used frequently in Book 8 of the *Odyssey*, no prizes were awarded for victory. The gifts that Odysseus received were rather due to the fact that he was a stranger of noble (perhaps even divine) birth and the Phaiacians wanted to show hospitality to such a guest. That is, they were more serious about hospitality than they were about sport.

Whereas previously it was hyperbolically asserted that the Phaiacians were the best competitors in the world, Alcinoos makes it clear that this boast cannot be redeemed. In fact, they were not at all very good at boxing and wrestling. Rather, their areas of expertise were dancing and oarsmanship. It should be noted here that rowing was not an ancient sport. The oarsmanship in question referred to the obviously serious and practical activity of seafaring, which was required if Odysseus was to return home with the help of 52 Phaiacian rowers.

The 'twinkling feet' of the Phaiacian dancers, including those of two of Alcinoos' sons, put a ludic end to the sport events and make us realize that the whole affair has something of a picnic aura to it. The Phaiacians, it turns out, loved music, dancing, plenty of clean linen (Nausicaa and her attendants were cleaning laundry and playing with a ball when she first encountered Odysseus in Book 6) and a warm bath more than any victory in sport. As part of their dance, one of Alcinoos' sons would toss a ball into the air and another son would catch it. There were no ancient sporting events that were what we would call ball games. The Phaiacians seemed to be saying, to put the point colloquially, 'we are not great at sports, but we like to play hackysack'. Their initial 'trash talking' about their prowess in sport was a bluff. They really liked frolic.

Before leaving the Phaiacians, I should mention the interlude in Book 8 provided by Demodocos, the blind minstrel who stood for Homer himself. He told the story of Hephaestus capturing with a net his wife Aphrodite and her lover Ares in the sex act. In addition to the obvious reference to Odysseus's future 'capture' of Penelope's suitors, the sport metaphor should not be lost. Hephaestus was lame and walked with a limp, but he had prodigious strength in his arms, much like Odysseus himself. The fact that Hephaestus nonetheless caught Ares, the quickest of the gods, with a clever net conformed to Odysseus's own wiles. And the fact that all of the gods (except Poseidon, Odysseus's enemy) laughed at the sight of Aphrodite and Ares caught (literally) in the act was indicative of the ludic character of the Phaiacian games in general in that the Phaiacians themselves were no doubt amused by Demodocos' tale.

Smothered in blood and filth

Back in Ithaca, Penelope's suitors were also engaged in frolic, specifically in draughts, quoits, or amusing themselves by frivolously tossing the discus or javelin (Rouse translation of the *Odyssey*: 6, 55, 214). When Odysseus did eventually make it home (in disguise) after his 20-year absence, his principal task was to find a way into his palace and then to find a way to eliminate the suitors who wanted to replace him both on the throne and in bed with Penelope. Actually there was a preliminary fight before the big fight in Books 21–22. In order to gain entry into the palace, Odysseus had to defeat the town beggar in a boxing match in Book 18. He won handily by striking the beggar's neck under the ear, thereby breaking his jaw and causing blood to gush out of the beggar's mouth. But this was merely a warmup bout, so to speak.

At the end of Book 19 Penelope revealed the contest that would have to be won in order to have her hand in marriage. The winner would have to string Odysseus's bow (which in itself was quite a task), then shoot an arrow through the open spaces in 12 axeheads, which would be lined up along the royal hall like trestles for a ship's keel. Little did the suitors know, however, that their 'prize' (*athlos*) was to be nothing less than death.

Book 21 of the *Odyssey* gives us a view of sport competition that is at the other extreme from that found in the ludic games of the Phaiacians. Even the origins of Odysseus's great bow involved blood: it was a gift to Odysseus from his friend Iphitos shortly before Iphitos was slaughtered by the great sport figure among the gods, Heracles.

Out of love for his parents, Odysseus and Penelope, young Telemachus tried to string the bow but failed. Then Antinoos and several of Penelope's suitors tried to do so but also failed, even after the bow was warmed and became more pliable. Finally Odysseus asked for a chance to string the bow. Because he was still disguised in rags, he was initially denied the opportunity to do so in that sport events in ancient Greece were the provenance of the nobility. But Penelope, who was playing the game well, insisted that the stranger in rags be given a chance. Wily Odysseus nonetheless also needed guile in order to achieve his goal; he had his old swineherd Eumaios deliver the bow and a quiver of arrows to him.

The rest, as they say, is history. With the ease of a harpist who strings a musical instrument, Odysseus strung the sheepgut over the pegs at each end of the bow. Then he took out an arrow from the quiver and on the first try won the contest by shooting the arrow through all of the axeheads.

With the bow and quiver in hand, his true purpose is evidenced in Book 22. The next shot in 'the great game' went directly through Antinoos' throat, bringing blood through his nostrils. The remaining suitors assumed that Odysseus had hit Antinoos by accident, hence they pleaded that the event should end, but Odysseus proceeded to let the arrows fly and to supplement his archery skill with his prowess at close fighting with spears and a sword that had been smuggled to him by Telemachus and Eumaios. Only the minstrel (a symbol of Homer himself) was spared.

When Odysseus saw all the bodies that were killed he momentarily smiled for the very first time in the epic. The suitors' bodies looked like a great haul of fish caught in a net, which reminds us of Hephaestus' device mentioned above. Even the women who had previously behaved disgracefully with the suitors were killed, indeed murdered.

Smothered in blood and filth, Odysseus took on the look of a lion that had just ripped apart a bullock. The most odious of the suitors, Melanthios, was stripped of his nose, ears and testicles, which were fed to the dogs. Even in this deadly game, however, there was a peculiar sense of propriety involved in that Odysseus refused to gloat over those who had been brought low, in partial contrast to the smile mentioned in the previous paragraph. The suitors' defeat was due as much to divine anger at their wicked deeds as it was to Odysseus's ability.

Fair play

Whereas the archery contest at the end of the *Odyssey* moved from sport competition to violence, the games dedicated to Patroclos in Book 23 of the *Iliad* involved the transition from violence to sport competition. Hence these latter games have a very different feel from the bloody archery contest described in the previous section and a somewhat different feel from the ludic games of the Phaiacians. The frolic on the beach with Nausicaa contrasts with the exhaustion and mourning on the beach after the fight against the Trojans. The context in the *Iliad* is the recent defeat of the Trojans by the Greeks, but at the expense of Patroclos' life. Because Patroclos was so admired by the Greeks, the sands were drenched with their tears. By contrast, Achilles desired that the slain Trojan warrior Hector be fed to the dogs, as in the aforementioned fate of Melanthios in the *Odyssey*.

Patroclos had come to live with Achilles' family as a youth after he had committed manslaughter as a result of a silly quarrel over knucklebones. So the overall context of Book 23 of the *Iliad* involves the contrast between the really serious (death in war) and the mistakenly serious (a dice game). After years of service as Achilles' attendant, Patroclos came to be loved by Achilles, such that when Patroclos died in battle Achilles mourned his loss the way a father would mourn the loss of a son.

How best to memorialize the loss of Patroclos? Achilles could think of no better way of doing this than through sport contests staged in Patroclos' name. It is these games that come closest in Homer to capturing the details and spirit of the ancient Olympic games in that the Patroclos games were energetic, yet friendly; the winners were given special prizes so as to call attention to their excellence; many of the games were the same as those in the Olympic games; and prohibitions against cheating were robust. I will argue that the Patroclos games, in contrast to the Phaiacian and Penelope games, best enable us to respond adequately to the two questions at the top of the present chapter.

Eight games are described, with the vast majority of attention given to the chariot race. Unlike the Olympic games, where only first-place finishers were rewarded, Achilles offered prizes out of his own coffers to all of the participants, signalling the cooperative character of the games. Although the fact that everyone received prizes seems to militate against the competitive nature of the games, the fact that the prizes were graded preserves the sense that excellence should be acknowledged. And Achilles' prizes were worth quite a lot, as they were in the Olympic games. In the chariot race, for example, he was prepared to award the participants cauldrons, tripods, horses, mules, cattle, and skilled women to perform household chores.

Achilles' magnanimity did not prevent him from presenting his own (perhaps accurate) assessment of his sport ability: if he were to compete in these games he and his horses would be the clear victors. But due to his grief over Patroclos' death, he sat out. As before, however, in contrast to the archery contest at the end of the *Odyssey*, where the ludic element is almost completely extinguished, there is definitely a play spirit that is present in the Patroclos games. The participants, along with Achilles himself, seem to be saying: Patroclos is dead, but we are alive, so let's race!

The chariot race was won by Tydeides, whose horses were the fastest, so he won by 'merit'. But the biggest drama and the most philosophically interesting part of the chariot race surrounded the competition for second place between Antilochos and Menelaos. The issue concerned cheating. Antilochos was given extended advice from his father, Nestor, regarding how to do better in the race than the speed, or lack thereof, of his horses would dictate. Nestor's advice was basically to use every trick of the trade in the search for victory. Specifically Antilochos was advised to have his horses turn the corner as tightly as possible, even if such a manoeuvre would endanger the driver and horses who would be passed at this crucial point in the course.

The joy of sport (see Novak, 1976), in contrast to the dread of war, was exhibited by the drivers at the starting point, who stood in their baskets with hearts beating high in hope. These hopes were dashed early for Eumelos, however, whose yoke was broken by Athena, leaving his horses to run away. That is, it was not only human beings who were known to cheat in sporting events, but also the gods. Athena was the ultimate cause of Tydeides winning and Eumelos finishing last, although there is still much that is of interest in tracing the proximate causation under the control of the human participants themselves.

But the joy of sport carried with it the possibility of defeat and of the anger that accompanied defeat if it was the result of foul play. Menelaos's complaint against Antilochos was that he engaged in reckless driving that endangered both Menelaos and his horses. Indeed, he thought that Antilochos played a dirty trick by squeezing around the turn in order to compensate for the fact that he had slower horses. He won by trick rather than by merit.

To complicate matters further, when Achilles proposed that the second-place prize be awarded to Eumelos rather than to Antilochos, the latter protested. The appeal to pity had no place in sport, he seemed to argue. In Antilochos' view, one's pursuit of victory ought not to be deflected by pity for one's opponents. Achilles relented and awarded him the prize for second place. Rapprochement between Antilochos and Menelaos was reached when the former, who had to swear to the gods that he had not cheated, exhibited a willingness to give his prize (and more) to Menelaos. Antilochos attributed his own excess to his youth and deferred to the age and wisdom of Menelaos, who, in turn, put aside his anger. A crisis was averted.

One might understandably expect that the tendency toward violence, and hence the elimination of the play spirit, would most likely occur in the contact sports, three of which were represented in the Patroclos games: boxing, wrestling, and a type of martial art involving spears. The winner of the boxing match, Epeios, had promised that he would smash the bones of his opponent to a pulp and that his opponent would need his relatives to carry him off. But this sort of talk was not so much a violation of the hypothesis of sport as competitive play as it was an affirmation of the fact that people play at or enjoy different things. Some people *like* to fight and an even greater number of people *enjoy* watching a fight. The ludic element of the boxing match was confirmed when, after the match, Epeios generously helped his pummelled opponent to his feet. That is, the real problem to be avoided is not so much physical contact per se but cheating.

The wrestling match was between Aias and Odysseus, who grappled to a draw, despite Odysseus's cunning. As in the story regarding Antilochos and Menelaos, there is a fine line between sport sagacity and cheating. Very often only those who are most knowledgeable in a particular sport can detect the line.

Although the winner of the martial arts event was to be the contestant who would first penetrate the armour of the opponent and draw blood with a spear, and although the two contestants (Aias and Diomedes) glared at each other terribly at the start (presumably so as to intimidate the opponent), the spectators at this event called the bout to a stop before blood was drawn. Thus the hypothesis of sport as competitive play was itself put to the test in the contact sports, but it came through these three ordeals unscathed.

It is also understandable that the hypothesis of sport as competitive play might be easier to detect in noncontact sport events, such as the footrace. The prize for the winner of this event was the most beautiful bowl in the world such that, in addition to the intrinsic value of participating in the event itself – the joy of sport – there was also the external reward of a valuable object. But none of these events were so important materially that the playful element was eradicated. This point was driven home in the hotly contested footrace, where Aias and Odysseus were in the lead until Athena tripped Aias, thus allowing Odysseus to win. (The Patroclos games took place before the long sea ordeal that diminished the power of Odysseus's legs.) The place where Aias fell was covered with offal from the beasts and Aias got his mouth and nostrils full of the stuff. Everyone present laughed, including Antilochos, the last-place finisher. Here we are reminded both of the Phaiacian games and the uproarious laughter of the gods at the time when Hephaestus caught his wife in an affair as well as the smile of Odysseus after he had killed the suitors. There are degrees of ludic lightheartedness. Although laughing at Aias's humiliation could be seen as odious, it does seem to mitigate an overly serious approach to sport competition.

An ancient version of the shot put involved an amicable *agon*. The same is true regarding the archery contest, in contrast to a very similar event at the end of the *Odyssey*, with the similarity consisting in the archery skills required in the two events. The Patroclos games were to end with the javelin throw, but before the contest began Agamemnon was awarded first place primarily as a sign of respect for his authority. This premature end to the javelin contest might seem to detract from the competitive spirit of the Patroclos games, but first place was given to Agamemnon not only out of respect but also due to his reputation *in this event*, built as it was on past success; hence the competitive spirit of the games is, in a way, preserved.

Philosophical implications: reflective equilibrium

It is the purpose of this section to articulate the *philosophical* benefit of understanding Homer's texts in terms of the method of reflective equilibrium. Indeed, my overall method is that of reflective equilibrium, which has a family resemblance to Aristotelian dialectic (see Rawls, 1999: 18–19, 42–5). We are most likely to achieve adequate responses to the questions at the top of this chapter by trying to achieve balance or harmony among several considerations. One does not so much *deduce* what sport is or ought to be as one tries to *understand* what sport is by bringing several apparently disparate considerations into some sort of equilibrium; deviations from this equilibrium negatively give us clues as to how one ought to engage in sport either as a participant or as an observer.

Nonseriousness

Consider the Phaiacians. I assume that I am not alone in thinking that there is something amiss in the Phaiacians' approach to sport: initially they proclaimed themselves to be the best competitors in the world(!), then Odysseus hurled the discus much further than any Phaiacian could, and finally they declared their lack of interest in sport and started dancing. They have thus trivialized sport competition. *If* we adopted this view of sport, I am arguing, then almost everything else that we care about in sport would be put into disequilibrium; hence, I conclude, we ought not to adopt this view of sport. The ancient Greeks themselves saw the problem here, which is why they distinguished athletics, competing for a prize, from children's games (*paizo*) and mere trifling with toys (*paignia*). Admittedly, if the Phaiacians had beaten Odysseus in some sport events they might not have trivialized them. The fact that the trivialization of the events came after Odysseus's discus throw perhaps signals a degree of cowardice in the Phaiacians.

The aforementioned problem faced by Odysseus was a literal di-lemma in the sense that there seemed to be only two roads and both of them had potholes. If he participated in sport competition he would be taking time and energy away from the very serious business of getting home, but if he ignored the taunts and prepared for his voyage home without entering into sport competition he would feel a strong sense of having missed something, of having given up on the excitement that is at the core of a sport event. Because he took sport events seriously, he chose to compete, a seriousness that was balanced by Alcinoos' nonserious approach. What is lacking in the Phaiacian games is a single person who embodies the serious nonseriousness of sport.

Contemporary examples of nonseriousness regarding sport are not hard to find. One can think of one's agitation when a talented teammate or a key player on one's favourite team does not practise hard enough in order to perform well in a big game. This agitation is easy to bring into equilibrium with the hypothesis I am defending, but it is not easy to bring it into equilibrium with some other views. Many of my colleagues in academe exhibit either an Alcinoos-like indifference to sport or even contempt for it. From *this* point of view the agitation makes no sense whatsoever.

Or again, the preponderance of moneyed interests in sport can also (ironically) lead to its trivialization in that one can become more concerned with the instrumental goods made possible by sport competition than with the intrinsic good of the competition itself.

Overseriousness

But it is equally clear that sport can be, and often is, taken too seriously. This is the greater danger, as I see things. Granted, there is the temptation toward anachronism when we (or at least I) cringe at the results of Odysseus's preliminary bout (a broken jaw, a probable concussion etc.) and victory in the archery contest (multiple deaths, torture and death of Melanthios, the murder of the female attendants etc.). It should be noted that there is no clear distinction in the text between 'sport event', on the one hand, and 'war', on the other. Even the arrow that went through Antinoos' throat was still part of 'the great game'.

No doubt some will object that Odysseus did not really care about sport at the end of the *Odyssey* in that his ultimate goal was to kill the suitors. Likewise, we would be reluctant to think of someone who entered a contemporary hockey game with the prior intention to kill an opponent as a player. But it should not escape our notice that the segue into Odysseus's violence *is* constituted by several remarkable sport feats: the convincing victory in the boxing match against the beggar, the muscular stringing of the bow and the incredible shot through the axeheads. In the Penelope games, at least, sport competition *is* preparation for war, or at least for widespread violence.

Despite the wide tolerance for violence in Homer, the other suitors realized (quite understandably) that the game had gotten out of control at the point when Antinoos was shot and that at that point the sport event should have ended. One is tempted to say that all of the deaths after this point were acts of war or murder rather than parts of the sport event itself. After all, a *com*petitive event is literally one where the participants ask *together* who is best; once the suitors dropped out, there was no longer a competitive athletic event. The point is a logical one.

Odysseus's refusal to gloat over the dead bodies shows some miniscule restraint on his part. But the preponderance of the evidence points toward lack of restraint. It should be noted that the motto for ancient Greek civilization in general was that found above the entrance to their most sacred site at the temple of Apollo at Delphi, which was also one of four sites for the stephanitic (i.e. crown) games, the most famous of which was at Olympia: nothing in excess. When judged against this standard, Odysseus seems quite immoderate at the end of the *Odyssey*. Perhaps he is to be commended as a warrior, but as a competitor he has taken the game far too seriously.

Contemporary examples of death as a result of sport are not hard to find. They occur not infrequently in boxing and American football, for example. They also occur more frequently than is commonly realized in marathon running, which would have struck the ancient Greeks as a type of excess. (Contrary to the popular myth, there simply was no 26-mile run by Pheidippides – see Miller, 2004a).

But death in sport is not the only sort of contemporary excess. Nor is it the most pervasive sort of excess. Odysseus's victory in the archery contest at the end of the *Odyssey* can be seen as a symbol for widely acknowledged excesses: that the Super Bowl has become the most important cultural event in the United States today, that sport is often the tail that wags the dog at a contemporary American university, etc. I am confident that similar examples could be found from other cultures in that sport fanaticism has become a global phenomenon. Odysseus's excess can act as a metaphor that spurs us to try to recover a sense of proportion with respect to sport.

On the hypothesis of sport as competitive play, we can easily understand why cheating in a sport event is bothersome in that it indicates that one takes sport competition too seriously such that one would be willing to lie or gain an unfair advantage over one's opponent in the pursuit of victory. By contrast, if one thought of sport competition on the analogy of war (as many sports commentators do implicitly with their metaphors regarding battles, killings, massacres and the like), then it would not be easy to understand why cheating in a sport event was wrong. That is, a view of sport competition as bellicose puts into disequilibrium one's aversion to lying and cheating. Of course in the method of reflective equilibrium it is possible that one would then give up the aversion to lying and cheating in that in this method nothing is fixed in advance. But this would be too great a price to pay, on my view, in that giving up on the aversion to lying and cheating would put into disequilibrium almost everything else that is crucial in ethical theory.

When a fight breaks out among sport participants or 'fans' (which is short for 'fanatics'), or when one football player headbutts another, or when hooligans hurl racial epithets at sport participants or attack fans from an opposing team, etc., something has gone wrong, on my view. I think most sport lovers agree with me here. But why? Because sport is a type of competitive play. By contrast, if we believed in the thesis that sport is to be understood as something like war or some fascist-like preparation for war (see Spivey, 2004; Tannsjo, 1998; Tamburrini, 1998), there would be nothing terribly wrong with any of these activities.

Reflective equilibrium

There is clearly no sure-fire *algorithm* for determining what sport is and what it ought to be. This is why reflective equilibrium is plausible as a fruitful *heuristic device*. Once we notice the problems involved in trivializing sport, on the one hand, and in taking it too seriously, on the other, we are then in a good position to calibrate our way to a moderate position between these two extremes. Such calibration is facilitated by a consideration of the games commemorating the death of Patroclos.

From the start these games were moving in the right direction (in contrast to the archery contest at the end of the *Odyssey*): away from war and toward pacific *com*petition (which is a partial redundancy). Further, these games are framed for us so as to encourage us to focus on moderation between really serious death in war and the mistakenly serious activity of playing a dice game. Sport competition is, I have alleged, serious nonseriousness. (To reverse this order by calling sport nonserious seriousness would be to risk exaggerating the importance of sport competition.) The fact that the Patroclos games were the closest of the three major sport competitions in Homer to the ancient Olympic games helps us to better appreciate the Olympic goal of *kalokagathia*, a compound word that refers to both physical excellence (*kalos*) and moral excellence (*agathos*).

Indeed, there is intense striving for excellence (*arete*) in both areas, and who wins and who loses is emphatically part of the equation in ancient sport, but *how* one strives for victory is also part of the equation. Achilles tries to preserve the ludic dimension of sport competition by awarding prizes to all participants, although the prizes were graded so that the winners would receive the best ones.

As before, something of a crisis arose in the dispute between Menelaos and Antilochos, but the former's strength of character was obviously normative. Menelaos acted as a lure for Antilochos to reach self-knowledge regarding his *hubris* and his transgression. This was no easy feat when it is considered that Antilochos was encouraged by his own father to do everything possible in the pursuit of victory. Even in the contact sports, however, there were signs of *kalokagathia*, so Antilochos' eventual accomplishment of self-knowledge should not surprise us. In the spearfight between Aias and Diomedes the spectators played a normative role somewhat like Menelaos's in that they prevented sport competition from going 'too far' toward hatred and violence. 'Spectator', it should be noted, preserves a sort of ocular distance, in contrast to the potential rabidness of 'fan'.

The laughter at Aias's fall into dung in the footrace put an exclamation point on the ludic element of the Patroclos games, a feature of sport competition that is at present under threat. Homer, I claim, can point us toward a better way. To such critics as Spivey, who see even in the Patroclos games a preparation for future war, I would emphasize the fact that there was no accuracy component in the javelin throw! (See Spivey, 2004: 27.)

Conclusion

Sport has conquered the contemporary world. Although there is no consensus regarding what sport is or what it ought to be, there *is* a remarkable convergence of opinion among morally reflective people that loss in a sport event, even a high-stakes sport event such as the World Cup, pales in comparison with the death of a child. I do not think that I hyperbolize here in using this example in that, in the sports world we live in at present, there is a disturbing tendency in popular culture to view sport victory and defeat in life-and-death terms, as listeners to sports radio can readily learn. By contrast, there is a remarkable convergence of opinion among morally reflective people that to think that a loss in a big-time sport event does not pale in comparison with the death of a child is to take sport competition too seriously. It has been one of the purposes of the present chapter to mine Homer so as to make better sense of this conclusion. The idea that it is possible to take sport competition too seriously (and hence be encouraged to cheat) is the key point in Homer's depiction of the Patroclos games, specifically in the ideas expressed by Menelaos and by the spectators at the footrace (see Dombrowski, 1979, 1987, 1995, 2009).

The task today, as it was in Homer's day, is to negotiate one's way between two 'monsters' (see Book 12 of the *Odyssey*): the fluent whirlpool of Charybdis, where sport is not taken seriously enough, and the rocklike sternness of Scylla, where sport is taken too seriously, as when the American football coach Bill Parcells declared with a straight face that football *is* life (see Feezell, 2004: 58; also see Huizinga, 1955).

For those who can successfully make their way through these dangers, there is the philosophical prize described by Porphyry in late antiquity, wherein one can 'enter the stadium … striving for the most glorious of all prizes, the Olympia of the soul' (Porphyry, 2000: I, 31; also see Dombrowski, 2006).

Note

1 An earlier version of this chapter appeared as Dombrowski (2012).

References

Dombrowski, D. (1979) 'Plato and athletics', *Journal of the Philosophy of Sport*, 6, 29–38.
Dombrowski, D. (1987) 'Asceticism as athletic training in Plotinus', *Aufsteig und Niedergang der Romischen Welt*, 36(1), 701–12.
Dombrowski, D. (1995) 'Weiss, sport, and the Greek ideal', in Hahn, L. (ed.) *The Philosophy of Paul Weiss*, LaSalle, IL: Open Court, 637–54.
Dombrowski, D. (2006) *Rethinking the Ontological Argument: A Neoclassical Theistic Response*, New York: Cambridge University Press.
Dombrowski, D. (2009) *Contemporary Athletics and Ancient Greek Ideals*, Chicago: University of Chicago Press.
Dombrowski, D. (2012) 'Homer, competition, and sport', *Journal of the Philosophy of Sport*, 39, 33–51.
Feezell, R. (2004) *Sport, Play, and Ethical Reflection*, Chicago: University of Illinois Press.
Homer (1954) *The Iliad*, Loeb edn, Cambridge: Harvard University Press.
Homer (1960) *The Odyssey*, Loeb edn, Cambridge: Harvard University Press.
Homer (2007a) *The Iliad*, transl. Rouse, W., New York: Signet Classics.
Homer (2007b) *The Odyssey*, transl. Rouse, W., New York: Signet Classics.
Huizinga, J. (1955) *Homo Ludens: A Study of the Play Element in Culture*, transl. Hull, R., Boston: Beacon Press.
James, W. (1984) 'The moral equivalent of war', in B. Wilshire (ed.) *The Essential Writings*, Albany: State University of New York Press.
Miller, S. (2004a) *Ancient Greek Athletics*, New Haven: Yale University Press.
Miller, S. (2004b) *Arete: Greek Sports from Ancient Sources*, Berkeley: University of California Press.

Novak, M. (1976) *The Joy of Sport*, New York: Basic Books.
Orwell, G. (1968) *Collected Essays, Journalism and Letters*, vol. 4, New York: Harcourt, Brace, and World.
Porphyry (2000) *On Abstinence from Killing Animals*, transl. Clark, G., Ithaca, NY: Cornell University Press.
Rawls, J. (1999) *A Theory of Justice*, rev. edn, Cambridge, MA: Harvard University Press.
Spivey, N. (2004) *The Ancient Olympics*, Oxford: Oxford University Press.
Tamburrini, C. (1998) 'Sports, fascism, and the market', *Journal of the Philosophy of Sport*, 25, 35–47.
Tannsjo, T. (1998) 'Is our admiration for sports heroes fascistoid?' *Journal of the Philosophy of Sport*, 25, 23–34.

Part III
Metaphysics and ontology

9 *Homo ludens* in the twenty-first century

Towards an understanding of Caillois's *paidia* in sports[1]

Imara Felkers, Ellen Mulder and Malcolm MacLean

Even among participants, physical activity and sport seem run through with paradox – the drive (rather than walk or cycle) to the club match or the gym, the joy of movement and the focus on repetitive regularity and performance in placeless stadia and fitness centres, the claims of an 'endorphine rush' and bliss in a sterile, emotionless place devoid of leisure and in many cases devoid of pleasure. The significance of this paradox may be seen in public health responses to the lack of physical activity as an issue connected to a global rise of obesity, diabetes and other health problems (Kohl *et al.*, 2012; Lee *et al.*, 2012). Many public health policies intended to stimulate physical activity, such as the WHO global physical activity strategy (WHO, 2010), do not deliver on expectations. Public health attempts to understand and solve the problem of inactivity tend to rely on the behavioral sciences that frame the issue primarily in terms of self-efficacy and self-motivation of individuals (Isen 2006), environmental factors (Van Lenthe *et al.*, 2010) or the bio-medical sciences that focus on physiological condition and motor skills (Hamilton *et al.*, 2008). These perspectives fail to unravel the phenomenon of becoming more physically active. Furthermore, some of the philosophical limitations of these approaches are suggested by MacLean's (2011) argument that the neo-liberal prioritization of choice makes physical *in*activity a legitimate response to exhortations to do more physical activity.

Paradoxically, it seems that we are physically active because we want to play. The joy of sport is within sport itself (in the game) and not in some abstract desire to move, so it is joy in specific movement, not generic movement. This chapter explores the nexus that is playfulness in movement, the rule-bound nature of play in-and-as sport and the limits of the regulation of joyfulness (i.e. playfulness) to argue that despite the exhortation to health-through-instrumentalized-activity we remain *homo ludens*. We do this by revisiting the relations between and meaning of key concepts in classic works by Huizinga and Caillois, focusing on agonic play. These paradoxes are highlighted where policy makers use athletes as key agents and frame sport as an instrument for health improvement. There is little evidence that athletes take up their sport because of the physical activity or other health issues. On the contrary, they take up a particular sport because of its play characteristics that produce a desire to move. In the words of one of the participants in our research, 'the game chooses you'. In this context, it is fruitful to look at the concept of play in relation to adults' physical activity. While play has often been considered as a means for children to become socialized into society, several authors have argued for broadening the concept of play in such a way that it escapes teleological ideas of development to put play back in the domain of adults (Eichberg, 2009; Lester and Russell, 2008). Johan Huizinga (1938) anticipated this argument when he stated that humans are *homo ludens*: people who play. Play is part of our existence.

As part of the project this chapter draws on, adults were interviewed about play in their life-span.[2] At first it seemed that adults hardly played at all. However, during the interviews it became clear that they did not call their play 'play', so attention shifted from *whether* they play to *what* they play: the activity. The presence of the verb to 'play' in sports activities such as 'playing' football or 'playing' tennis indicates that a sport activity cannot exist without being 'played', yet much sport is regulated in ways that undermine playfulness. This discursive characteristic demands that we unravel the concept of play to clarify the role of play in physical activity.

Play: the truth and the problem

Although there is a growing body of approaches to the study of play (e.g. Bateson, 2005, Sutton-Smith, 1997, Pellegrini, 2011), we have returned to its foundational text in modern scholarship. The Dutch historian and philosopher Johan Huizinga argues that the *fun* of playing 'resists all analysis, all logical interpretations' (Huizinga, 1950/5: 3), suggesting that the presence of play in sport, itself a version of physical activity, is at odds with the vision of sport and related forms of physical activity as instrumental and rational practice – hence our turn to phenomenological sensibilities. Furthermore, in asserting that 'play is older than culture' Huizinga (1950/5: 1) opens his analysis in *Homo Ludens* with a demand to resist a human-centred perspective. There is play, whether humans are playing or not. Huizinga states that play extends beyond the sphere of human and animal life, so the human individual frame disappears and a larger cosmopolitan perspective arises.

Huizinga presents challenges for analysts, especially given some seemingly subtle but significant translation issues. In the Dutch original Huizinga (1938/2008: 45) observed that: '*in* den vorm en *in* de functie van het spel, dat een zelfstandige kwaliteit is, vindt het besef van's menschen begrepen zijn in den kosmos zijn eerste, zijn hoogste, zijn heiligste uitdrukking' (in our translation: '*In* the form and *in* the function of play, which is an autonomous quality, man grasps his situation in the cosmos, his first, his highest, his sacred expression'). In the published translation, however, the second 'in', and therefore 'play' as an autonomous quality, has been omitted: 'in' is only used once and is not highlighted, so that the passage reads: 'in the form and function of play ... man grasps his situation in the cosmos' (Huizinga, 1950/5: 17). In emphasizing 'in' on both occasions, Huizinga separates form and function so that play-as-autonomous may occur where the activity form does not seem to allow it and therefore to suggest play's transcendental potential.

If play is non-logical, as Huizinga states, and goes beyond any human perspective, we need to look carefully at his claim that 'any thinking person can see at a glance that play is a thing on its own' (Huizinga, 1950/5: 3). Huizinga underpins his vision by referring to Plato's work *The Laws*. This immediate recognition of play is explained by Plato as given. The place of play is, de facto, transcendental: it goes beyond humans and animals. It is precisely this articulation of play in Plato's work that makes it possible to conceive the place of humankind in the cosmos. Huizinga further refines Plato's work by distinguishing 'play' as an autonomous quality and being played where we grasp our situation in the cosmos.

According to Plato, the identity of play transports the participant to another world.[3] With the precondition that all things are human, it seems reasonable that it is the player who transports or causes the transformation of 'real' life. However, seen from the cosmos's point of view, it is exactly the opposite: the play transports. That is why Huizinga emphasizes what he first calls 'speelruimte', literally translated as 'play-space', by naming it 'a temporary world'. Huizinga's choice of these words is important. A play-space, rather than the word 'play-ground' (as used in the English version), connotates also a sphere of its own rather than being just a physical playground. Seen from this view it is understandable why it is possible that participants play their sport or fitness activities in the joy of movement in sterile, emotionless places. 'All play moves and has its being in its play-[spaces]' (Huizinga, 1955:10: 'Elk spel beweegt zich binnen zijn speelruimte'; 1938/2008: 17). From this perspective it is logical that Huizinga takes this 'play-space' one step further to a world. The word 'world' instead of 'play-ground', and our phenomenological concerns, take us beyond the limitations of rules, space and time to a holistic, affective experience resulting from 'play'. Plato did not hesitate to understand these sacred meanings involved in the category of play. In play a person realizes their human-ness, which makes them *homo ludens*. In order to understand the role of play in adult life, Huizinga and Plato make clear that in play we can identify and be ourselves.

To make sense of this issue of self-realization in adult 'play' we reflect on French philosopher Roger Caillois's work on the relation between self-identity and play. Although Caillois rejected Huizinga's notion of play as seen from a cosmopolitan perspective, his thoughts about self-identification are of value to Huizinga's framework of play. Caillois's work has often been interpreted as opposing Huizinga's ideas, but for our purposes it is a necessary addition to Huizinga's legacy rather than its opposition. In *Les jeux et les hommes* (1958, translated as *Man, Play and Games*) Caillois distinguishes between *paidia* and *ludus*. Caillois was impressed by *Homo Ludens* but argued that it was concurrently too broad and too narrow. Hence Caillois categorizes play into four categories: *agon*, *alea*, *mimicry* and *ilinx*. The category *agon* has as its main principle 'competition'. There is always rivalry, based on equality. In *agon*, play is about winning the contest by showing superior skills. All sports belong to this category. In contrast to *agon*, the category *alea* is much more physically passive. Its outcome is based on the result of chance and, as such, has little to do with the skills of a player. In the category *mimicry*, players accept a temporary imaginary universe, where they play at being somebody or something else. *Ilinx* is about a pursuit of vertigo, which consists of an attempt to destroy the stability of perception and self-awareness.

In all four categories the players have their own motive to play, while noting that a play experience may incorporate several or all categories, even while one is dominant. The attraction for the player in *agon* is 'for each player to have his superiority in a given area recognized' (Caillois, 1958: 15). This explains the drive to train, develop and improve skills for a game. *Alea* reveals that players favour destiny, where in mimicry the pleasure for the player is in becoming another. *Ilinx* shows the desire for disorder and destruction, a drive that is normally repressed. In these four categories Caillois distinguishes *paidia*. Each category encompasses play without any restrictions through to more structured and regulated games. It is by this continuum that Caillois distinguishes both *paidia* and *ludus* in play: 'Inside each section different games are arranged in a rank of order of progression'(Caillois, 1958: 13).

Caillois uses the Greek tradition as the starting point in his distinction between *paidia* and *ludus*. The Greek word *paidia* means 'play activities that children play'. In Greek, however, the accents make clear whether it is about child play – *paidía* – or childishness – *paidiá*.[4] *Paidia* is a derivation of *paizein* – to play – and can involve all kinds of games yet remains connected to the child. At the same time the ancient Greeks saw many similarities between the divine muse forms, such as music and dance, and child-play, *paidía*. This *paidía* and divine music have the same core characteristics in rhythm and harmony. Many children's games fully or predominantly consist of rhythm: for example, games that do not even have proper names other than 'counting games'.

Caillois identifies *paidia* as an expression of energy, or a burst of energy, a drive of the senses. The main motive in *paidia* is lust, as in 'lust for life', where 'free improvisation, and carefree gaiety is dominant' (Caillois, 1958: 13). Features of this lust are strength and the uncontrolled power of eruption. Eruption is always accompanied by force: an uncontrolled power that escapes (this is most obviously so in *ilinx*, where lust dominates the play form). *Paidia*, in itself, is unsustainable as a singular play form for adults where the conventions of 'grown-up-ness' limit *paidia's* lustful excess, but exists in tense and contradictory relation with *ludus* and arises during ludic activity; most of the time people are unaware of its occurrence, or where and how it ends.

Caillois proposes that during the first of three stages of *paidia*, disturbance and tumult are an elementary need: this is remarkable, as normally disturbance and tumult are repressed. According to Caillois, the first primarily body-oriented stage includes embodied forms such as impulses to touch, yell, grasp, taste and smell that are ways of giving substance to this need. The need is dominant, and it seems there is an absence of morality when he discusses these embodied forms of *paidia*: 'It readily can become a taste for destruction and breaking things' (Caillois, 1958: 28).

After disturbance and tumult comes a desire to mystify or defy, the second stage of *paidia*. In this stage, fantasy and imagination arise. To mystify and to defy assumes that there is the presence of an Other. This implies that awareness is extended to the outside world. Notably, imagination and appearance of the other arise at the same stage.

In both these stages some elements of play are already recognizable as either voluntary or agreed upon. It is not about good or bad behaviour, it is about the child's self-expression: 'for the child it is a question of expressing himself, of feeling he is the cause, of forcing others to pay attention to him' (Caillois, 1958: 28).

Progress through the first and second stages of *paidia* shows the development of this eruption of energy to self-expression leading finally to self-realization in the third stage. *Paidia's* lust starts with a primitive joy of 'making' but also destruction. This need for turbulence and disturbance leads to a form of self-expression, where fantasy arises, making it possible to mystify and defy. These two stages are invisible during the last stage, 'self-realization'. Caillois calls this third stage *ludus*: where broad forms of self-expression emerge into a desire to demonstrate skills explicitly.

The development of *paidia* ends, according to Caillois, in *ludus* which is 'complementary to and a refinement of *paidia*, which it disciplines and enriches' (1958: 29), and which contains and seeks to control *paidia*. Caillois emphasizes that *ludus* is not about rules but about self-realization, stating: 'Soon there is born the desire to invent rules, and to abide by them whatever the cost' (1958: 28). Hence self-realization is possible through abiding by rules. Abiding by rules, according to Caillois, enables a person to show mastery and solve problems, so the rules belonging to *ludus* facilitate self-realization. He describes this as an advantage of *ludus*, in contrast to *paidia*, where self-realization through rule compliance is not possible.

In *ludus*, because of play's rules players can show their skills and what they are able to do: this explains the tendency to follow rules which are in essence arbitrary. That is why people run a marathon and do not take the bus to cover the 26 miles. *Ludus* creates opportunities for optimal self-realization and the possibility of performance: after all, you can be a champion in *ludus* activities but not in *paidia* activities. Paraphernalia such as medals and cups are trophies that show superiority and confirm identity. These performances can also be shown in less substantial forms, such as on souvenir t-shirts with texts such as 'London Marathon Finisher', including the date of accomplishment. Where elements of *paidia* arise in uncontrolled and spontaneous forms, it takes patience and endurance to win a game or to give a perfect performance of *ludus*, according to Caillois. Therefore training and discipline are essential. It is an important part of *ludus* to refine your skills and experience the joy of *ludus*. It is not by coincidence that Caillois places all contests, including sport, in *ludus*. *Ludus* is always permeated 'with an atmosphere of competition' (Caillois, 1958: 32).

There are two significant aspects of *paidia* that are not addressed in Caillois's work. One element that limits the usefulness of Caillois's case in our context is the weakness in his claim that *paidia* is for adults, which he hesitates to elaborate: 'Within each class, I have not distinguished between children's and adults' games.... The point of doing this was to stress the very principle of the proposed classification' (Caillois, 1958: 13). However, he illustrates his examples of *paidia* only with children's activities: embodied shapes such as grasping, smelling and feeling, typical behaviour of infants and toddlers. If *paidia* is also about bodily energy that escapes from the body, like a scream, a yell or a kick, it is a missed opportunity that Caillois does not provide examples of *paidia* during adult life. Who does not recognize the joy of being the fastest vehicle when the traffic light turns green? Or the pleasure when your fingers slide across fine fabric, or making doodles during a meeting? Or of the uncontrolled imagination that emerges while strolling?[5] Since Caillois does not provide these adult examples, this awareness disappears quickly to the background, suggesting that *paidia* is solely childlike.

With this linear approach, the second unaddressed aspect becomes more evident. Namely that Caillois puts *paidia* and *ludus* on a continuum: 'this frolicsome and impulsive exuberance is almost entirely absorbed or disciplined' (Caillois, 1958: 13), in which only the word 'almost' provides a margin of further interpretation. However, this is neglected by how these two elements are represented. The model where Caillois presents *paidia* and *ludus* is the representation of a continuum that stresses linearity: in each of the four categories of *agon*, *alea*, *mimicry* and *ilinx*, 'games are classified in such an order that the *paidia* element is constantly decreasing while the *ludus* element is ever increasing' (Caillois, 1958: 36). There are two crucial points here: the first is that *paidia* is *almost* but not *fully* absorbed; the second is that his case leaves unexplained the extent to which the degree of absorption may vary between the four categories of play. *Paidia* retains the connotation for adults of childishness, the first unaddressed issue. However, the two aspects of *paidia*, one noted by Caillois, the second unaddressed, mean that we reject this emphasis on childishness to argue (below) that *paidia* arises from gaps created by players between the formal rules, so *paidia* is always a potentiality in *ludus*, the form that adults play the most.

The potential for *paidia* in *ludus*

To explore the role of lacunae in the rules and elaborate this potential for *paidia* in *ludus* we consider the relation between a game and its players. The need to play a game and to obey the rules is discussed by Mary Midgley (1974) in 'The Game Game'. In raising these questions she focuses, in line with Huizinga, on the position of the player. Midgley states that a player brings himself into a game, meaning that games are not closed systems after all. She explains this by indicating that although there are many books containing the rules of a game, none mentions when the player has to start or quit a game. Rules suggest that the behaviour of the players is set by the formal instructions of a game, but there is nothing in these rules that requires someone who has not *chosen* to play to submit themselves to the rules of the game; that is, the rules of a game do not compel anyone to enter the world created by the game to play (dystopian science fiction aside). Furthermore, and depending on the game, there are different levels of bringing yourself in as a player, varying from the first stages of *paidia* through to fully developed self-realization.

By way of example, consider Diego Maradona, who while warming up for the 1989 UEFA cup final engaged with the song *Live is life* (Opus) that was playing throughout the stadium. His action shows a contradiction between him, his bootlaces untied, keeping the ball high on the rhythm of the music, and his teammates, who seem to do their standard warm-up. The public recognizes and appreciates Maradona's actions and begins clapping along with the rhythm of the music, which is shortly afterwards followed by Maradona himself.[6] Although some might argue that the warm-up lies outside the official game, we suggest that the warm-up is both symbolically a transition into the game and physiogicicly an essential part of the game designed to minimize risk to player well-being. The interesting thing is that Maradona *plays* unlike his teammates, so the unprepared and lustful experience becomes visible. Games can be presented as a closed system because (rule) 'books take obvious points for granted' (Midgley, 1974: 237). There are no rules describing that there must be spectators watching a game; or the way players encourage themselves and each other while playing; or that the movements on the court have to be purely functional.

From this perspective, many recognizable moments within a game belong unmistakably to that game but are not part of the rules. The celebratory behaviour of an athlete after a scored point during a match underlines Midgley's point. There are explicit regulations about behaviour during these celebrations which are mandatory but these do not require that these celebrations occur or prohibit many of the forms these celebrations take. For instance, a football player taking his shirt off will be punished with a yellow card: this regulation indicates that celebrating is axiomatic in a football match and is another example of sport as more than a closed system that cannot contain the moments of excess associated with triumph within the game. Moreover, when we take a closer look at the structure of a football match, it is strange that football players celebrate after they have scored a goal while the game is still going on. After all, if the lusory goal (Suits, 1988: 43) of football is to pass the ball with your foot across the goal line *more often* than the opponent, then cheering should only take place at the end of the match. In-match celebration underlines Midgley's assertion that all players bring themselves to the game. In these moments, an eruption of energy is noticeable, which seems similar to the description that Caillois provides of *paidia*: gaiety and frolicsome behaviour that is not attached to a conventional rule but which has been practised.

These football-related examples show that there is much more to a game (*ludus* activities) than what is or can be written down in a rulebook. From Caillois's perspective we also notice that the categories of play are permeable, so it is possible for a player that plays in the *agon* category to draw elements from the other categories of *alea*, *mimicry* and *ilinx* in the same game. For mimicry there is the notion that the second stage of *paidia* includes fantasy and imagination as well, so the mimicry element is included in each category. We illustrate this drawing on our interview with professional basketball player Jamal Boykin. 'Imagination is the whole game', states Boykin.

> The value of imagination is, like right now, there is a player: Blake Griffin ... he is a beast. When he goes to the basket, he dunks over people, I am nowhere near his caliber, nowhere near.... I have been watching his videos.... During practice this week ... I am telling you, I was attacking them. I could have broken the room by the way I was dunking the basketball. Trying to be like him, watching him, thinking, feeling like Blake Griffin: I was Blake Griffin, now am I jumping as high as Blake Griffin.

Boykin's imaging of self mimics Griffin. This mimetic participation brings us back to the problem that playing only in *ludus* leaves open Midgley's problem of what is absent from the rulebook of a game; when does the player start a game? It is too naive to answer 'when the whistle blows', as we see from a narrative in Eamon Dunphy's book *Only a Game* that illustrates how a professional footballer changed in the course of a game from a reluctant participant to someone enjoying himself. During the 1973–4 season with Millwall, Dunphy was relegated to the reserve team:

> Back in the bloody Midweek League again ... there is no one there, absolutely nothing at stake except your own pride.... You have got to think of a million different ways to motivate yourself. Really it is down to personal pride.... And if you go out there not too bothered about the whole thing, thinking you will play it of the cuff, all of a sudden you will find you are two–zero down, which we did. And you feel sick as a pig, you think now you really have got to work, because there is an hour to go, and unless you absolutely stop altogether, you are going to get a horrible chasing. So why not go out and have a go.
>
> And you begin to enjoy it. It is amazing the pleasure you can get out of it. It is just your own pride and you begin to enjoy the game.... We won four–two. We came of the park really pleased. It is meaningless, the Midweek League. They hardly even bother to print the result in the paper. But you come off with a little glow of satisfaction because you have got a little bit of self-respect back.
>
> (Dunphy, 1977: 144–6)

Whereas Boykin may be seen as starting to play well before the first whistle, Dunphy suggests he began to 'play' 30 minutes after that whistle was blown. The constitutive rules of the game may say that it begins at the opening whistle, but this is not the phenomenological experience.

Midgley states that the origin of a game arises from human desire:

> The restraining rules are not something foreign to the needs or emotions involved, they are simply the shape which the desired activity takes [here she stresses Huizinga's statement that '*in* the form and *in* the function of play, which is an autonomous quality, man grasps his situation in the cosmos his first, his highest, his sacred expression']. The Chess Player's desire is not a desire for general abstract intellectual activity, curbed and frustrated by a particular set of rules. It is a desire for a particular kind of intellectual activity, whose channel is the rules of chess.
>
> (1974: 243)

Seen from this perspective, playing indicates that a sport activity cannot exist without being played: that is, playing by the rules creates the game.

Similarly, Caillois states that self-expression in *ludus* is not about the rules but about complying with them, a view clarified by Midgley: 'Until we understand the reasons for playing, I do not think we understand the abidingness of the rules' (1974: 236).[7] These reasons are according to Huizinga and Caillois not a quest, which lies in a sociological or biological sphere: they lie in play. In this light Boykin's statement that 'the game chooses you, you know' takes on a fuller meaning. Looking beyond (or through) sports codification, we have a set of rules that closely connect to these primary fluid game forms that develop in the first two stages of *paidia*, but although *ludus* enriches and disciplines *paidia*, the first two stages of *paidia* cannot disappear.

Rethinking the *ludus–paidia* continuum

The current dominant health paradigm of physical (in)activity as a meta-discourse of rational, instrumental play and physical activity is characterized by a focus on behaviour instead of identity; trust in the power of the individual mind to steer the body unless the body is physically incapable to move, and a rationalist goal-oriented approach where the goal is to become more healthy. The suggestion that play, given this rational, instrumental discourse, is an underestimated vehicle for stimulating physical literacy, for identity change, for increasing 'I can' must be unpacked, because the play of adults is often invisible: 'I can', but because I am an adult 'I don't'. Moreover, play is connected to feelings and thus is embodied. For a human being to exist there needs to be space for the unprepared and the uncontrolled, since *paidia*, in which lust and tumult are the antithesis of rational instrumentalism, has not disappeared, but the 'rules of adulthood' mean that it has become invisible, noting that our focus on agonic play is likely to make tumultuous lust less visible than in other forms of play. This invisibility is hard to recognize because of the implict, totalizing character of *ludus* in rationally instrumental, agonic play. We can explain this by a mathematical, semiotic example. In daily life when you buy an apple, you ask for one apple. More precisely, you ask for one out of one apple (i.e. $1/1$). The numerator is the one apple that you want and the denominator is the unit that represents the whole apple. Because the denominator is equal to the numerator, the denominator becomes invisible. In daily life the denominator is not mentioned anymore; therefore you think the one apple is a singularity 'one', the denominator disappears and the 'world' and its component become one. In daily life we only think about the numerator. Imagine that you change the denominator of the apple to 2; suddenly you are asking for half (1/2 parts) of an apple, or one of two whole apples in the bowl. The role of the denominator becomes crucial in this case: it defines the whole of which the numerator is a part, the 'world' in which that part exists. The dominance of *ludus* in rational instrumental play, as exemplifed by agonic play, obscures the link between *ludus* and *paidia*, suggesting that they may be seen as discrete.

When viewing *ludus* as an enrichment of *paidia*, *ludus* may be seen as the numerator and *paidia* the denominator. Suppose the same mechanism arises as described above with the apple, than we forget that *paidia* is the denominator of *ludus*. We disregard the denominator, so *paidia* becomes invisible and we get used to only talking and thinking about sport and adult play in *ludus* terms, so *ludus* becomes the 'world' of play. This leads to a view that the institutionalized rules of *ludus* cover the entire game, which can be caught in a book of or ageement about rules. As a result, *paidia* disappears from the constitution of *ludus*. Caillois has depicted the *paidia–ludus* model into a continuum as follows:

$$Paidia \rightarrow Ludus$$

Consequently, due to this form the invisible denominator results in an unintended distinction between child and adult: *paidia* is for the children and once arrived at *ludus*, one takes on adult characteristics.

Adapting this continuum to highlight its (whole) world by including the denominator '*paidia*' decreases the chance that the constitution of *ludus* changes significantly. It is important to make the denominator visible, especially because *paidia* is hard to grasp due to its uncontrolled forms and outcomes. For instance, many *paidia* forms have no names. It is difficult to capture the daydreaming moments you experience while riding your bike, or the nice smell of fresh mown grass of a sports field which transports you while playing, or the moments of feelings of spontaneous triumph within a game that includes elements of competition. Including the whole 'world of play' means that we suggest adjusting Caillois's continuum as follows:

$$\frac{Paidia}{Ludus} \rightarrow \frac{Ludus}{Paidia}$$

This retains both *paidia* and *ludus* but makes explicit those moments of gaeity, improvisation and lust while removing (or minimizing) the distinction between adult and child. Play is the principle, no matter who starts to play. Adults play most of the *ludus* forms. The proposed model incorporates *paidia* by including *paidia* as a denominator (world-maker and determining the existence) of *ludus*. This means that the connotation of childishness (understood as play-by-children) that is attached to *paidia* disappears.

Hence *paidia* arises in the gaps the actuality of play finds in the formal rules of a game. This explains why people start playing. It is *paidia* that gives impetus to *ludus*; in this form, the game starts and provides lust and turbulence during the game. *Paidia* is enclosed within *ludus* but paradoxically creates the play-world within which *ludus* comes into existence. In adult life *paidia* mostly happens in *ludus*, while in the lives of children *paidia* can exist singularly. This implies that most of the *paidia* in adult life takes places in institutionalized forms. *Ludus* makes it possible for adults to experience *paidia*. These institutions allow adults to play the way children play and remove the connotation of childishness that belongs to *paidia*, as, for example in the way sports fans dress up when attending a game, or when people join carnival, or in the pleasures of triumph that lead to moments of celebration.

The connotation of childishness that is attached to *paidia* constrains adults' abilities to participate openly in the first two stages of *paidia*. The specific energy that originates from *paidia*, the need for turbulence, the eruption of energy, the frolic outburst is in conflict with the adult's fear of being identified as a fool. Activities in *ludus* are not conceived as childish, and until *paidia* is labelled it stays invisible and is difficult to identify or communicate: its invisibility and the 'rules' of adulthood mean that it cannot be an active presence in 'proper' adult life. According to Caillois, *paidia* has disappeared within institutionalized play; however, our argument is that the opposite applies: *paidia* creates the world for adult play and continually forces its way through the interstices in the rules created by the experience of playing the game.

Leaving the uncontrolled and the unprepared out of *ludus* takes away the lust for playing which is the start of self-expression and with it the stimulus of the desire to play and the creator of the view that 'I am' rather than the call to 'I do'. The fundament of *ludus* is lust (*paidia*), which is invisible in the rules and the actuality envisioned by the regulations. We therefore are *homo ludens*, but not quite in the way Huizinga envisaged.

Sport activities are a key vehicle in the drive to reduce health issues such as obesity; we argue that while the focus is often on sport activities, people's involvement is more likely to be as a result of the possiblities for playfulness and joy. The rational instrumentalism of the health paradigm's dominant meta-discourse means that these activities should be evidence-based within the goal-oriented health frame and measured by visible outcomes. In the Netherlands, for instance, the measurable time indicator for appropriate levels of physical activity is 30 minutes a day. This is seen from a rational and anonymous perspective, where there is reluctance to ask about lust, bodily experiences or imagination, the indicators that a person is (self)expressing during play-based physical activity. All sport activities are *ludus*, but it is *paidia*, the unregulated and unprepared form of bodily energy, that brings the player into play. It is this energy that expresses lust, fun and creativity. The fluidity of *paidia*, which gives impetus to *ludus*, provides the motivation for starting and continuing to play. Reconsideration of the goal-oriented health frame is needed. A focus on *paidia*, the power that starts and keeps players playing, can make a valuable contribution to this rethink. It seems clear that the public health debate has won the argument that we *should* be more physically active; perhaps an emphasis on *paidia* will help us become so.

Notes

1 This chapter draws on research carried out as part of the project *The Power of Play: A Philosophical Anthropological Investigation of the Relation between Play and Physical (In)activity among Adults in Various Body Cultures*, PR 13–01, Maastricht University, Department of Health, Ethics and Society (Horstman, 2013).
2 *The Power of Play.*
3 Other forms of this argument may be seen in Bateman (2011) and Fuchs (in this volume).
4 Following Caillois, we do not maintain this distinction.
5 Consider for instance Gros (2009/14).
6 See *YouTube*, www.youtube.com/watch?v=Cdf6D19Etmc (accessed 6 December 2014).
7 See also Dönmez in this volume regarding freedom and rule compliance.

References

Bateman, C. (2011) *Imaginary Games*, Winchester: Zero Books.
Bateson, P. (2005) 'The role of play in the evolution of great apes and humans', in Pellegrini, A. and Smith, P. (eds) *The Nature of Play: Great Apes and Humans*, London: Guildford Press.
Caillois, R. (1958) *Man, Play and Games*, transl. (1961) Barash, M., New York: The Free Press of Glencoe Inc.
Dunphy, E. (1977) *Only a Game? The Diary of a Professional Footballer*, ed. Ball, P., Harmondsworth: Penguin Books.
Eichberg, H. (2009) 'Sports in the life cycle: Diversity in and of ageing', *Sport, Ethics and Philosophy*, 3(3), 325–45.
Gros, F. (2009/2014) *A Philosophy of Walking*, transl. Howe, J., London: Verso.
Hamilton, M. T., Healy, G. N., Dunstan, D. W., Zderic, T. W. and Owen, N. (2008) 'Too little exercise and too much sitting: Inactivity physiology and the need for new recommendations on sedentary behavior', *Current Cardiovascular Risk Reports*, 2, 292–8.
Horstman, K. (2013) *The Power of Play: A Philosophical Anthropological Investigation of the Relation between Play and Physical (In)activity among Adults in Various Body Cultures*, research proposal, Maastricht University, Department of Health, Ethics and Society.
Huizinga, J. (1938/2008) *Homo Ludens: Proeve eener bepaling van het spelelement der cultuur*. Amsterdam: Amsterdam University Press.
Huizinga, J. (1950/1955) *Homo Ludens: A Study of the Play-element in Culture*, Boston: Beacon Press.
Isen, A. J. (2006) 'The influence of positive affect on intrinsic and extrinsic motivation: Facilitating enjoyment of play, responsible work behaviour and self-control', *Motivation and Emotion*, 29(4), 297–325.

Kohl, H. W., Craig, C. L., Lambert, E. V., Inoue, S., Alkandari, J. R., Leetongin, G. and Kahlmeier, S. (2012) 'The pandemic of physical inactivity: Global action for public health', *The Lancet*, 380(9893), 294–305.

Lee, I.-M., Shiroma, E. J., Lobelo, F., Puska, P., Blair, S. N. and Katzmarzyk, P. T. (2012) 'Effect of physical activity on major non-communicable diseases worldwide: An analysis of burden of disease and life expectancy', *The Lancet*, 380(9893), 219–29.

Lester, S. and Russell, W. (2008) *Play for a Change, Play, Policy and Practice: A Review of Contemporary Perspectives*, London: National Childrens Bureau.

MacLean, M. (2011) 'Choosing ill-health: Aspects of a critical sociology of physical activity', in Schultz, H., Wright, P. R. and Hauser, T. (eds) *Exercise, Sports and Health*, Chemnitz: Universtätsverlag Chemnitz, 184–92.

Midgley, M. (1974) 'The Game Game', *Philosophy*, 49(189/July), 231–53.

Pellegrini, A. (ed.) (2011) *The Oxford Handbook of the Development of Play*, New York: Oxford University Press.

Plato (1967–68) *Plato in Twelve Volumes*, volumes 10 and 11, transl. Bury, R. G., Cambridge, MA: Harvard University Press; London: William Heinemann Ltd.

Suits, B. (1988) 'The elements of sport', in Morgan, W. J. and Meijer, K. V. (eds) *Philosophical Inquiry in Sport*, Champaign, IL: Human Kinetics, 39–48.

Sutton-Smith, B. (1997) *The Ambiguity of Play*, Cambridge, MA: Harvard University Press.

Van Lenthe, F. J., Kamphuis, C. B. M., Giskes, K., Huisman, M., Brug, J. and Mackenbach, J. P. (2010) 'Sociaal-economische verschillen in recreatief bewegen: De rol van de fysieke en sociale leefomgeving', *Tijdschrift voor gezondheidswetenschappen*, 88(1), 32–40.

WHO (2010) *Global Recommendations on Physical Activity for Health*, Geneva: World Health Organisation Press.

10 Locating rhythms

Improvised play in the built environment

Dani Abulhawa

In his text on seeing Manhattan from the hundred-and-tenth floor of the World Trade Centre, Michel de Certeau describes the relationship of walkers to the city as being like 'lovers in each other's arms' (1984: 93). He writes,

> the ordinary practitioners of the city live 'down below', below the thresholds at which visibility begins ... they are walkers ... whose bodies follow the thicks and thins of an urban 'text' they write without being able to read it.
>
> (1984: 93)

Although de Certeau's perspective is from a literal position above the street, his reference to 'down below' suggests a metaphor – below the level of consciousness – to describe how walkers accustom themselves to the flow of the city and negotiate their routes through corporeal rather than cognitive means: we move and are moved in ways that are beyond our conscious awareness.

The flows we follow in urban spaces, often unthinkingly, derive from the 'perceived', 'conceived' and 'lived' elements of space that Henri Lefebvre articulates as constituting the production of space (1991). In contemporary urban spaces, these flows often serve the smooth transacting of capital in relation to productive human behaviour – from one shop to another, or from home to place of work and back again. These dominant practices, which are established over time, become embedded in space and bodies leading to tacitly understood rules of movement and behaviour. Our seemingly free movement in public spaces is better understood as freedom within the confines of an already established, embodied and therefore ubiquitous (and invisible) set of regulations.

In relation to this, Lefebvre's final work on space, titled *Rhythmanalysis* (2004), looks at how we can understand space as consisting of rhythms – the interaction of expenditures of energy in time and space. Alongside dominant movement there are also practices that sit in dialogue – those that critique, subvert and interrupt the flow of dominant spatial practice. This chapter considers this idea of rhythmic interruption, through a focus on my own version of a playful performance practice I have undertaken in various cities and towns throughout the UK as part of a practice-as-research project. The chapter begins by outlining Lefebvre's theory of rhythmanalysis as part of his broader theory of the production of space, which is followed by my rhythmanalysis of three moments of playful practice and the knowledge produced through exploring the practice in this way. These three moments are addressed in two sections: the first discusses the relationship of play to dominant ordinary rhythms, and the second explores a moment of flow with another person and the rhythmic connection experienced in this encounter.

The play in this project was developed as a transformation of skateboarding, following my own history of involvement in the subculture. I questioned why there was a lack of female involvement in skateboarding and identified other playful urban practices, such as rollerblading and parkour, where there appeared to be a similar lack of female involvement. Understanding this issue as one concerned with the relationship between gender and play, and freedom of behaviour in public urban spaces, I began my research with the question: how and why might a woman choose to play in the public built environment? In order to address this enquiry, one aspect of the research involved me adopting a type of play in urban spaces as a form of social and physical experimentation (Figures 10.1 and 10.2).

The form that my play takes is improvisatory, in relation to both the more permanent elements of space and the temporal presence of people. In the moment of playing, an offer that comes from an external source is either accepted and incorporated or blocked. In order to develop my improvisation

Figure 10.1 Image from *Unknowable*, performed in Sheffield, 2014 (photo: David Penny).

Figure 10.2 Image from *Unknowable*, performed in Sheffield, 2014 (photo: David Penny).

skills, it has been necessary for me to adopt openness with regards to my surroundings, in which I occupy a state of not being attached to a fixed notion of self, space and place. It requires an ability to see the world and the body as containing possibilities for a range of actions and experiences, rather than adhering to a system of already established habitual patterns and rules.

The notion of 'play' encompasses a wide range of different activities, but this chapter is focused on free improvised play, as opposed to playful practices of a more rule-bound or structured nature. In my practice, this playing is primarily movement-based, involving my interaction with street objects, people or paving patterns, or simply my moving through or occupying of sites in an unusual way. The practice is very much not dance, involving unskilled and vernacular or easy physical expression. In actuality, the practice does have clear skill to it, particularly around improvisation and the ability to respond creatively and spontaneously, but the movement itself does not bear any markers of virtuosic or formal movement practices.

The multi-modal practice-as-research process also integrated critical reflection on these performances of play and an engagement with existing theory during and after the event of play. Lefebvre's theories of spatial production became central to this, because they offer a way to understand how my playing functions *within* the everyday, at the micro level of movement and the slightest physical gestures, as an important contribution to 'spatial practice'. The interaction of Lefebvre's theories with 'real-life' experiences raises an awareness of the importance and power of the instant of play in the public built environment.

Rhythmanalysis

Lefebvre embraces the knowing body in his theories of space, but particularly in *Rhythmanalysis*, in which he explicitly critiques philosophical enquiry that understands thinking only as something located in the mind. He writes:

> the Cartesian tradition has long reigned in philosophy. It is exhausted, but remains present ... what *we* have thought over the course of the preceding pages implies another concept of *thinking*. It is to think that which is not thought: the game and the risk, love, art, violence, in a word, the *world*, or more precisely the diverse relations between human beings and the universe.
>
> (2004: 17)

For Lefebvre, then, omitting bodily knowing from the project of philosophy denies the opportunity to fully explore the world of knowledge.

This knowing is inherent in the 'screaming monumentality' of the steps of Gare Saint Charles in Marseille, as described by Regulier and Lefebvre in their 'Attempt at the rhythmanalysis of Mediterranean cities' (2004). The steps are navigated through a muscular negotiation of the weight of the body, they initiate the body into the city, they offer a particular vantage, and they set a pace that must be reconsidered at the point of the next rhythmic engagement with the built environment. They explain,

> [t]hey are for the traveller the obligatory – one could say initiatory – passage for the descent towards the city, towards the sea. More than that of a gate or an avenue, their screaming monumentality imposes on the body and on consciousness the requirement of passing from one rhythm to another, as yet unknown – to be discovered.
>
> (2004: 97)

The notion of passage is also important; the steps mark an exiting from an enclosure and the rhythms contained within it. The descent places the city at a tonal depth from the station and point of arrival. All of these things can be described perfectly well, but the experience of them – in situ – is integral to a full understanding because of the complex and embodied way that space is produced.

Lefebvre sets up a basic framework for the analysis of rhythms, which involves a consideration of the following from the perspective of the individual:

(a) repetition (of movements, gestures, action, situations, differences);
(b) interferences of linear processes and cyclical processes;
(c) birth, growth, peak, then decline and end.

(Lefebvre, 2004: 15)

Repetition is an important, identifying feature of rhythm. Also, Lefebvre makes a distinction between linear and cyclical rhythms, arguing that cyclical rhythms derive from nature, whereas linear rhythms are a product of social practice. He writes:

> [t]he cyclical originates in the cosmic, in nature: days, nights, seasons, the waves and tides of the sea, monthly cycles, etc. The linear would come rather from social practice, therefore from human activity: the monotony of actions and of movements, imposed structures.
>
> (Lefebvre, 2004: 8)

This distinction does not attempt to articulate human beings and their actions as unnatural, but rather emphasises how human activity sets out to rationalize and measure. For example, time as a linear construct is a fiction that allows human beings to measure their existence, but it compartmentalizes experience and places a marker on the end point of a process sometimes to the detriment and disregard of an experience of the process itself, or to any notion of a continuity of experience. For Lefebvre these two rhythmic dynamics – the linear and the cyclical – exist together as an 'antagonistic unity' (2004: 8). He writes, '[t]ime and space, the cyclical and the linear, exert a reciprocal action: they measure themselves against one another; each one makes itself and is made a measuring-measure; everything is cyclical repetition through linear repetitions' (2004: 8). This antagonistic relationship between cyclical and linear repetitions is revealed in the playful practice of this research; linear repetitions are connected with a rational and economic practice of the public built environment, while cyclical repetition is more closely connected with the rhythms of the body and playful practices occurring in these sites. As my research practice shows, the dichotomy between linear and cyclical repetitions becomes muddled when commodified forms of playful movement are also considered.

Lefebvre's final point in his framework for analysing rhythm – its building and eventual dying out – is a way to understand rhythm from the embodied perspective as a sequence that is determined by the individual in a moment of interaction of 'a place, a time and an expenditure of energy' (2004: 15). Lefebvre's theory does not work when considered from an abstracted position – the fly-on-the-wall perspective of watching space from 'nowhere'. There is no such space in which to determine when rhythm begins, peaks, declines and ends, unless within the present.

Therefore space is experienced from an individual, embodied perspective. For someone who crosses the road and begins walking across Albert Square in Manchester, their rhythm will begin from their first step on the cobblestones and end when they step onto the flagstones at the other side. Their 'peak' might be nothing more than reaching the centre of the square, or the walker might reach a peak of their heart rate. Or this person's peak might occur as their movement intersects suddenly with three other walkers, who are also crossing the square. On the other hand, for the person who sits on the outskirts of Albert Square during their lunch break their experience of beginning, middle and end of rhythm is in the witnessing of other expenditures of energy, in time and in this square. The rhythmic peak for this watcher might come as three or four walkers exchange paths like two waves colliding in the centre of the square, or when the watcher witnesses a sudden downpour that speeds up the pedestrians and scatters them quickly out of the square. Therefore, there are not only different perspectives of rhythm in space but also different knowledges and ways of knowing spatial rhythms.

While the play activity of my research does not constitute ordinary, everyday movement performed in public spaces, its rhythms are still born from within the ordinary spatial practice of specific places. Playful practices connect with space in oblique ways, absorbing rhythms from people, objects and architecture and expressing them in heightened or more elaborate ways that serves to create a dialogue between Lefebvre's triad of the 'lived', 'conceived' and 'perceived' elements of space.

The power of the instant

Lefebvre's theories on the production of space are conceptually located in his triad consisting of 'spatial practice', 'representations of space' and 'representational space'. This tripartite structure of space is conditioned by the history of a particular site, what Lefebvre describes as 'the "etymology" of locations in the sense of what happened at a particular spot or place … all of this becomes inscribed in space' (1991: 37). 'Spatial practice' refers to the 'perceived' elements of space – the tangible, permanent elements of space; what we understand as the 'built' environment. These permanent elements are planned and built over time in response to the ostensible needs of society; they typically support functional, often capitalist purposes of commercial exchange and profit. 'Representations of space' refers to the 'conceived' elements of space – our symbolic understanding of spaces, mental images, as well as the physical enactment of these images of space in the form of maps. These conceived elements are subject to the influences of a dominant cultural ideology; maps are always a projection of the real and as such represent a particular viewpoint. 'Representational space' is the 'lived' elements of space – the ephemeral, physical activities and movements, and here is where the great possibility of space lies. Lived space is the immediate and fluid context within which practices of resistance and play are possible (Lefebvre, 1991: 38–9).

Importantly the three parts of Lefebvre's schema are not to be thought of as separate from one another – each part contributes to another, while examples of activity occurring in spaces are likely to fit into each of these categories in different ways. Lefebvre's theory does not suggest that there is a fixed, unchangeable, built environment; rather his model acknowledges the interrelationship of ostensibly more permanent elements, alongside the ephemeral and the psychological, bearing in mind that space is experienced always from an individual's embodied perspective.

Explaining the way in which these three points might fold into one another, Marco Cenzatti writes,

> the physical space of, say, a square does not change when it is occupied by a market, a political rally, or a carnival. Yet the social relations taking place in the different instances produce different 'lived moments' – different spaces of representation ... [these] may leave traces in the built environment and change the physical space.... They are a modification of the physical space and, therefore, a spatial practice. They can also change our perception of space ... thus fitting into Lefebvre's second 'moment' [his representation of space].
>
> (Cenzatti, 2008: 80–1)

Skateboarders, for example, in their occupation of a city square, create a 'representational space' in which they perform their skateboarding activity. This impacts on the environment in physical and symbolic ways: first, the act of skateboarding causes markings on the physical parts of the space, which adds to the perceived elements of space. Second, for the skateboarder performing this activity as well as for people occupying a site at the moment of performance and witnessing skateboarders' markings after the event, this experience is likely to affect how spaces of the built environment are conceived (Borden, 1999, 2001). Therefore, as Lefebvre theorizes, ephemeral moments in space are actually very powerful indeed. While the more permanent, enduring features of space (buildings, maps, memories) might seem to occupy the most importance in a common conception of space, they are documents of our physical occupation and use of the environment.

Our ephemeral performances often adhere to dominant flows of movement and behaviour, but they can also be transformative interruptions of spatial production. Stuart Elden, writing in the introduction to *Rhythmanalysis*, explains how early in Lefebvre's work he had been influenced by a particular concept of Nietzsche's – his 'Augenblick', the blink of an eye. Elden writes:

> [f]or Lefebvre, moments are significant times when existing orthodoxies are open to challenge, when things have the potential to be over-turned or radically altered, moments of crisis in the original sense of the term. Rather than the Bergsonian notion of *durée*, duration, Lefebvre was privileging the importance of the instant.
>
> (Elden, 2004: x)

Actions undertaken within the instant either adhere to the perceived and conceived elements of space, often unconsciously, or else they function as a resistance and challenge to space, which results in changes to conceived and – over time and repetition perhaps – to perceived space. As an extension of his theory in *The Production of Space* (1991), Lefebvre's swansong – his theory of rhythmanalysis – delves deeper into his triad and his interest in the present moment, through considering it as composed of rhythms.

The rhythmanalytic project is a fundamentally embodied one. The ephemerality of the lived moment places the body at the centre of the enquiry among the 'polyrhythmia' of the everyday. Lefebvre writes:

we know that a rhythm is slow or lively only in relation to other rhythms (often our own: those of our walking, our breathing, our heart) … spontaneously each of us has our own preferences, references, frequencies; each must appreciate rhythms by referring them to oneself, one's heart, or breathing, but also to one's hours of work, of rest, of waking and of sleep.

(Lefebvre, 2004: 10)

The findings of my research practice result from my consideration of the similarities and differences between the rhythms of my play activity compared with other rhythms within these spaces, or between my play activity and my memory and experience of ordinary rhythms I have performed in these spaces of the public built environment. The two examples of play discussed within this chapter explore moments that illustrate these kinds of rhythmic relation and the knowledge that results from them. This knowledge of rhythm, then, is situated and local, and likely to shift as spaces alter through the dialectical engagement of Lefebvre's spatial triad.

This foregrounding of an embodied, phenomenological perspective of space, alongside the interrelationship of Lefebvre's triad of 'spatial practice', 'representations of space' and 'representational space', forms the foundation of theories that considers space and place as, in the words of Edensor, 'always in a process of becoming' (2010: 3). Ingold's notion of the 'dwelling perspective' relates clearly with Lefebvre's concept of rhythmanalysis. He writes:

the world continually comes into being around the inhabitant, and its manifold constituents take on significance through their incorporation into a regular pattern of life activity. It has been rather more usual, in social and cultural anthropology, to suppose that people inhabit a world – of culture or society – to which form and meaning have already been attached.

(2000: 153)

Ingold privileges an ongoing practice of place and objects as the project of weaving existence – places, buildings, artefacts and natural objects are always in a state of being made by their occupation and usage, rather than being conceived of as finished, completed things that form the setting or backdrop for life.

The presence of features such as desire lines[1] in landscapes, the curved wearing away of hard stone steps in mill factories over hundreds of years, or the markings made by skateboarders from grinding and sliding against planters, curbs and benches demonstrate some of the ways that objects and buildings are transformed over time through different types of use (Borden 1999, 2001). Similarly, environments and practices transform the bodies of people – for example, the popular complaint of veteran skateboarders having 'shit knees' refers to the wear and tear of joints through high-impact jumps down sets of steps.[2]

Rhythmanalysis (2004) includes a chapter in which Lefebvre discusses 'dressage' to explain how human beings are broken in to the ways of moving and holding themselves that are common within a society or nation through repetition of acts, gestures and movement that serve to perpetuate, rather than challenge, the conceived and perceived elements of space. Dressage is also a term adopted by Foucault in *Discipline and Punish* (1977), in which the body is seen as a site in which power is enacted through the training and disciplining of the human body. Lefebvre is, in a similar thread to Foucault, critical of our 'urban–state–market society' (Lefebvre, 2004: 6), remarking '[t]he commodity prevails over everything' (2004: 6). Because rhythms are the means by which 'dressage' is activated, and therefore power is performed, this chapter examines the ways in which play might be understood as operating within everyday rhythms as a powerful instant that disrupts productive, commercial space.

The sites in which the practice takes place are of key importance. The built environment is increasingly a place in which people's rhythms (their expenditures of energy in space and time) serve a dominantly commercial aim, to get them from one place of consumption or production to another. In his book, *Performance and the Contemporary City* (2010), Nicolas Whybrow asserts that an increasing interest in urban space as a site for performance and art derives from 'the perception that increasingly the behaviour of individuals in urban space is becoming restricted in fact to little more than the 'right to shop' (2010: 195).

Therefore this chapter refers to my practice as an example of a type of play that is best characterized as representative of an unusual and critical form of spatial practice in the public built environment: a lived space moment in tension with conceived and perceived space. It allows the player to consider the built environment as grounds for open physical improvised expression, and in doing so critiques dominant spatial rhythms. Rather than seeing this approach to play as a frivolous and unimportant interruption, Lefebvre's theory of rhythmanalysis opens up a theoretical case for the ephemeral playful moment to be seen as a powerful instant that accentuates the elements of lived space. Reflections on my own practice articulate how an instance of play might work as a critique of space in practice.

Play as intra-ordinary rhythm – cyclical and linear repetitions

The body is the means by which rhythms are experienced and responded to tacitly in ways that are not preconceived by the individual. This capacity of the body to organise itself rhythmically, in a way that is quite unknowable to the individual, can be seen in the way that the menstrual cycles of women who live or work together sometimes synchronize over time. In terms of space and place, Edensor argues that 'corporeal capacities to sense rhythm ... organise the subjective and cultural experience of place' (2010: 5), acknowledging how the body is drawn into patterns and speeds of movement within specific locales.

There have been several moments during my practice when a rhythmic engagement with a specific site was revealed to me. On one occasion, I was

Locating rhythms 145

playing on a set of railings that line the edge of the Shena Simon building on Whitworth Street in Manchester. Standing with the right side of my body closest to the railings, I grabbed a spike with my right hand and hauled my right foot onto the bottom rung of the railing. Tipping my body forward slightly, I allowed my left side to fall in towards the railings, grabbing a new spike with my left hand further along and setting my left foot down on the bottom rung of the railing. Then I would switch my left hand for my right, and my left foot for my right foot and repeat this movement again until I had reached the end of the railings.

Moving gradually in this way, I made a linear progression across the railings, similar to the movement of pedestrians around me, but in a way that was inefficient and slower, incorporating a cyclical action of swinging and dipping (as I switched hands and feet). The action of swinging reminded me of the swing of a person's arm as they propel themselves forward to walk. The repetition of a dipping motion also felt as though it resembled the slight dipping and rising of hips during an ordinary walking action, which can be noticed more clearly when slowed down. Therefore, the play action was not absurdly 'out of the ordinary', but can be more accurately described as entirely 'within the ordinary' – a pattern of behaviour and actions born out of the ordinary rhythms exhibited (and performed by myself) within this type of space.

This instant of play utilized an aspect of the space – the railings – that are designed in the conceived space of planners and in everyday spatial practices to keep people out, but also to dissolve out of public consciousness. My playing on the railings both underlines the fact that they are there, and undermines their status as a symbol of authoritarian control. In this way, my playing can be understood as a subversion of the dominant movement performed within this space, and a critique of authoritarian control; therefore it is an instant that opens up a dialectical interrelationship with perceived and conceived space.

As a subversion of dominant rhythms, the playful action I developed on these railings also demonstrates the 'antagonistic unity' of linear and cyclical rhythms. The act of walking is dominantly understood through the propelling of a person forwards in space and time. The action of walking, however, integrates many cyclical repetitions activated thorough the mechanics of the body, which are commonly not paid attention to and are seen as ancillary to the linear rhythmical process of walking. The swinging and dipping of my playful action on the railings heightened the cyclical aspects of this movement and relied upon the transfer of weight as my body became hinged against each railing.

This heightening of cyclical repetition through play can also be seen in another intervention in Manchester's Exchange Square. I was experimenting with video recording my practice, which provided me with a unique view that captured an interesting moment. I was located at the side of the Harvey Nichols building at the top of a gradual sloped walkway that links Exchange Square with Deansgate. At this time, the square housed a 'big wheel' tourist attraction, allowing public to view the city from 60 metres above ground.[3] I had positioned the camera on a tripod at the bottom of the slope, closest to Deansgate, and angled the camera upwards, so that it would capture me performing at the top of the slope and making my way down. This vantage also captured several of the buildings in the background as well as the top of the big wheel.

The slope has a stone-columned railing on one side. Facing this rail and slotting my feet into the gaps between these pillars, I took hold of the handrail and began a movement that involved placing my right toes into a gap, followed by my left toes, and then turning 180° (so that my back was against the rail) and placing my right heel, followed by my left into gaps further along. This (rather awkward) action was repeated as I moved slowly down the slope towards the camera.

When I reviewed the footage my movement was very slow. The wheel in the background – also moving very slowly – appeared static, much like the buildings surrounding it. I became bored watching my slow progression and decided to fast-forward the footage. As I watched the rate of my circling increase rapidly on the screen, I was surprised and fascinated to see the big wheel in the background of the image speed up at a very similar rate. Not only was my movement reciprocating the turning of the wheel, but I was also moving at a very similar speed. With the image sped up, I was able to notice the synchronicity between myself and the wheel, in comparison with the speed and movements of other objects and people within the frame.

In this example, my bodily absorption of rhythm came from a connection made to the imposing mechanical wheel that occupied so much of Exchange Square, rather than from pedestrians walking, as could be inferred in the previous example. It is interesting that in this example of play, as with the previous one, there is a heightening of and connection with cyclical repetition. While there is this rhythmical similarity between my act of play and the Big Wheel, there is also a stark ideological contrast between the two, since The Big Wheel represents an activity of commodified play in the built environment through its association with tourism and leisure time.

Play as intra-ordinary rhythm – connecting with other bodies

Many play theorists have explored the unification that play engenders (particularly Csikszentmihalyi and Bennett, 1971, Schechner and Schuman, 1976, Turner, 1982 and Sutton-Smith, 2001). It is mainly discussed in relation to organised play, such as games, sporting events and festivals, in respect of how individuals become part of a collective playful culture that involves a temporary removal from everyday life and a range of social engagements within that play world. Schechner and Schuman state:

> a play community generally tends to become permanent even after the game is over ... the feeling of being 'apart together' in an exceptional situation, of sharing something important, of mutual withdrawing from the rest of the world and rejecting the usual norms, retains its magic beyond the duration of the individual game.
>
> (1976: 54)

This suggests that play bonds individuals through the shared experience of an extraordinary event or encounter and that the connection felt during play is retained.

Therefore the unifying power of play tends to be discussed in terms of its function of developing community. Following a description of a Catalan festival (citing Noyes, 1995) in which a participant explains his feeling of becoming part of the mass of bodies, Brian Sutton-Smith remarks that 'festivals bring a renewal of community identity' (2001: 110), acknowledging the communal bond that a play-space brings and the expression of an identity played out by that community. This perspective echoes that of Carl Seashore – writing as far back as the beginning of the twentieth century. He articulates play as a social tool, stating 'we become like those with whom we play' (1910: 514) and thus suggesting that play homogenizes through shared identity. These perspectives posit play as a tool in the production of a dominant community identity or ideology, which does not quite explain the type of connection made in my own performances of playing.

In contrast to these notions of play, Csikszentmihalyi's theory of attention and flow relates more to the rhythmic ontology of play as distinct from ideological connections between participants of a community. He describes attention as a form of 'psychic energy' (1990: 33), which is invested and spent in the process of engaging in tasks. Flow is the state of being held within this kind of deep attention as part of a given task. Being in a state of flow is understood as not exclusive to play, but many of the examples used by Csikszentmihalyi are drawn from a wide range of play activities and events.

As Csikszentmihalyi explains, during the experience of flow, participants experience a weakened sense of self and gain a feeling of union with fellow participants and/or environments. He states that

> when a person invests all her psychic energy into an interaction – whether it is with another person, a boat, a mountain, or a piece of music – she in effect becomes part of a system of action greater than what the individual self had been before.
>
> (1990: 65)

In Csikszentmihalyi's theory, the focusing of attention allows for 'self-transcendence' (1990: 64) where the body is operating in a state of being in total cooperation with another person or object. The notion of selfhood, then, is to be understood as contingent upon 'presence': the self is constructed over and again in each instant of space and time and in relationship to other people and rhythms within that instant.

An instant of play in Plymouth demonstrates how such a connection can be experienced in practice. I was located in one of the main pedestrian shopping streets in the city centre, stepping from one paving stone to another to avoid the cracks and sometimes using the linear gaps between stones as a pretend tight-rope, trying to balance my feet while moving forwards and backwards.

While I was playing, a boy about 16 years of age walked up and stood next to me. I paused as I registered his presence and then began to continue with my activity. As I shifted my foot to the right, he copied me. I moved to the left, and he followed. I began to try and catch him out, shifting my weight quickly, but an intense concentration developed between us such that we began to move in almost perfect synchronicity.

Although I was directing our movement, I kept pausing, hoping that he might take the lead. After what was only a minute of play but seemed to me like a much longer period, he dropped his attention and ran away. Neither of us made an attempt to converse in any way, and we didn't ever look at each other, as we moved entirely on the basis of a peripheral vantage of the other person's actions. Despite this lack of visual contact, I felt close to the body of this stranger and our interaction was based on miniscule details apparent from close proximity.

As an instant of play, it was mildly competitive; a playful resistance that developed into synchronicity and appeared like an impromptu choreography between two different people. When he walked up and stood next to me, my engagement with the site was split between the paving stones and him. When he broke from the 'communitas' (Turner, 1982) we had created – indeed, it felt like the space was suddenly shattered – I remember feeling that I had to adjust myself, to make a connection internally, in order to go back to playing on my own. My attention, which had been focused on him, was refocused back on my feet, those stones and those cracks (Figure 10.3).

Figure 10.3 Film still from *Alice in Plymouth*, Plymouth city centre, 2009 (image: David Penny).

In this example of play in direct connection with another person, my consciousness was extended to incorporate the person standing next to me out of a desire to respond to him as much as the rhythms of the pattern of paving stones or the actions of walkers. If a notion of the 'self' is understood as fluid, then we (myself and this boy) developed a connection in the present that was 'me', 'him' and 'us' simultaneously. This was our peak of rhythmic connection – a brief instant of synchronized movement – and the boy's breaking of attention and running away signalled the end of our interaction.

Though people in public places interact in lots of ways, holding doors open for each other, saying 'good morning', and through the interaction between customers and business owners, play in many forms is able to generate spaces of rhythmic synchronicity between people in the public built environment that is not primarily concerned with the flow of capital, the generation of profit, the productivity and efficiency of individuals, or the creation of an ideological community identity. It also operates at a deeper corporeal and rhythmic level than the superficial communication and interactions required to ensure the smooth flow of capital in commercial spaces.

Conclusion

Lefebvre's theory of rhythmanalysis provides a theory and framework for understanding an embodied experience of space and the interrelationship of elements in his spatial triad, as well as raising the status of the instant as having great powerful potential. An instant has the potential to function critically as a site of resistance to the otherwise smooth flow of dominant spatial rhythms in the public built environment, which increasingly serves a commercially driven conception of space. Lefebvre's theory contributes much to the study of improvised forms of play, offering a suitable framework within which to gain access to the knowledges contained within improvised practice of the public built environment. His theories are also particularly useful in illuminating an understanding of the connection felt in moments of flow during play.

Free improvised play is a particular type of playing that avoids formalization and rules. It involves the absorption of rhythms in space and suggests the possibility of alternative movement. It highlights dominant pedestrian movement through its contrast, and it draws attention to exclusionary objects (such as railings) that delineate space but that are designed to sit quietly in the background.

Forms of play often respond critically to the commercialized, alienating features of the public built environment. In terms of linear and cyclical rhythms, free improvised play adopts a non-regulated mode of attention and behaviour in these spaces that interrupts the smooth flow of productive and efficient linear rhythms. My experience of free improvised playful practice highlights how play heightens the cyclical rhythms of space, though this is, perhaps, compromised by commodified forms of play, which adopt cyclical rhythms for a commercial aim.

This chapter has also considered a rhythmic ontology of play as distinct from ideological or instrumental conceptions of play, which are concerned with how play functions as a tool for learning necessary skills and behaviours or establishing personal and community identity. Referring to Csikszentmihalyi's theory of flow, the rhythmic ontology of free improvised play is understood through the way that it produces deep connections between players and between players and objects. In this way it challenges the dominant spatial practice of public space, particularly the way that the perceived and conceived elements of space engender lived practices that partition people through the avoidance of physical closeness and contact and achieve productive pedestrian rhythms that serve the flow of consumption and capital. Play, therefore, functions as dialectic practice within Lefebvre's triad.

The activity of playing in a free, improvised way with objects and others can be understood in relation to Lefebvre as an instant of engagement that creates deep rhythmic interaction and synchronicity. These instants – of connection and critique of space – are vital rhythmic interruptions in the public built environment.

Notes

1 A path created through the gradual deterioration of the land due to persistent use by pedestrians or cyclists.
2 Jumping sets of steps is a popular skateboarding trick and most skateboarding videos feature stair jumps. The number of steps and their depth is proportionate to the level of difficulty. The terrain on which the steps are approached and landed also adds to the difficulty.
3 The 'Big Wheel' was removed in April 2012 and has since been relocated to Piccadilly Gardens.

References

Borden, I. (1999) *A Theorised History of Skateboarding with Particular Reference to the Ideas of Henri Lefebvre*, unpublished thesis, University of London.
Borden, I. (2001) *Skateboarding, Space and the City: Architecture and the Body*, Oxford and New York: Berg.
Cenzatti, M. (2008) 'Heterotopias of difference', in Dehaene, M. and De Cantor, L. (eds) *Heterotopia and the City: Public Space in a Postcivil Society*, London and New York: Routledge.
Csikszentmihalyi, M. (1990) *Flow: The Psychology of Optimal Experience*, New York: Harper and Row.
Csikszentmihalyi, M. and Bennett, S. (1971) 'An exploratory model of play', *American Anthropologist*, New Series, 73(1), 45–58.
De Certeau, M. (1984) *The Practice of Everyday Life*, Berkeley, Los Angeles and London: University of California Press.
Edensor, T. (ed.) (2010) *Geographies of Rhythm: Nature, Place, Mobilities and Bodies*, Farnham and Burlington: Ashgate.
Elden, S. (2004) 'Rhythmanalysis: An introduction', in Lefebvre, H., *Rhythmanalysis: Space, Time and Everyday Life*, London and New York: Continuum.

Foucault, M. (1977) *Discipline and Punish: The Birth of the Prison*, transl. Sheridan, A., Harmondsworth: Penguin.

Ingold, T. (2000) *The Perception of the Environment: Essays on Livelihood, Dwelling and Skill*, London and New York: Routledge.

Lefebvre, H. (1991) *The Production of Space*, transl. Nicholson-Smith, D., Oxford and Malden: Blackwell.

Lefebvre, H. (2004) *Rhythmanalysis: Space, Time and Everyday Life*, transl. Elden, S. and Moore, G., London and New York: Continuum.

Regulier, C. and Lefebvre, H. (2004) 'Attempt at the rhythmanalysis of Mediterranean cities', in Lefebvre, H., *Rhythmanalysis: Space, Time and Everyday Life*, transl. Elden, S. and Moore, G., London and New York: Continuum.

Schechner, R. and Shuman, M. (eds) (1976) *Ritual, Play and Performance: Readings in the Social Sciences/Theatre*, New York: Seabury Press.

Seashore, C. (1910) 'The play impulse and attitude in religion', *The American Journal of Theology*, 14(4), 505–20.

Sutton-Smith, B. (2001) *The Ambiguity of Play: Second Edition*, Cambridge, MA and London: Harvard University Press.

Turner, V. (1982) *From Ritual to Theatre: The Human Seriousness of Play*, New York: PAJ Publications.

Whybrow, N. (ed.) (2010) *Performance and the Contemporary City: An Interdisciplinary Reader*, London: Palgrave Macmillan.

11 Weltentzug und Weltzerfall (world-withdrawal and world-decay)

Heidegger's notions of withdrawal from the world and the decay of worlds in the times of computer games

Mathias Fuchs

World-withdrawal

This chapter investigates whether the concepts of 'world-withdrawal' and 'world-decay' that German philosopher Martin Heidegger elaborated for traditional works of art in the 1930s have any currency for contemporary cultural artefacts such as computer games. It is tempting to apply Heidegger's terminology to the player-game-world triangle, as it seems to describe in a very literal way, and very close to 'the things', a situation that we can observe today when a gamer puts a computer monitor on a table, watches a world in front of his eyes and notices that the world he is watching has withdrawn. The world has decayed. Albert Hofstadter calls Heidegger's method 'the most concrete thinking and speaking about Being' (Heidegger, 1971: xi, translator's introduction). A statement such as 'the work puts up a world' ('stellt eine Welt auf') sounds as if a simple object – that which we call world – is about to be put on its feet, like a monitor upon the table. For a gamer a world is in most cases first of all the entity of game levels in a videogame and not a philosophical concept. The language of the phenomenological thinker works on two levels at the same time. It actually talks about palpable things and it talks about ideas as well. That is why Heidegger calls his work the work of a poet ('Dichter'). In German a 'Dichter' is a poet, somebody who condenses things.

A computer game is a visual, acoustic or textual artefact ('angefertigtes Ding', Heidegger, 1960: 10) that claims some relation to the real world outside the game-world. This relationship might be mimetic or constructed otherwise, yet it always refers to the world we live in at a certain point in time. The problem with the game is that it has been created at a certain moment, a certain decade, a historic context and with a certain place in mind, but at the moment we look at the game, listen to it or experience it spatially, the time and place of its origin have gone. Ubisoft's recent game *Assassin's Creed® Unity*, for example, is staged in Paris and takes place during the years following the revolution in 1789 (Figure 11.1).

Figure 11.1 Assassin's Creed® Unity (© 2014 Ubisoft Entertainment. All Rights Reserved. Assassin's Creed, Ubisoft and the Ubisoft logo are trademarks of Ubisoft Entertainment in the US and/or other countries. All other rights are reserved by Ubisoft Entertainment.)

But this year has long since gone and contemporary Paris definitely looks, smells and sounds completely different from they way it did some 200 years ago.

We try to understand a game with a spatio-temporal reference to a world that does not exist any more. The game has been withdrawn from the world it refers to and world has been withdrawn from the work.[1] In this respect the videogame shares a problem with a referential painting or with any work of art. Heidegger sarcastically remarks that 'Hölderlin's poems have been put into the soldiers' rucksacks as has the shoe-shine set, and Beethoven's quartets are stored in the publisher's archive like potatoes in the cellar' (Heidegger, 1960: 9). The work of art therefore does not contain relevance that is unaffected by time; it is on the contrary the artist's attempt to condense the specific truth of a historic moment within a work of art. By analogy, a computer game is designed to contain a multitude of aspects of the world that it refers to: sounds, architecture, climate, garments, hairstyle, vegetation, movement patterns and many more. The game designer attempts to capture a historical setting as a whole and present it as a game. This is what Heidegger describes as 'putting the particular truth of a historical period into the oeuvre'[2] (Heidegger, 1960: 34).

> Looking at van Gogh's shoes in the painting, we cannot say where these shoes have been standing. There is nothing about these shoes that would tell us to whom these shoes belong to and where they belong. There is nothing there except for a space without specific properties. Not even traces of soil are attached to these shoes, that might tell us which path they have been walked upon and what they have been used for.
>
> (Heidegger, 1960: 27)

Heidegger calls the work of art a 'thing' (Ding). The shoes in a real world context would be best described as 'tool' (Zeug). A work of art is a thing, like a stone, a dog or 'even God Himself' (Heidegger, 1960: 12), as opposed to a 'Zeug'. 'Zeug' is usually translated as 'tool' and sometimes as 'product'. In German however, it also carries the connotation of 'Zeuge' (witness) and of 'erzeugen' (to create). The shoes that van Gogh depicted have been a tool to somebody else some time ago. For this person the shoes were an extension of the body and a tool that was used unconsciously. The shoes served a purpose and served the person and possessed their Being – 'Zeug' – via this mode of usage. In analogy to that, it makes sense to call computer games works of art and things, as they have been withdrawn from the world and turned into lifeless objects. As we will see later, some form of life – or 'earth' – can be created from the objects that have been deprived of earth in the first place.

Many contemporary computer games seem to work on the basis of *mimicry* and seem to capture a realistic socio-historic situation that the players can get immersed within. *Call of Duty* seems to drop us into World War II as if we were there, *Assassins's Creed*® *3* leaves us in between opposing parties in the battles of the American Civil War. The games are therefore highly suggestive of us interacting with a world, and do not tell us that this very world has been withdrawn and that the corresponding real-life world has decayed. In regard to the work of art, Heidegger thought that the world that has been captured by a photographer or the landscape that has been painted by a painter suggests some worldliness, or even some life of its own. (Benjamin would have said that the auratic moment when the painting looks back at the observer is a moment of magic where the dead object seems to live for an instant.) But the world that we see in the work of art has stopped 'worlding'. This might sound ridiculously trivial,[3] but I think what Heidegger does not want to point out here is that we should be surprised that a deer on a painting cannot jump out of the frame and canvas. What he rather wants to tell us is that the observer is inclined to accept an illusion of worldliness within the artefact. This is the case for works of art and even more so for computer games. The etymological roots of the word 'illusion' (Latin *ludus, ludere*) connect play with pretending and self-delusion. It is surprising, though, that we often accept a state of 'half-belief' (Pfaller, 2002) or of 'as if' when looking at artworks' worlds. In an analogy that links works of art to computer games, I'd suggest that we half-believe that game worlds are worlding and half-believe that game worlds are not worlding any more.

World-decay

Heidegger clearly states that the decay of world can never be reversed.[4] The worlds that have decayed have done so for good. When we visit the Greek temple today we cannot revive ancient Greek society, the polis, the people, the gods and half-gods. Neither watching films nor visiting the ancient sites and the temples will enable us to partake in a world that was once worlding but has stopped worlding now. The promises of tourist agencies and the suggestions of heritage organizations that we will 'experience a stunning theatre of the fourth century BC – as it was right then' just by booking a fly-drive to a former Spartan city is a lie. This is not a moral statement: I just follow Heidegger's suggestion that a work of art, like the theatre mentioned above, does not and cannot convey truth. In his 1955 essay 'Über die Sixtina', Heidegger briefly and minimally characterizes the relation of a painting and truth: 'the image errs' ('Das Bild irrt'; Heidegger 1955). The reason for the aberration of the painting lies within its displacement ('Versetzung') from the original place of production and from the world-decay of the artist's world: the world of Raphael and the church of San Sisto in Piacenza that the painting was painted for. Heidegger commented upon the exhibition of Raphael's *Madonna* in Dresden in the year of 1754. He opposed the idea of his contemporary Theodor Hetzer, who stated that the fact that the *Madonna* impressed everybody in Dresden was evidence that this work of art could be shown anywhere and that the painting has to be considered to be 'at home' in every place of the world. For Hetzer, masterpieces such as Raphael's *Madonna* were universal works of art that did not require a particular space or time to reveal absolute truth. Obviously computer games like *Assassin's Creed*® build upon universal intelligibility and intercultural, affective compatibility to guarantee global vendibility. Works of art that claim to be of an absolute nature must work independent of location and time. But according to Heidegger this says little about their truthfulness to the world they originated from. We cannot re-experience the French Revolution by playing *Assassin's Creed*® *Unity*. All we can do is to be immersed in an environment that resembles the one it alludes to and get enthused ('uns begeistern' Heidegger 1960: 35) for a world that has long since decayed.

World-decay and world-withdrawal both contribute to the aberration we are bound to experience. We believe we see something that does not exist any longer as a consequence of world-decay. We believe we see something that does not exist where we think it should be as a consequence of world-withdrawal.

Problem A: Where is the world in Tetris, and where is the world in abstract art?

One of the premises of my argument so far is that many contemporary computer games work on the basis of *mimicry*. This can be said for many games, but not necessarily for all computer games. Games such as *Tetris*, or more recent examples such as *Dyad*, have little reference to the physical world we live in and they are void of representation or mimesis. There have been attempts to decipher *Tetris* as a representation of conveyor belt factory labour or of transport logistics, but these explanations usually fall short in explaining what players experience when playing those games. Most of the players do not connote *Tetris* with working in a factory.[5] This poses the question of what the relationship of such games with the world is. If there is not a relationship with the physical world around us, then the notion of world-withdrawal would make little sense. Heidegger's observations on the work of art and its 'Weltentzug' face a similar problem: what about abstract art? Heidegger has been criticized for always having referred to the traditional fine arts, architecture and poetry, but never to modern art (Wallenstein, 2010). His explanation of 'Weltentzug' takes as examples the fifteenth-century statue of Aegina by Nikolaus Gerhart, a painting by van Gogh, and rather vague and pathos-driven descriptions of Greek temples. Heidegger planned a sequel to the *Origin of the Work of Art* that was supposed to deal with the possibility of art in a technological world and to non-representative art in particular, but according to Wallenstein 'this project failed to materialize since it was contrary to his own philosophical presuppositions' (Wallenstein, 2010: 163). I think, however, that even an abstract painting such as a composition by Mondrian has a relationship to the world. This relationship might not be representative, but it can still capture elements of a historical situation with very specific gestural stereotypes, expressive motives, or a habitus of a group of people within society.

A painting by Mondrian suffers from 'Weltentzug' and 'Weltzerfall', when the painting is taken from its original place and time of creation. The painting is, however, not unrelated to the world it was painted in. It carries a rich set of references to the past that can be seen and felt in the present. That is why we have a strange feeling of conflict between a strong expressive force and a historical distance when we look at a Mondrian or an abstract painting from the 1920s in a museum of the twenty-first century. In analogy to that, I would argue that abstract computer games have a relation to the world that they have been created in: very much like abstract paintings they are not resistant to the ageing of this world. An abstract painting by Mondrian, Kandinsky or Klee is not an artistic statement of eternal truth, it ages just the way a representative painting does. In the very same way *Tetris*, when played and looked upon nowadays, has assumed a remoteness that is a consequence of former world-withdrawal.

Problem B: Are all videogames withdrawn from the world?

In a discussion with British philosopher and game designer Chris Bateman[6] he made the point that my assumption that Heidegger's proposition of art works relating to the world can be easily transferred to computer games is questionable.

> It seems that Heidegger says that art works have a direct relationship to the world they appear in, but in the moment of 'capture' these worlds-of-origin cease to be 'worlding'. I recall he mentions this in 'The Origin of the Work of Art' ...
>
> But I'm not sure how true it is that the fictional worlds of videogames are not worlding – this may be the case for, say, a retail game on a disc, but is it true for a MUD[7] or another kind of game with continuous renewal and revision of content? It seems to me there are kinds of videogame that are worlding (are capable of worlding? Not sure how to word this!), and in

particular my favourite example, the tabletop role-playing game. Worlding is the essential action of the play of such a game – at least as I (dimly) understand this term! – since the players are constantly discovering, inventing, revising, and creating the fictional world they are playing within.

(Bateman, 2013)

Bateman has a point there. I would however argue that what Bateman calls 'worlding' in regard to tabletop role-playing games or for MUDs is what I would refer to as setting forth and producing earth. I will explain these Heideggerian notions in more detail later, but I want to point out here that the continual process of 'discovering, inventing and revising' that Bateman correctly attributes to MUD games does not take place in the world that the game designers referred to when they originally built the game, but to an instance of 'earth'. If the MUD was based on a medieval story of knights and castles, the MUD players do not contribute to the medieval landscape but to a physical reality that they produce. This earth contains pens and papers, friends and neighbours and computers that are completely non-medieval. A closer look at mimetic computer games might explore the matter further.

The examples below reflect upon a specific historic situation in the country of Iraq in the year 2003. The images on the left show photographs from a war scenario; the images on the right show computer games content based on the photographs that has been built using 3D software (Figures 11.2 and 11.3).

The computer game suggests that the simulated world would be 'worlding' ('Welt weltet') but this is an illusion, in a very literal sense of the word. World does not world in the computer game. The game is characterized by its 'having been' ('Gewesen sein'). Heidegger tells us that the process of world-withdrawal and world-decay is irreversible. The game with all of its assets has lost its 'standing to itself' ('Zu-sich-stehen'). Therefore the computer game can only be encountered in the dimension of tradition and of conservation. The computer game establishes a relation to world ('Welt') and to earth ('Erde'). This is

Figure 11.2 Left: Ramadi, Iraq, US soldiers with tank (photo © John Cantlie; right: screenshot from Arma 2: Operation Arrowhead, copyright © 2015 Bohemia Interactive. All Rights Reserved. ARMA® and Bohemia Interactive® are trademarks of Bohemia Interactive).

Figure 11.3 Left: Ramadi, Iraq, militia in the Ta'meem district (photo © John Cantlie; right: screenshot from Arma 2: Operation Arrowhead, copyright © 2015 Bohemia Interactive. All Rights Reserved. ARMA® and Bohemia Interactive® are trademarks of Bohemia Interactive).

constitutive of its work-being: computer games put up a world ('Aufstellung einer Welt'; see Figure 11.4), but not in the sense of attaching it somewhere, rather by erecting it ('Errichten') in terms of dedication ('Weihen') and praise ('Rühmen'). In the process of being put up the works lose their 'springing-power' ('Sprungkraft').

The power to spring up is a notion that Heidegger develops further in a reflection on Hölderlin's 'holy wildness'. Different from an inherently consistent development, springing-power would enable complex processes to 'create' ('schaffen und schöpfen') unpredictable outcomes. The fact that the work of art has lost its springing-power does not, however, imply that the work of art is dead or completely static. As we will see, the production of world creates a new

Figure 11.4 Gamers in front of a game world that has been 'put up' (Copyright holder: Mathias Fuchs).

dynamism that is driven by the physical environment and the product of its very physicality. Heidegger seems to hint here but does not say it *expressis verbis* that earth has some autopoietic and self-defined end or purpose (τέλος) that makes it almost an autonomous agent in the interplay of work, world and earth. (Zimmerman, 1990: 122) There is a contradiction in Heidegger's system when it comes to things. On the one hand he defines things as 'what is without life in nature and in daily use'[8] (Heidegger, 1960: 12), but on the other hand the mysterious springing-power seems to transform things into entities that have willpower: 'Colour glows and intends to do nothing but glow'[9] (Heidegger, 1960: 43). This is indeed a strange viewpoint for a phenomenologist.

Problem C: Do computer games inform us about the world?

Computer games, like movies, often try to refer to the real world in a narrative manner. We know that Gérard Depardieu is not Georges Danton in the 1983 movie *Danton*. We also know that we are not in 1789 Paris when playing Ubisoft's *Assassin's Creed® Unity* game in the year 2015. Yet without us believing that there is some information about the world that the movie or the game is referring to, we would not want to watch or play them. There is an assumption that computer games inform us about the world. The world that they inform us about has however been abandoned and the movie and the game have been 'ripped off' ('entrissen') (Heidegger, 1960: 36) from their respective worlds and their essences. Heidegger's suggestion is that the work of art can therefore not inform about the world, but that it rather transforms the world (Heidegger, 1976: 36). The act of creating a film or a computer game is best understood in terms of formation and not of form. In Heidegger's terminology this leads to an understanding of the artwork as 'trans-formation' rather than 'in-formation' (Heidegger, 1976). When looking at the informational content of a computer game in this way, the popular discussions about political correctness of certain games or the violence of scenes staged within them has to be reframed: an action undertaken or observed in a game has connotative meaning, but no denotative meaning about the world it refers to – it transforms the real world. According to Espen Aarseth the meaning of the game is a ludeme – as Aarseth and others have called gameplay elements[10] – and not the physical word it is connotative of. We should therefore not conclude that properties or qualities such as violence, dirt, peacefulness or cleanliness can be mapped from the game to the world they might refer to – as some have argued (Anderson, Gentile and Buckley, 2006).

Destruction of worlds, production of earth

Computer games are both appearance and reality. The appearance is the aspect of the world that the game has been withdrawn from. Reality is what Huizinga calls 'the common world' and what Heidegger refers to as 'earth'.[11] Frissen, de

Mul and Raessens (2013) point out that Johan Huizinga's attempt to separate sacred space of play and the rather profane world of everyday life was based on two ontologies that were mutually exclusive, the real and the virtual. Huizinga's dilemma arose from the assumption that play would have to reside outside the common world. A demarcation line would have to protect the area of play from the common world. Functions and spaces to create this separation of play and common world have been described as playgrounds, gameboards, arenas or 'toovercirkel' (Dutch for a circle where rituals of witchcraft have been performed) by Huizinga. Salen and Zimmerman (2003a, 2003b) simplified and translated Huizinga's enumeration and named the demarcation line the 'magic circle'. Huizinga is not responsible for the wording, but most likely for the idea and the conceptual implications created therefrom (Günzel, 2012: 331). The reason for creating the concept of a magic circle was the attempt to avoid the embarrassing problems of the 'common world' leaking into the 'sacred earnest of play' (Huizinga, 1950: 24) or even into the cosmos of 'sacred play' (Raj and Dempsey 2012: 22).

It is clear from *Homo ludens* (1950) that Huizinga wanted to create a distinction between what he called the 'sphere of play' and the 'common world'. He was certainly apprehensive about his ideas such as 'free activity standing quite consciously outside "ordinary" life' (Huizinga, 1950: 17). There are a few sections in *Homo ludens* where Huizinga struggles with his own concept. Is war of a playful nature? Huizinga says: 'Modern warfare has, on the face of it, lost all contact with play' (Huizinga, 1950: 210). On the same page he speaks about his 'gnawning doubt whether war is really play'. He comes to the conclusion at one point that 'war has not freed itself from the circle of witchcraft', but leaves the reader in the dark why this is 'despite appearances to the contrary'. Considerations such as these show Huizinga's awareness that the materiality of the physical world was in a complex and ambiguous relationship with his idealistic 'sphere of play'. I have developed elsewhere how Huizinga might have solved the conflict of a hermetic playsphere versus the common world if he had rewritten *Homo ludens* (Fuchs, 2014).

Heidegger did not fall into the trap of mutually exclusive ontologies for world and earth. He developed the concept of earth from the Greek notion of *physis*[12] (Heidegger, 1960: 38). But earth and physicality – or $Φύσις$ – cannot be thought without world. 'World is rooted in earth and earth permeates world' ('Die Welt gründet sich auf die Erde und Erde durchdringt Welt'; Heidegger, 1960: 46) is how Heidegger describes the dialectics of earth and world. In a language that very much refers to spatial metaphors, he proposes that world cannot vanish from earth, using the word 'entschweben', which means both 'to float away' and 'to evaporate'. There is no antagonism between world and earth. World is neither an anti-earth nor the antithesis of earth. Heidegger observes that the work of art can instigate contention of world and earth, but he also says that the work-being of the work of art ('Werksein des Werkes') consists in the impeachment of quarrel, or 'Bestreitung des Streites' (Heidegger, 1960: 47). Once more the German language provides the philosopher with the means to

Weltentzug und Weltzerfall 161

express his ambiguous position. 'Bestreitung' means both disputing and defray, as in defray of livelihood.

Computer games seem to work in this respect as works of art do. They are mediators between world and earth. Games such as *Assassin's Creed® Unity* put up worlds as the complex network of ideas, images, text and references, for example those that the French Revolution is constituted of, but they are withdrawn from this world that has decayed. Yet they start producing earth once the world has decayed. The production of earth happens when material things get involved and when fantasy and imagination get replaced by *physis* (*Φύσις*). A computer game could easily be misconceived as a completely fictional world,[13] but there are still DVDs and joysticks, consoles and mice, table desktops and fingerprints on touchscreens. There are also sounds of cooling-fans, biscuit crumbs and coffee stains on keyboards that produce earth. For Heidegger, production of earth happens when the work 'pulls itself back' ('das Werk sich zurückzieht'; Heidegger, 1960: 42), when 'the brightness and gloom of colour, the timbre of sound and the power of the word'[14] (ibid.) become significant.

On the one hand computer games present decayed worlds, as we have seen, yet on the other hand games are setting forth and produce earth ('Herstellung der Erde') as the self-secluding ('das Sich-verschliessende'). This product, earth, is that special constituent in the games which adds itself to the world in order to complement the presentational achievement of the world by keeping the presented things from becoming customary. Earth is secluded in its 'unusualness'. Heidegger's notion of earth is difficult to translate and probably rooted in ideas that made sense at the time, when he wrote 'Der Ursprung des Kunstwerks' (1935/6). Already at that time, and even more so after the war, the notion of earth seems to be a high-risk term, if not a term that it is impossible to use. The notion of earth was corrupted by Nazi ideology when they celebrated 'blood and soil' ('Blut und Boden') and threatened scorched earth ('verbrannte Erde'). For Heidegger earth refers to a notion of dense and semantically loaded materiality. He talks about the earthen mug that has been made from earth and that can be placed on earth – mediated through a table. In *Poetry, Language, Thought*, he says:

> The potter makes the earthern jug out of earth that he has specially chosen and prepared for it. The jug consists of that earth. By virtue of what the jug consists of, it too can stand on the earth, either immediately or through the mediation of table and bench. What exists by such producing is what stands on its own, is self-supporting. When we take the jug as a made vessel, then surely we are apprehending it – so it seems – as a thing and never as a mere object. Or do we even now still take the jug as an object? Indeed.
>
> (Heidegger, 1971: 165)

Heidegger's earth is a nostalgic attempt to find a counterpart to civilization and human activity. 'Earth is effortlessly indefatigabile without purpose and goals'[15] (Heidegger, 1960: 43). No wonder that Adorno, Heidegger's philosophical arch-enemy, polemicized that those who talk about a nature that is untouched by man evoke the image of nature's destruction by industry. In 'Dialektik der Aufklärung', Horkheimer and Adorno refer to a nature that is 'without purpose and goals' when they say:

> Nature, that is conceived as an opposing remedy to society by the mechanisms of the ruling classes, pulls it into the calamities of this very society and sells the former off to the latter. Pictorial affirmations of the trees being green, the skies being blue and the clouds moving gently, turn nature into a cryptogram of industry chimneys and gasoline stations.[16]
> (Horkheimer and Adorno, 1947: 157)

Horkheimer and Adorno address the culture industry directly with the aforementioned statement, but they have Heidegger in mind for holding some responsibility for such an ideological framing of nature – even though Heidegger used the term earth for what is usually called nature. For Adorno, Heidegger's interplay of earth and world and the impeachment of contradictions under the umbrella of the work of art belonged to what he detested as 'jargon of authenticity' ('Jargon der Eigentlichkeit'; Adorno, 1964).

In order to stick to Heidegger's notion of earth and earthern things for objects like works of art and computer games, one would have to extend the notion of materiality considerably. Maybe a 'network of things' might be one direction that such thoughts could be leading us to.

Conclusion

For computer games, 'Herstellung der Erde' – setting forth and producing earth – is accomplished not in the game that works on the monitor screen but in the network of actors and in the physicality of a gaming environment. To put it bluntly, when gamers create habitual modes of playing, surrounded by pizza-boxes, cola bottles, friendship rituals and a jargon of the gaming community, then earth is produced. At the same time world is withdrawn, because the objects that are played with are no longer worlding. The objects, the tanks, soldiers and airplanes, have been withdrawn from the world. The process of producing earth reinforces withdrawal from world, because the earthen environment increases consciousness of the game not being mixed up with allegedly authentic worlds. What I want to suggest here is that a social setting that is abundant in what Heidegger calls earth is counterproductive to illusion. When games produce earth they accelerate the process of becoming aware of the decay of worlds. The decay of worlds is under such circumstances no longer an inhibiting factor for an understanding of the work and the world. On the contrary, works of art and computer games might accomplish a deeper understanding about decayed worlds when realizing that world-decay is an irreversible process. As Heidegger put it: 'World-withdrawal and world-decay can never be undone' (Heidegger, 1971: 40). This need not lead towards disquiet and lament that 'the image errs' (Heidegger 1955). The image might tell us that what we see is not a worlding world. The image might truthfully report of its being withdrawn from the world.

Notes

1. In a discussion with German philosopher and Heidegger specialist Markus Rautzenberg (Berlin, Barcomis's Café on 21 November 2014) Rautzenberg suggested that Heidegger would not have thought that world has been withdrawn from the aforementioned computer game. The reason for that is that Heidegger sketched his examples of world-withdrawal from works of art that have been produced in the very moment they refer to. A computer game about the French Revolution was, however, not designed in between 1789 and 1794 – the years *Assassin's Creed*® is supposed to happen. I am thankful for Rautzenberg's comment, but I would like to suggest that Heidegger's concept of world-withdrawal makes also sense for work that is built upon distant times and places. A piece such as Jacques-Louis David's 'Napoleon at the Saint-Bernard Pass' was painted in different versions in between 1801 and 1805, but never on location at the time of Napoleon's crossing the alps in May 1800. I would like to suggest that first it is almost impossible to find work that is created completely on location and in time. Even Heidegger's Ancient Greek temple at Paestum was not completely built where it was erected. Van Gogh did not sit in front of the farmer's shoes for each and every brushstroke Heidegger refers to. Second I think that insisting on a singularity of time-space of the act of creation and a worlding world around it would create a completely artificial separation of authentic artworks and of second-class pieces that has nothing to do with the quality and nature of the works of art.
2. Translated by the author; German original: 'die jeweilige Wahrheit eines Geschichtsabschnitts ins Werk zu setzen'.
3. I am grateful for Chris Bateman's response to my rather floppy comment on the triviality of such an assumption:

   > I can see why you would warn me that this 'might sound ridiculously trivial', but it doesn't at all – on the contrary, it dances close to something very relevant to my work in philosophy, namely the relationship between worlds (fictional or otherwise).
   >
   > Chris Bateman, in an email from 8 June 2013

4. 'Allein, Weltentzug und Weltentwurf sind nie mehr rückgängig zu machen' (Heidegger 1960: 36).
5. Some non-players do however: cf. Theoder W. Adorno's statement of play as 'the afterimage of unfree labour' in *Aesthetic Theory* (Adorno 1970: 421).
6. Email from Chris Bateman, 8 June 2013.
7. A MUD is a Multi-user Dungeon.
8. Translated by the author; German original: 'das Leblose der Natur und des Gebrauches' (Heidegger, 1960: 12).
9. Translated by the author; German original: 'Die Farbe leuchtet und will nur leuchten' (Heidegger 1960: 43).
10. Espen Aarseth in an unpublished lecture on 11 April 2014 at AG-Games Workshop 'Cutting Edges and Dead Ends', in cooperation with Gamification Lab and the Centre for Digital Cultures at Leuphana University, Lüneburg.
11. There are differences between earth and reality – as we understand it – but let us for the moment say that modern physical reality and Heidegger's earth are closely related.
12. German original: 'Dieses Herauskommen und Aufgehen selbst und im Ganzen nannten die Griechen frühzeitig die $\Phi\acute{v}\sigma\iota\varsigma$' (Heidegger, 1960: 38).

13 For a radical deconstruction of the understanding of computer games as fictional worlds, cf. Aarseth (2013).
14 Translated by the author; German original: 'das Leuchten und Dunkel der Farbe, der Klang des Tones, die Nennkraft des Wortes' (Heidegger, 1960: 42).
15 Translated by the author; German original: 'Die Erde ist das zu nichts gedrängte Mühelose-Unermüdliche' (Heidegger, 1960: 43).
16 Translated by the author; German original:

> Natur wird dadurch, daß der gesellschaftliche Herrschaftsmechanismus sie als heilsamen Gegensatz zur Gesellschaft erfaßt, in die unheilbare gerade hineingezogen und verschachert. Die bildliche Beteuerung, daß die Bäume grün sind, der Himmel blau und die Wolken ziehen, macht sie schon zu Kryptogrammen für Fabrikschornsteine und Gasolinstationen.
> (Horkheimer and Adorno, 1947: 157)

References

Aarseth, E. (2013) 'Fictionality is broken: Ludo-realism and the non-fictionality of game worlds', keynote lecture at conference 'The philosophy of computer games', Bergen, 3 October.
Adorno, T. W. (1964) *Der Jargon der Eigentlichkeit*, Frankfurt am Main: Suhrkamp.
Adorno, T. W. ([1970, 1995] 1984) *Ästhetische Theorie/Aesthetic Theory*, Frankfurt am Main: Suhrkamp.
Anderson, C. A., Gentile, D. A. and Buckley, K. E. (2006) *Violent Video Game Effects on Children and Adolescents: Theory, Research, and Public Policy*, New York: Oxford University Press.
Bateman, C. (2013) 'Heidegger in a rucksack', email, 8 June.
Frissen, V., de Mul, J. and Raessens, J. (2013) 'Homo ludens 2.0: Play, media and identity', in Thissen J., Zwijnenberg, R. and Zijlmans, K. (eds) *Contemporary Culture: New Directions in Art and Humanities Research*, Amsterdam: Amsterdam University Press.
Fuchs, M. (2014) 'Ludoarchaeology', in Tremmel, A. and Gilbert, A. (eds) *Extending Play: Games and Culture Journal*, 9(6), 528–38.
Günzel, S. (2012) 'Die Ästhetik der Grenze im Computerspiel', in Prange, R., Engelke, H. and Michael, R. (eds) *Film als Raumkunst. Historische Perspektiven und aktuelle Methoden*, Marburg: Schüren, 331–50.
Heidegger, M. ([1951], 3rd edn 1967) 'Bauen Wohnen Denken', in *Vorträge und Aufsätze*, volume 2, Pfullingen: G. Neske.
Heidegger, M. (1955) 'Über die Sixtina', in Putscher, M. (ed.) *Raphaels sixtinische Madonna. Das Werk und seine Wirkung*, Tübingen: Hopfer Verlag Tübingen.
Heidegger, M. (1960 [1935/36]) *Der Ursprung des Kunstwerks*, Stuttgart: Reclam.
Heidegger, M. (1971) *Poetry, Language, Thought*, transl. Hofstadter, A., New York: Harper and Row.
Heidegger, M. (1976 [1927]) *Sein und Zeit*, Tübingen: Max Niemeyer Verlag.
Horkheimer, M. and Adorno, T. W. (1947) *Dialektik der Aufklärung*, Amsterdam: Querido.
Huizinga, J. (1950 [1938]) *Homo ludens. Vom Ursprung der Kultur im Spiel*. Reinbek bei Hamburg: Rowohlt.
Pfaller, R. (2002) *Die Illusionen der anderen. Über das Lustprinzip in der Kultur*, Frankfurt am Main: Suhrkamp.
Raj, S. J. and Dempsey, C. G. (2012) *Sacred Play: Ritual Levity and Humor in South Asian Religions*, Albany: State University of New York Press.

Salen, K. and Zimmerman, E. (2003a) *Rules of Play: Game Design Fundamentals*, Cambridge, MA: MIT Press.

Salen, K. and Zimmerman, E. (2003b). 'This is not a game: Play in cultural environments', DIGRA 2003 Level Up conference, Utrecht, 4–6 November, www.digra.org/dl/db/05163.47569 (accessed 12 March 2014).

Wallenstein, S. (2010). *The Historicity of the Work of Art in Heidegger*, www.diva-portal.org/smash/get/diva2:217475/FULLTEXT01.pdf (accessed 27 September 2014).

Zimmerman, M. E. (1990) *Heidegger's Confrontation with Modernity: Technology, Politics, and Art*, Bloomington: Indiana University Press.

12 The paradox of rules and freedom
Art and life in the simile of play

Damla Dönmez

> God created every living creature that now moveth, and one was man. Mud as man alone could speak. God leaned close to mud as man sat, looked around, and spoke. 'What is the purpose of all this?' he asked politely.
> 'Everything must have a purpose?' asked God.
> 'Certainly', said man.
> 'Then I leave it to you to think of one for all this', said God.
> (Kurt Vonnegut, 1963: 153)

This question of the meaning of life and the quest for a purpose is a recurring theme for Vonnegut and one that we struggle with. In this chapter I explore this mind-boggling question by means of the concepts of art and play. My argument has two parts: first, art as a play-activity can present freedom by means of having rules, and that can help us transcend the bondages of life, i.e. time, space and mortality. Second, via art's introduction of an 'extraordinary realm of experience', the meaning of 'ordinary life' can acquire a novel interpretation; it can be experienced in the mode of play and with the spirit of art. In the first part, initially I define what play is following Huizinga: (1) auto-telic, (2) pleasurable, (3) voluntarily chosen and (4) structured by internal rules. Consequently, I argue 'All art is play' and explain the common characteristics shared by play and art with reference to Kant and Nietzsche. However, I claim 'not all play is art' but art is a specific subset of play, since art is a context-dependent and dialogic interaction. Last, I analyse the paradoxical relation of rules and freedom with reference to Kant and Seward and the parasitic dependence of freedom on rules is emphasized and examined. Building on this foundation, I consider the proposition that due to having a concrete constrained area, namely rules and a play-arena, art can raise the individual to non-spatiality and atemporality. This, then, allows exploration of the claim that as long as the individual surrenders him/herself to the rules of each particular art form, life can acquire an alternative meaning: it can be experienced in the mode of play with the spirit of art; i.e. as an end-in-itself, pleasurable, existing only in the 'present' as an authentic artwork.

What is play?

Play and its relation to art has for centuries attracted the attention of philosophers. Following this tradition, in this chapter I defend the view that art is a play-activity; however, I argue that 'not all play is art' but 'all art is play'. This has been formerly asserted by philosophers such as Schiller,[1] Kant and Nietzsche. However, before moving into the discussion of what I mean by 'all art is play', we must explore definitions of play. For the purposes of this chapter, Huizinga's (1955) definition that it is: (1) auto-telic, (2) pleasurable, (3) voluntary and (4) structured by rules. Let us see what is meant by each.

(1) *Auto-telic:* play's[2] aim is in itself (Huizinga, 1955), not a means for something else (Drake, 1921) but enjoyed for its own sake (Hein 1968). In other words, it is 'self-sufficient' (Seward, 1944: 178). The motivation to play and importance of play lie in the experience and the meaning of play itself (Sheets-Johnstone, 2003). Therefore, we should get rid of 'teleological explanations of play' (Seward, 1944: 179). However, play might bring forth by-products. These by-products do not point to its essential features but rather refer to its secondary, accidental properties.

(2) *Pleasurable*: play is 'pleasurable' (Hein, 1968: 67; Huizinga, 1955). Even studies of the neurochemistry of animals' play support this. For example, 'play in rodents is associated with and regulated by the neurotransmitters that are known to have roles in other pleasurable activities' (Allen and Bekoff, 2005: 128). Moreover, 'the relaxed open-mouthed face of most primate species, what is termed as "play-face", is homologous to human laughter and the silent, bared-teeth face is homologous to human smiling' (Sheets-Johnstone, 2003: 419).

(3) *Voluntary:* play is a voluntary activity. When there is an instruction to play, it is no longer play but a 'forcible imitation of it' (Huizinga, 1955: 7). The existence of pleasure is also dependent upon this characteristic.

(4) *Determined by rules*: all play has rules (Huizinga, 1955) which are necessary to determine its form. It has its own time and space and according to 'its fixed rules' it works in 'an orderly manner' (Huizinga, 1955: 13). Homan states that though 'play is non-purposive, it is not simply arbitrary' (2013: 100):

> Play is always carried out with a certain play space (*Spielraum*) and within the realm of different rules and boundaries.... When engaged in play, persons take seriously the play space and activity at hand. Not only do they choose to play, but they choose to play in this way.... The rules and boundaries of play thus do not inhibit or stifle the movement; rather these boundaries are what enable play in the first place.

For the rest of the chapter, I will concentrate upon this characteristic of play. There have been some opposing arguments; however, I consider them to be invalid. For example, Burke (1971: 37) claimed that play could be defined with 'intrinsic completeness, artificiality and freedom' and not all play should be defined 'with rules'. He gave the examples of 'a one-year-old child rolling a toy across the floor or wearing his cereal on his head instead of eating it' and/or 'a five-year-old engrossed in building a tower by himself or a girl making a dress for her doll' (1971: 36). However, there are still rules governing these instances of play. For example, the one-year-old child needs to place the cereal on the head firmly and fixedly in order to see it *as* a hat, because that is the way the hats are. As a matter of fact, his play has the rule of *placing-the-cereal-on-the-head-firmly-without-letting-it-fall* and in the second case, the boy tries to build the tower by means of placing the pieces in a determined pattern which would rise up to resemble a tower, in short his play has the rule of *placing-the-pieces-on-top-of-one-another-vertically-and-not-letting-them-fall.* Moreover, Burke's definition of play as 'artificial' and 'intrinsically complete' implies that play can be acquired only via some limits that would primarily designate, separate and specify the playground and second constitute what *that* play is about. Play would be acquired on the basis of some fixed, determinate, particular rules which give a structure and impose a form. Burke does admit that 'discipline' is a feature of play (1971: 47). Hence, his ideas seem to be suffering from an ambiguous usage of terms which ultimately are not a threat to the principle of Huizinga that play is formed and governed by rules.

Art as play-activity

All the abovementioned features of play are embraced in art, justifying the statement 'all art is play'. However, art is a subset of play, therefore 'not all play is art'. First I would like to point to the characteristics of art that are in commonality with play, and then indicate what makes art a subset of play and leads me to claim 'not all play is art'.

Let us start with the first statement: 'All art is play'. In this case, we claim that art is an activity that finds its aim in itself (i.e. auto-telic), pleasurable, voluntary and formed by intrinsic rules.

The first characteristic, that art is an auto-telic activity whose end is in itself, has been asserted by Kant: 'Beautiful art is a representation that is purposive in itself' (Kant, 2000: 306).[3] According to Kant, 'aesthetic judgements' differ from 'determining judgements' in the sense that they lack a determinate concept (Kant, 2000: 204). He defines it as 'purposiveness without representation of an end' (Kant, 2000: 236). In aesthetic judgements, imagination presents 'a manifold of intuitions', but because there is not 'a determinate concept', 'the faculty of understanding' cannot unify them. It receives them *as if* to have a specific end, but fails to fulfill that purpose; hence, it is 'purposive with no end'; 'purposive' because it exists *as if* to fulfill a purpose for the subject; but 'with no end' because it lacks an objective concept. However, since we can find purposiveness with respect to an object's form without ascribing any objective end, we can call it 'subjective formal purposiveness'. This also lays the ground for the subject to gain pleasure: since the subject is presented with a supposed cognition in general but finds out that s/he is not restricted to a particular end, the cognitive faculties, imagination and understanding result in a free play and the feeling of pleasure (Kant, 2000: 222). Kant explains 'feeling of pleasure and displeasure' as the faculty of the mind responsible for the aesthetic judgements (Kant, 2000: 246). 'Purposiveness with no purpose' and 'pleasurable' are characteristics of art that cause Kant to differentiate it from craft; this distinction is maintained by its ontological feature that it shall be voluntarily practised.

> The first [art] is regarded as if it could turn out purposively only as play, i.e. an occupation that is agreeable in itself; the second [handicraft] is regarded as labour, i.e. an occupation that is ... attractive only because of its effect (e.g. remuneration) and hence as something that can be compulsorily imposed.
>
> (Kant, 2000: 304)

Art cannot be 'compulsorily imposed'; it is a *voluntary* activity. The spirit which animates the work of art must be 'free'; otherwise it would be a mere 'mechanism'. Hence, art can best be promoted when all compulsion is lifted and it is transformed 'from labour into mere play' (ibid.).

Similar to Kant's emphasis on *pleasure*, Nietzsche mentions that the Greek theatre is born out of the encounter of 'the joyous necessity of the dream experience' of Apollo and Dionysus, which is 'the most intimate one by the analogy of intoxication'. They grace 'all nature with *joy*' (1967: 35ff.). Nietzsche's *Gay Science* is another example of art's 'joyful' and 'free' characteristics. Nietzsche had borrowed this name from the Provençal troubadours, the first poets of modern Europe, whose poetry was named 'gay science' (Kaufmann, 1974: 6).

Last but not least, the fourth characteristic of play shared by art is its feature of being structured by rules. Each art form has some particular and definite determined limits. Every artwork has an internal pattern that requires the agent to commit him/herself to that 'order' of the art form.[4] Kant and Schiller stressed these 'orderly' characteristics of art 'as a necessary, if not sufficient condition of the lawful self-determination' (Hein, 1968: 68). This characteristic is very important for the first argument of the chapter, namely that art can help us experience freedom and transcend the bondages of life. Therefore, before going into detail about this issue, let me justify the statement that 'not all play is art'.

Art has something peculiar to itself when we contemplate all forms of play such as sports, law, etc. We can visualize play as the main set and art as one of the subsets of play. Huizinga presented all culture as developing through the characteristics of play. 'Culture does not come *from* play like a babe detaching itself from the womb: it arises in and as play, and never leaves it' (1955: 173); in addition to art Huizinga includes sports, war and law as other forms of play. With respect to his theory, if we state 'All play is art' then all these areas would be encompassed as art forms, which is an undesirable conclusion. Moreover, common sense also cautions us that not all types of play can be art, for example children's games such as hide-and-seek or the abovementioned one-year-old's play which has the rule of *placing-the-cereal-on-the-head-firmly-without-letting-it-fall*. Then, what makes art different from other forms of play? There are many parameters to be considered, but I will clarify only the most significant ones due to lack of space. First of all, art has to exist within an 'artworld' in Danto's (2007) words, namely within a context and historicity; second, it is a 'dialogic interaction' between the spectator and the creator.

Danto claims that what makes modern artists' works 'works of art' is the fact that 'their work belongs in this atmosphere and is part of this history' (2007: 420). However, for some forms of play this is not a necessary condition. I can invent as many ways of playing as I want as long as its aim is in itself, it gives pleasure, it has some rules and it is voluntarily chosen. However, in the case of art there are some norms of appreciation such that some objects are classified to be non-art in contrast to art. Danto exemplifies a layman who might have difficulty in distinguishing some works to be important artworks, such as the case in Rauschenberg's bed which had paint on it or Oldenburg's disproportional bed (ibid.). What makes these works entitled to be art is that they are in 'an atmosphere of artistic theory, knowledge of the history of art – an artworld'. This is related to the second feature of art, that it is a dialogue. There have to be audiences for any artwork to exist. No work can be characterized as art if it has never been seen by anyone. But many forms of play can take place without an audience, only with the existence of a player and play materials. In contrast, art requires multiple subjects, the 'doers' and the 'undergoers': the author and the reader, the actor and the spectator. It requires and invites the other's answers, unlike some forms of play, provoking him/her to contribute to the subject, either by 'opposing or by joining' (Patterson, 1985: 135). In every form of art, unlike every form of play, the changing positions of author and reader, or artist and spectator, are necessary (Dewey, 1980). That is the essential characteristic of its being a dialogic interaction. Therefore, art is a specific subset of play and 'Not all play is art'.

Paradox of rules and freedom in art

I have said above that every art form is regulated and formed by some determinate rules and that this is an ontological necessity for something to be called art. Now I want to move to the discussion of how these rules can provide freedom. Rules and the concept of freedom seem to be mutually exclusive at the surface level. However, I argue that the inverse applies, that the subject can attain freedom from the bondages of life via the rules of art, despite this seeming paradox.

First of all, the subject surrenders him/herself to the rules of art voluntarily and, upon deciding to take part, accepts the exposition of its rules which define and structure its play-sphere. This, in other words, implies a contract previously made between the subject and the relevant, particular art form. By means of these imposed rules or limits, the numbers of possible activities which are permissible within it are reduced. The rules predetermine only 'a limited number of situations to arise during the creation process whose character can be foreseen and methods of dealing with them can be decided upon in advance of their occurrence' (Seward, 1944: 183). As a result, the choice of means in order to cope with a particular situation is regulated. The surrendering of the subject to the limitations of rules makes this particular play-activity, i.e. art, distinct and 'less complex than ordinary experience' (ibid.). In art 'a heightened feeling of responsibility' takes place due to the submission to voluntarily-surrendered-to rules and this 'heightened feeling of responsibility' is the gate to 'the sense of freedom' (Seward, 1944: 184). Chance or chaos is avoided by these voluntarily-surrendered-to rules of play. In short, the real hindrance to freedom is not the *rules* but rather the *set of infinite possibilities*.

Stravinsky also asserts that 'the more art is controlled, limited, worked over, the more it is free' (1947: 63). The fact of imposing limits upon itself is the activity of creating. He confesses that he experiences 'a sort of terror' when he finds himself facing 'the infinitude of possibilities ... that everything is permissible' while composing (ibid.). He asks himself if he would 'lose himself in this abyss of freedom ... to what shall he cling in order to escape the dizziness ... before the virtuality of this infinitude?' For him, consolation can be found in something 'concrete' that is 'finite, definite' such as the 'notes of the scale and its chromatic intervals', 'the strong and weak accents' that can provide 'a field of experience ... presenting itself ... together with its limitations'.

> Here we are ... in the realm of necessity. And yet which of us has ever heard talk of art as other than a realm of freedom? My freedom thus consists in my moving about within the narrow frame that I have assigned myself ... I shall go even further, my freedom will be so much the greater and more meaningful the more narrowly I limit my field of action and the more I surround myself with obstacles. Whatever diminishes constraint, diminishes strength. The more constraints one imposes, the more one frees one's self of the chains that shackle the spirit.
>
> (Stravinsky, 1947: 65)

If the paradox has not yet been sufficiently illuminated, we need to refer back to the history of philosophy. The debates about freedom have generally been emphasized by many prominent figures to be not an unlimited ability and space of action but to be able to act within determined but self imposed rules. Since freedom is a huge subject with implications of politics and morality, due to lack of space and in order to retain a focus on rules, I will not deal with them at length. However, Kant's explanation of the intricate link between rules and freedom in relation to ethics is relevant to this discussion. He presents the idea of *autonomy* in the discussion of free will and morality, which is the combination of *autos-nomos*, 'self-imposed laws' (Kant, 1996: 433).[5] Will, for Kant, is free as long as it is able to obey the laws that it imposes upon itself. In other words, the subject has a free will as long as s/he becomes both the author and executer of his/her own rules (Kant, 1996: 431-3).

Although the same conceptual schema could be applied to the discussion of art, there remains a debate about whether the rules of art are self-imposed or defined beforehand by others. Hence the rules of art should not be explicated by means of a comparison with morality, which might cause an equivocation. However, we should remember the play-element of art, i.e. it is a *voluntary* activity. If there is any coercion, it is no longer play, and no longer art. This is an important point to which we should pay careful attention. Therefore, when a subject enters into a play-arena of any art form, s/he voluntarily submits him/herself to the rules or limits which have been predetermined and opens him/herself to the new possibilities these limits would create. Just on that occasion s/he can be transported to another level of experience distinct from the ordinary one: that is, to an *extraordinary realm of experience*.

Transcending the bondages of life

Now we can move to unravel the argument that art helps us transcend the bondages of life and introduces an extraordinary realm of experience. But what do we mean by *extraordinary realm of experience*? Let us define it from its contrast: ordinary experience. We experience life *ordinarily* by means of two basic parameters: time and space. In this sense, in referring to ordinary experience, we mean experiencing time in the context of our normal, pragmatic life such as when we say 'we have time for something' or 'we don't have time'. This is the same for space: we mean a determined physical existence in a determined place as our five senses provide relevant data of perception.

However, the temporal structure of life differs in art when we surrender ourselves to its play-arena. With respect to the parameter of time, there is a totally different experience of it. Gadamer (1986: 42) calls this ordinary experience of time 'empty' in contrast to 'fulfilled' or 'autonomous' time in the extraordinary experience of art where it 'fulfils every moment of its duration'. When you watch every child and every artist who plays enthusiastically, you see someone who is immersed and deeply involved with the activity. I take this 'autonomous temporality' to be the closest experience of eternity where the limits of time are transcended and overcome. However, this experience is dependent upon the existence of rules. There have to be rules so that one shall be limited but move within them with various possibilities freely. In case of music, one has to limit oneself within some specific notes, rhythm and duration; in dance, within the limits of some specific movements and rhythms of music; and in painting, within some particular range of specific colours, a painterly surface and particular emotional determinations, etc. As a result of surrendering to these rules, the intensity of concentration and focus would alter the perception and experience of time. The time which we *ordinarily* experience is not any more 'managed and disposed of' but 'brought to a standstill' in an atemporality (Gadamer, 1986: 42). Art would 'proffer time, arrest it and allow it to tarry' (ibid.).

A parallel to this art-focused power of concentration and its relation to the transcendence of time may be seen in Eastern philosophies. Patanjali, who was the author of *Yoga Sutras* in 500 BCE, explains the state of *samadhi* as the state of 'supreme meditation' where the flow of consciousness merges with the object of meditation. This state is defined as the dissolution of the subject into the object so that s/he can transcend the conditioning of time and live in atemporality where there is only 'the moment'. Iyengar, a famous yoga guru, in his interpretations compares it to the play of children and mentions the 'passionate interest' of a child which 'fuels his concentration' and makes him 'totally absorbed in his task, oblivious of his surroundings' while playing (1993: 168). Iyengar also indicates that not only play but also experience of art has a similar link to atemporality:

> When a musician loses himself and is completely engrossed in his music, or an inventor makes his discoveries when devoid of ego, or a painter transcends himself with colour, shade and brush; they glimpse *samadhi*. So it is with the yogi: when his object of contemplation becomes himself, devoid of himself, he experiences *samadhi*.[6]
>
> (Iyengar, 1993: 170)

As a result, 'perhaps art is the only way that is granted to us finite beings to relate to what we call eternity' (Gadamer, 1986: 45) unless we are a devoted yogi who gains it by *samadhi*.

The same goes for spatial limits. We are restrained by spatial conditions in our ordinary life. We are always in one single place due to physical determinations. However, in art the spatial experience differs; any artist, like any child who is deeply immersed in any form of play, would be able to transport themselves to the virtual reality of their play-arena. This is in connection with the power of concentration and imagination respectively. As we surrender ourselves completely to the rules of play, our power of concentration and focus increases and the power of imagination intensifies proportionally, letting us transport ourselves to the experience of a novel place. However, I want to emphasize the fact that imagination can deepen as long as one can surrender oneself to the rules of that particular art form. Therefore, one can go beyond the spatial limits of one's existence as long as *one is absorbed by the art form that one is in*. The actor who is playing Hamlet is able to move beyond the limits of the stage and transport his/her experience to Denmark, feeling the cold or the rain of the graveyard as a real experience.

In the same vein, this extraordinary realm of experience is interpreted in contrast to 'reality' by many psychoanalysts. Freud described play as 'rearranging and creating a world in a new way' (1959: 143). Thus he has rejected the notion that 'serious' is the opposite of play, but rather insisted that play is opposed to 'reality'.

> Might we not say that every child at play behaves like a creative writer, in that he creates a world of his own, or, rather, rearranges the things of his world in a new way which pleases him? It would be wrong to think he does not take his play seriously, on the contrary he takes his play very seriously and he expends large amounts of emotion on it. The opposite of play is not serious but what is

real. In spite of all the emotion with which he creates his world of play, the child distinguishes it quite well from reality; and he likes to link his imaginary objects and situations to the tangible and visible things of the real world. This linking is all that differentiates the child's 'play' from 'phantasying'.

(Freud, 1959: 144)

In short, art, as a form of play, can uplift and raise us beyond our everyday existence if we surrender ourselves to its particular rules. Our experience of life differs and is elevated to a kind of universality, infinity and eternity. By infinity and eternity, I mean going beyond the limits of being determined, where there is not a separation of 'past' and 'future' but union of them in the 'now'; and not a strict bondage to 'here' but a capacity to be 'anywhere'. When time is suspended in art due to its playful essence, past, future and present become one and spatial barriers are surpassed. This introduces us to the *extraordinary realm of experience* because in the ordinary realm of experience we are bounded by temporal and spatial limits. In Gadamer's words, 'art transforms our fleeting experience, into the stable and lasting form of an independent and internally coherent creation' (1986: 53). The flow of time and the 'cosmic rhythm' of existence are held for a brief period and the smell of immortality is acquired; as Hölderlin states via art 'something can be held in our hesitant stay' (quoted in Gadamer, 1986: 53).

A novel meaning to life

What can we gain from this discussion of art and its ability to transcend bondages of life? Why do we seek it or become advocates of it? In connection with the above argument, we can move to the second part of the thesis. The answer is because it is an illuminating means for us to reflect back on our ordinary experience of life and the question of how we shall experience it. Life in its ordinariness does not have to be strictly separated from the extraordinary realm of experience introduced by art and inferentially by play. Upon having the taste of it, we can endeavour to enlarge its sphere of influence. The extraordinary experience introduced by art and play can transform our ordinary experiences in life and provide intuitions to reshape and restructure them into extraordinary realms. This offers an answer for the initial question posed at the beginning: what is the meaning of life? I think at this point we need to reformulate the question as *how can we give meaning to our lives?* The answer is by means of experiencing it in the mode of play and with the spirit of art.

If we can obtain freedom from the constraints of life by means of art and play, we would also recognize the satisfaction that exists 'now' and 'here': i.e. life has a meaning in itself and has to be experienced as play. To put it differently, the experience of art can illuminate our life as a playful activity and attribute an intrinsic meaning to it that is non-consequentialist, an end-in-itself. Schlick (1993: 135) in the same manner claims that 'a life dealt with distant goals' at all times will lose all its creation power. Therefore, he suggests that we should take 'present' as our sole reality without ultimate purposes and experience it in the form of 'play' as an end in itself. In this respect, only 'the moment' has reality. The same viewpoint can also be traced in the aforementioned Eastern philosophies. Iyengar explains that the yogi who attains *samadhi* realizes that the 'moment in time is timeless and that this timelessness is real and eternal, while its movement is confined to the past and future'; since 'the moment is everlasting, changeless and sacred', the yogi who attains *samadhi* lives only in the moment (1993: 220). Therefore, when we encounter a gazelle and think why her life is 'not a hell of fear and insecurity' although 'knowing that the inevitable end will be in the lion's maw', the answer is because 'they can live in the present moment *as it* is and not as it might be' (1993: 221).

Experiencing life in the mode of play can also be assisted with the spirit of art. The ordinary experience of life can be recreated and reconstituted with creativity and authenticity in which each subject's life becomes a unique masterpiece. The play sphere of art constitutes a realm of creativity in which 'one can give style to one's character' (Homan, 2013: 104). The life of each person will be their own self-creation. Nietzsche states that 'to be an artist in the fullest sense requires the translation from creativity in art to creativity in life' (quoted in Homan, 2013: 105), which means that the form and content of each person's life has to be adorned autonomously in accordance with the spirit of art. This reminds us of Foucault's inspiring question: 'Art should not be something that has been specialized by experts who are artists. But couldn't everyone's life become a work of art?' (quoted in McNay, 2005: 147).

Conclusion

I have argued that art is a play-activity. I have defined play as an activity that (1) finds its aim in itself, (2) is pleasurable, (3) is voluntary and (4) is structured by intrinsic rules. All features of play are embraced in art and therefore 'All art is play', although 'Not all play is art' since art is context-dependent dialogic interaction. However, the most important characteristic for the chapter is the fourth one, to have rules. I have proposed that by means of surrendering oneself to the rules of the specific art form, one transcends the bondages of ordinary life, i.e. time, space and mortality. Upon this extraordinary experience, art with its playful essence can present a novel viewpoint for the meaning of life and give intuition in how to experience it: in the mode of play, with the spirit of art; i.e. an end-in-itself, pleasurable, existing only in the 'present' as an authentic artwork.

Notes

1 Due to lack of space, I will not deal at length with Schiller in this chapter; for more information see Schiller (1982, 79–84).
2 Although this noun 'play' could have some similarities with the noun 'game', game is a form of play. Games are generally a type of play that includes competition and rivalry, but play introduces a more general theme.
3 For more information see Kant (2000).

4 I am not following a strict formalism that limits each art form into a tyrannical, one-sided view, but rather want to point to its rule-governed ontology.
5 For more information see Kant (1996).
6 However, of course Iyengar states that there is a difference between a yogi and an artist. Whereas the artist or musician reaches this state by effort and cannot sustain it, the yogi experiences it as natural, continuous and effortless (1993: 170).

References

Allen, C. and Bekoff, M. (2005) 'Animal play and the evolution of morality: An ethological approach', *Topoi*, 24, 125–35.
Burke, R. (1971) 'Work and play', *Ethics*, 82(1), 33–47.
Danto, A. (2007) 'Artworld', in. Cahn, S. and Meskin, A. (eds) *Aesthetics: A Comprehensive Anthology*, Malden: Blackwell Publishing.
Dewey, J. (1980) *Art as Experience*, New York: Perigee Books.
Drake, D. (1921) 'Philosophy as work and play', *Journal of Philosophy*, 18(16), 441–4.
Freud, S. (1959) 'Writers and daydreaming', in Strachey, J. (transl. and ed.) *The Standard Edition of the Complete Psychological Works of S. Freud, 1906–1908*, volume 9, London: Hogarth and Institute of Psychoanalysis.
Gadamer, H. G. (1986) *The Relevance of the Beautiful and Other Essays*, ed. Bernasconi, R., transl. Walker, N., Cambridge: Cambridge University Press.
Hein, H. (1968) 'Play as an aesthetic concept', *Journal of Aesthetics and Art Criticism*, 27(1), 67–71.
Homan, C. (2013) 'Whoever cannot give, also receives nothing', in Ryall, E., Russell, W. and MacLean, M. (eds) *The Philosophy of Play*, Abingdon: Routledge.
Huizinga, J. (1955) *Homo Ludens: A Study of the Play Element in Culture*, Boston: Beacon Press.
Iyengar, B. K. S. (1993) *Light on the Yoga Sutras of Patanjali: Patanjala Yoga Pradipika*, New Delhi: Harper Collins Publishers India.
Kant, I. (1996) *Groundwork of the Metaphysics of Morals* (G.), in Gregor, M. J. (transl. and ed.) *Practical Philosophy*, Cambridge: Cambridge University Press.
Kant, I. (2000) *Critique of the Power of Judgment* (CroJ), ed. Guyer, P., transl. Guyer, P. and Matthews, E., Cambridge: Cambridge University Press.
McNay, L. (2005) *Foucault: A Critical Introduction*, New York: Polity Press.
Nietzsche, F. (1967) *The Birth of Tragedy and the Case of Wagner*, transl. Kaufmann, W., New York: Vintage Books.
Nietzsche, F. (1974) *Gay Science*, transl. Kaufmann, W., New York: Vintage Books.
Patterson, D., (1985). 'Mikhail Bakhtin and the dialogical dimensions of the novel', *Journal of Aesthetics and Art Criticism*, 44(2), 131–9.
Schiller, F. (1982) *On the Aesthetic Education of Man: In a Series of Letters*, ed. Wilkinson, E. M. and Willoughby, L. A., Oxford: Clarendon Press.
Schlick, M. (1993) 'Philosophical papers', in Westphal, J. and Levenson, C. (eds) *Life and Death*, Cambridge: Hackett Publishing Company.
Seward, G. (1944) 'Play as art', *The Journal of Philosophy*, 41(7), 178–84.
Sheets-Johnstone, M. (2003) 'Child's play: A multidisciplinary perspective', *Human Studies*, 26, 409–30.
Stravinsky, I. (1947) *Poetics of Music in the Form of Six Lessons*, transl. Knodel, A. and Ingolf, D., London: Oxford University Press.
Vonnegut, K. (1963) *Cat's Cradle*, New York: Dell Publishing Co.

Part IV

Ethics of work in play and play in work

13 Philosophy, play and ethics in education

Sandra Lynch

Philosophers working with children and adolescents in classrooms recognize the pleasure their students take in philosophical exploration using the methodology of Philosophy in Schools or Philosophy for Children,[1] which is underpinned theoretically by the work of Matthew Lipman, John Dewey and Lev Vygotsky. Within the literature, one less frequently discussed aspect of this methodology is its emphasis on *playful* engagement with ideas and the impact that form of engagement has on the social dimensions of classroom inquiry, on students' developing senses of themselves and the world, and on learning (Weber, 2011).[2]

This chapter aims to provide a theoretical foundation for the playful engagement typical of the Philosophy in Schools (hereafter 'PinS') classroom. Such classrooms emphasize the centrality in school education of learning to think, where thinking is conducted within a classroom 'Community of Inquiry' (hereafter 'CoI') and understood as a process of collaborative inquiry, distinguished by particular practices which draw attention to the ethical dimensions of playful philosophical engagement (Cam, 2006).

Play, educational development and philosophy

Educators generally agree that play, as a dynamic, creative and constructive activity, is an essential and integral part of all children's learning. Most defend the need for play, while recognizing that the results of research have not been well articulated in policy or in curriculum documents (Isenberg and Quisenberry, 1988). The view that play is trivial, frivolous and without social purpose is challenged by research and theory arguing that play assists children in social development, integration of selfhood, development of intelligence, shaping of moral judgement, dealing with everyday and traumatic experience, and coming to enjoy learning (Piaget, 1962; Vygotsky, 1978; Erikson, 1963; Matthews, 1980; Garvey, 1997; Creasey *et al.*, 1998; Fleer, 2010).

In most instances, the PinS lesson is like play in that it steps outside normal, literal daily routines, taking a different and imaginative orientation, and signaling a change in the everyday structures of classroom experience. While it is purposeful, philosophical inquiry in the classroom context is without particular 'purpose' since with the teacher as facilitator, students are encouraged to imaginatively explore ideas and to take the initiative in opening discussion to possibility. Bateson (1973: 155, 166) argues that in playing, we create a frame or context around actions and interactions that has a distinct, paradoxical 'real but not real' premise; without which 'the evolution of communication would be at an end. Life would then be an endless interchange of stylized messages, a game with rigid rules, unrelieved by change or humour.'

Bateson's theory of play focuses specifically on the nature of communication within play and on the way play contexts or frames are set up. Matthews (1980) reports a discussion between two brothers and their mother about being 'early' or 'late' for school. James grumbles to his mother about 'the fuss people make about getting up early, and things' (Matthews 1980: 14).[3] Denis (his younger brother: just over six years old) responds saying that 'early and late *aren't* things. They're not things like tables and chairs and cups ...!' Denis seems to be defining what philosophers call material objects to indicate that tables, chairs and cups are material objects, but he rightly points out that 'early' and 'late' are not. Clearly, his brother did not mean to imply that early and late were material objects and Denis surely realized this, but he wants to pretend otherwise so that he can play with words in a way that raises interesting conceptual or philosophical questions. The frame that Denis has established temporarily liberates him from literal, routine conversation and allows him to explore concepts.

For Bateson, the value of this kind of liberation lies partly in the fun it provides but also in the opportunities that arise for the evolution of human communication through the use of humour. As an aspect of play, humour punctuates the serious and routine passages of everyday life, bounded by the paradoxical 'real but not real' premise. The play frame can both liberate us from the routine structures of the everyday life world and release tension or respond to some form of incongruity.[4]

Similarly, Donald Winnicott appreciated the liberating effects of play. '[I]n playing and only in playing the individual child or adult is able to act creatively and to use the whole personality, and it is only in creativity that the individual discovers the self' (Winnicott, 1971: 73). The association between play, humour and the creation of what Winnicott calls 'a transitional space' in which creativity can flourish can be usefully applied to the methodology of PinS. Barbara Weber explains that we learn to interpret the world and give it shape through play: young children use a table as a cave; older children begin to play with words, concepts and meanings to 'create their own interpretations of reality; they abandon their immediate instincts or learned habits and re-enter the realm of possibilities and creativity, [creating] alternative meaning and usage of the world' (Weber, 2011: 246).

Weber argues that Winnicott accords with Schiller in arguing that in play the human embraces two extremes of being fully immersed in the world and simultaneously separate from it. The notion of the 'in-between'[5] can be applied here, since these theorists see creative play as symbolizing the effort both to be connected with the sensuous world and simultaneously to construct concepts and interpretive structures that lift the continuous stream of being into the world of ideas and reason. Play with the world becomes play with concepts.

(Weber, 2011: 246)

While philosophers have questioned the wisdom of encouraging philosophical play with concepts among children, critical commentary of the content and the methodology of PinS reveals misunderstandings. PinS practitioners are censured for attempting to introduce the work of crucial figures in the Western philosophical tradition to school students, when this is neither their objective nor their practice. Richard Smith (2011: 223) has criticized practitioners for their recognition of the PinS methodology as 'Socratic' in approach and for encouraging the kind of playfulness to which Socrates refers in the Platonic dialogues. Smith argues that it is 'the very *playfulness* of the young, who behave like puppies, that is said ... [in the Platonic dialogues] to make them unsuitable for philosophy'.

The distinction that is important to Smith's argument is made in the *Theatetus* (167e), where playfully (*en men tōi paizéi*) scoring points – and tripping up one's opponents – is contrasted with engaging in serious dialectic (*en de toi dialegesthai spoudazéi*). In the Platonic Dialogues, Socrates does urge caution with regard to introducing philosophy to the young. But Smith overstates this in applying it to the methodology of PinS, since he fails to recognize the difference between that methodology and the kind of playfulness to which Socrates refers in the *Theatetus*. Playfulness in the *Theatetus* is more akin to competition and one-upmanship than to creating the kind of rule-bound community that is the hallmark of the PinS classroom.

Martha Nussbaum also suggests that philosophy conceals dangers, if not for children, then at least for adults, but her critique of its dangers can be read as supportive of PinS.

> Philosophy, a profession that usually demands not only sanity but also a high degree of order and rationality, is always at risk of allying itself with society's repression of the true self. Perhaps it can avoid this risk, if it learns to listen more than it usually does to the voices of disorder and play, to the childlike within the adult.
>
> (Nussbaum, 2006: 376)

Nussbaum's risk avoidance strategy is precisely what the PinS methodology provides. For Nussbaum, a focus on conformity typically stifles creativity, forcing people to hide rather than unfold themselves; a focus on order conceals the messiness of individuality. By contrast, the playfulness of PinS allows for what she refers to as 'the messy self' (Nussbaum, 2006: 375). It encourages creativity and the use of the imagination, which are crucial to the development of a capacity to put oneself in the place of the other and hence to develop moral feeling and concern. Nussbaum's exploration of Winnicott leads her to argue that even the moral life of an adult stands 'in continual need of nourishment of the playful and imaginative capacities, [which are] so easily suppressed by the demands of "the real world"' (Nussbaum, 2006: 375).

The benefits of sustained practice with PinS have much to do with encouraging playful engagement with ideas. Within the 'Community of Inquiry' (CoI), students are encouraged to bring an attitude of exploration to the classroom, to hold their views tentatively; to be prepared to play with ideas and change their minds in the face of good reasons for doing so; and to try to build on one another's ideas. The methodology allows students to set the agenda for discussion, as the teacher adopts the role of facilitator of discussion and champion of the development of the cultural context definitive of a CoI (Lipman *et al.*, 1980: 45).

Play, playfulness and intentionality

The discussion in this chapter follows John Dewey in distinguishing between 'playful engagement' and 'play'. For Dewey, playfulness is a more important consideration than play, because while playfulness is foundational and defines 'an attitude of mind', play is 'a passing outward manifestation of this attitude' (Dewey, 1977: 162). Dewey goes on to argue that 'the playful attitude is one of freedom. The person is not bound to the physical traits of things, nor does he [*sic*] care whether a thing really means (as we say) what he takes it to represent' (Dewey, 1977: 162). The playful attitude as characterized by Dewey is accommodated by Piaget (1962), who argues that play is a cognitive process in which assimilation takes precedence over accommodation.[6] This means that for Piaget, play and playfulness are portable and not confined to a particular space or time. In fact, as Csikszentmihalyi (1975) argues, play can occur at or outside of work, since it depends on the cognitive and intentional engagement a person has with the challenges of a situation and the person's capabilities and motivation to meet these challenges.

The particular kind of intentionality revealed in playfulness has been referred to elsewhere as indirection or 'purposefulness without purpose' (Kant, 1952: 159–69)[7]; and the literature on play addresses this in different ways. Simmel (1950), for example, sees play idealistically as a primary category or social form of society in which social reality is open to playful reinterpretation in the context of sociability, which is the 'pure' form of social interaction given that ideally, 'purely sociable conversation' has no ulterior motive, no content and no determinate result outside of itself. Sociability is the play form of social interaction and is valued for its own sake (having purposefulness but being without particular purpose). This focus on the nature of intentionality is important to successfully engaging students in the PinS classroom, since it implies engagement in communal discussion for its own sake and for the enjoyment students experience when playing with ideas.

Huizinga (1955: 13) describes play as a non-literal orientation to behaviour in the sense that what is done in play is not literally intended: the players may follow rough scripts but they are not bound by any clearly defined set of rules. Rather they agree to a play frame in which rules are implicit and unarticulated, although play can break down if these implicit rules are flouted. In the PinS classroom, a student can destroy playful engagement by throwing the cush-ball, which identifies the speaker, to the next speaker with too much force.

However, within the PinS classroom we are not only playing with ideas. As a pedagogical approach, PinS does have certain serious objectives, such as the development of students' critical and creative (higher-order) thinking skills, independent thought, and a socially supportive classroom environment. Dewey (1977: 162) recognizes that play and seriousness are not mutually exclusive categories; playfulness is a valuable attitude of mind, but in order that it 'may not terminate in arbitrary fancifulness and in building up an imaginary world alongside the world of actual things, it is necessary that the play attitude should gradually pass into a work attitude'. The usual way of distinguishing between play and work is to say that in play activity, we are interested in the activity for its own sake (e.g. as Simmel suggests above), while in work, it is the product or outcome of the activity which is of interest to us. So play is regarded as being purely free and work is regarded as tied to outcome and 'the adequate embodiment of meaning ... in some objective form through the use of appropriate materials and appliances' (Dewey, 1977: 163). On Dewey's view, this fails to appreciate that playfulness and what we take to be work depend on attitudes of mind. It creates an unnatural separation between process and product, between activity and achieved outcome.

> The true distinction is not between an interest in activity for its own sake and interest in the external result of that activity, but between an interest in an activity just as it flows on from moment to moment, and an interest in an activity as tending to a culmination, to an outcome and therefore possessing a thread of continuity binding together its successive stages.
> (Dewey, 1977: 164)

Like Dewey, Csikszentmihalyi (1975) does not focus on the distinction between work and play but rather argues that it is the intensity (or 'flow') of the engagement that is the key element in explaining human enjoyment of particular activities and by analogy the enjoyment students and teachers experience in the PinS classroom. On Dewey's view, there are two unfortunate consequences of the tendency to sharply contrast play and work. The first is that the early years of schooling are associated with play, which is seen as unduly symbolic, fanciful, sentimental and arbitrary, while the later years are associated with work and with externally assigned tasks. The second is that the unnatural separation of play and work is usually associated with false notions of imagination and utility and a false opposition between imagination and utility. For Dewey, the healthy imagination is not characterized by a flight into the unreal and the purely fanciful; rather its exercise is a method of expanding and filling in what is real, constructing experiences of wide social value and meaning (Dewey, 1977).

Dewey's rejection of the oppositions between play and work and between imagination and utility in educational contexts provides a theoretical foundation for the kind of work undertaken in the PinS classroom. We take a playful orientation to philosophical inquiry, but one that can have positive and serious benefits – intellectually, socially and morally. The benefits are part of what might be referred to as the 'hidden agenda' of the PinS methodology from the perspective of the student – particularly the young student – since it is the playful engagement with ideas which is emphasized to them. For example, while discussing a story such as *The Bunyip of Berkeley's Creek* (Wagner and Brooks, 1978), which students have read together, the concepts of stereotyping and personal identity (required curriculum topics) come up naturally in discussion. The teacher as facilitator draws attention to the use of higher-order thinking skills that students employ in exploring these concepts during discussion, e.g. by encouraging students to recognize and identify assumptions and implications, to consider the quality of reasons offered, to explain ideas and to consider alternatives. In this way, students implicitly rather than explicitly engage with aspects of mandatory quality teaching frameworks,[8] via their participation in the development of the CoI, a playfully rule-bound cultural form that is central to the PinS classroom (Cam, 1995: 34–54).

The literature suggests that benefits in the development of intelligence, in the evolution of communication and in social and moral development do occur through play and playful engagement, as well as through the playing of games (Matthews, 1980; Wohlwend, 2011). The next section discusses the support that the literature on play theory contributes to these suggested benefits.

Theoretical foundations of playful engagement

For Piaget, play has a crucial role in intellectual development; he uses the concepts of schema, assimilation and accommodation to describe the cognitive processes involved. For example, the child at play assimilates a schema (a well-defined, regularly repeated sequence of mental or physical actions) such as handclapping or sucking to a variety of new objects. However, the child may be forced to accommodate or adapt a schema if it meets with negative responses from carers, e.g. when she sucks a shoe. Within this conceptual framework, Piaget conceived of play as the process in which assimilation takes precedence over accommodation, since in play, the player is more likely to assimilate the external world to fit in with her way of 'seeing' or perceiving the world, rather than to adapt herself to or accommodate the external world. So the child pretends that the cardboard box is a row-boat; in this way, play becomes symbolic as the child enjoys a subjective reality, using and developing language to articulate her experience and express her feelings.

Thus through play and games children are assisted in undertaking the transition from sensory-motor stages of intellectual development to conceptual and operational (imaginative) thinking (Piaget, 1962).[9] PinS offers a methodology that encourages such conceptual and imaginative thinking, where imagination is used in Dewey's (1977) sense of the term to describe not only thinking that is entirely speculative and fanciful but also thinking that expands and fills in what is real and in so doing constructs experiences of wide social value and meaning.

Social and moral development in play and games

The rules that define a social or an individual world that players of games agree to enter when they choose to play a game are to that extent entwined with the learning of moral values and ethical behaviour. But, as Piaget explains, games are significant in the moral development of children in part because they are explicitly rule-bound in a way that play is not. The child beginning to play games must learn to accommodate herself to new schemas, as she discovers that the game environment does not respond to the schemas she already holds. Piaget makes the following comment about games.

> Children's games constitute the most admirable social institutions. The game of marbles, for instance, as played by boys [*sic*] contains an extremely complex system of rules, that is to say a code of laws, a jurisprudence of its own.
>
> (Piaget, 1965: 13)

Piaget's studies of children led him to conclude that there are two sources of morality for children: a 'sacred' morality learnt from parents and older children; and a second, negotiable morality developed on the basis of mutuality. Play and games are both implicated in the development of the child's sense of moral judgement, since they provide an arena in which the child learns to negotiate and argue rules and conventions. Through the process Piaget describes, the child becomes an autonomous moral agent who recognizes her connection with and responsibility toward others and is able to renegotiate the previously learnt, 'sacred morality'.

Mead (1962) also emphasizes the role of play in the socialization and moral development of children, noting that in play children initially acquire the ability to take on the attitudes of individual significant others; they then display the ability to take on the attitudes of generalized others, i.e. of a community of others. Like Piaget, Mead argues that play and games are important to the development of both these stages. In play, children take on and incorporate elements of the roles and attitudes of significant others, e.g. those of mother, father, nurse, shopkeeper or teacher. In doing so, the self is socialized and at the meta-level children learn the concept of a role. Individual play at role-taking is followed developmentally by the playing of games, which are seen as a context both for the development of the self and for the development of morality. Mead explains that the rule-bound nature of participation in games and role-play requires that children learn what they and other players are expected to do, and in particular how their own roles in the game can fit in with those of other players. This organization of the roles of a community of others allows individual children to appreciate and to choose how to conduct themselves within a group according to the attitudes and conventions that apply to that community. It also makes it possible for individual children to reflect on themselves as objects from the standpoint of the community to which they belong and to explore the extent to which they respond to the demands of the generalized other. The point I wish to emphasize in this chapter is that the development of a CoI within the PinS classroom is clearly an example of such a community of others. It has both playful and game-like features that help to explain both the enjoyment that students and teachers experience in the PinS classroom and the value of the methodology in terms of its contribution to intellectual, social and moral development.

The game-like features of the PinS methodology, which are found in the rules of conduct applying within the CoI established in the classroom, are analogous to the rules of a game and are made explicit to students. For example, rules about taking turns in contributing to discussion and sharing participation involve game-like strategies for encouraging students to respect these rules. Props such as balls, string, match-sticks and toy microphones are used in this context; and memory cards are used to reinforce the habit of not interrupting – unless doing so is judged to be absolutely necessary. The use of the props is designed to take the explicit focus off the learning of rules and to make it more fun than it might otherwise be.

These game-like features imply that the views of Piaget and Mead on the connection between games and moral development can apply to participants in the CoI. As their views suggest, the players as members of the CoI must take on the roles and attitudes which membership implies. They must learn the rules of conduct within the CoI and practise acting according to those rules. More specifically, they must develop a conception of the way in which the different roles they will take as members of the community (as listener, speaker/initiator, interlocutor, supporter or challenger, evaluator) fit together; they must also develop an understanding of their responsibilities as members and participants in the CoI – including an understanding of how to respond appropriately and respectfully within the various roles they take on. The methodology emphasizes the equal worth of each participant in the CoI and includes a set of playful strategies used to help participants evaluate the CoI after a lesson. Thus students rate the quality of their participation and that of others, as well as the success of the lesson generally, on intellectual, social and moral criteria, as appropriate to their capacity for judgement.

While this discussion has focused on the role of the playing of games in moral development, some theorists, notably Simmel (1950) and Csikszentmihalyi and Bennett (1971), suggest that play is also to some extent socially constrained and that this constraint accounts for the ethical significance of play. Their view is that the pleasure the individual finds in play is closely tied up with the pleasure of fellow-players. As Csikszentmihalyi and Bennett (1971: 51) put it, play 'combines in an experiential unity both social constraints and spontaneous behaviour'. This view undermines a separation between play and games, at least in some respects, and so reinforces the claims made in this chapter about the appeal of the PinS classroom. It recognizes the connection between the playful attitude that is crucial to the PinS classroom and the use of rules enacted via playful strategies. These strategies, which include the configuration of the room where students are seated and the use of props, set the play context or provide a play frame. They signal the intention to begin a playful engagement with ideas – indicating that we are in class, but we are in class in a different way.

Huizinga (1955) appreciates nuances that are relevant to the PinS classroom in the interaction between play and games as regards students' social, moral and intellectual development. He explicitly defends the intellectual and moral values of play, arguing that these values can raise play to the level of culture and enhance social life; and in the context of philosophical inquiry, he emphasizes play's capacity to move beyond the demands of conformity to the rules of a game to encourage the exploration of novel ideas.

Without this kind of playful exploration, philosophical inquiry in the classroom is likely to face the dangers Nussbaum identifies by overemphasizing rationality and stifling imagination and creativity. Within the PinS classroom, students ought to be encouraged to play with ideas; to set the agenda by reflecting upon and discussing anything they find interesting or puzzling about the stimulus material used; and to express their own ideas in ways that respect the rights of each of their peers to do the same. Similarly, without the methodology's focus on the participant's responsibility to support peers in the process of inquiry and dialogue, which underpins the social and moral dimension of the PinS methodology, the discussion could degenerate into one of competition and one-upmanship, as Smith (2011) suggests.

Playful engagement in the philosophy classroom

While some commentators have argued that the PinS methodology is rationalistic and deontological in its approach (Weber, p. 240), one can as easily argue that an ethics of care or a virtue ethics approach is equally implicit in the methodology. The conception of ethics that underpins the PinS methodology is dependent on the approach that teachers – as facilitators of CoI – adopt. The possibility to which I am referring can be demonstrated via Piaget's reference to the game of marbles in his treatment of the development of moral judgement through games. Piaget refers to the complex system of rules (prescriptions) that apply to the game of marbles, as noted above. However, he describes a situation in which the moral sensitivity of the subjects of his research went beyond the stated rules. A system of honesty beyond the rules was clearly present.

> When a player places a marble of superior value in the square, thinking he has put down an ordinary marble (say an 'ago' instead of a 'coilleau') he is naturally allowed, if he has noticed his mistake, to pick up his 'ago' and put an ordinary marble in its place. Only a dishonest opponent would take advantage of his partner's absent-mindedness and pocket the 'ago' after

having hit it. The children were unanimous in pronouncing such procedure equivalent to stealing.

(Piaget, 1965: 18)

Equally, while the CoI does have a set of rules or prescriptions for participation, the ethical responsibilities of the students are not limited to complying with those prescriptions. Students are encouraged to develop an ethic of care in relating to others, in which they respond sensitively to one another; listen carefully so as to be able to build on the ideas of others; imaginatively put themselves in the place of the other; exercise the principle of charity in understanding the other's perspective; and disagree respectfully. These are ways of relating that have more in common with what legal ethicists refer to as 'fuzzy laws' than 'black letter', deontological prescriptions. They have more to do with consideration of the kind of character traits or virtues that members of the CoI, ideally, ought to possess to ensure optimal functioning of the community.

My argument is that the game-like features of PinS, while increasing enjoyment, also can contribute to or accommodate a broad notion of ethics, one which goes beyond 'black-letter' law prescriptions such as 'don't interrupt others' to an understanding that behaving ethically requires a consideration of what taking the perspective of the other might entail. Equally, one could argue, as Csikszentmihalyi and Bennett do, that play has its own ethical dimensions associated with the shared enjoyment of the activity being undertaken. On this view, a playful attitude in the classroom cannot be sustained without reciprocity, which requires a recognition of and responsiveness to the enjoyment of other participants.

Conclusion

The teacher as facilitator is central to the possibility of sustaining the playful attitude this chapter recommends and hence must be alert to the dangers that theorists such as Winnicott, Nussbaum, Schiller and Weber have identified. As philosopher-teachers in the PinS classroom, we would do well to listen more than we usually do to the voices of disorder and play and to use those voices as the basis of discussion; to engage with concepts and ideas that relate to the actual problems of our students' lives; and finally to recognize that we cannot avoid the messiness of individuality that will emerge within these processes. Encouraging elements of playfulness and attitudes of exploration and experimentation requires that teachers adopt the requisite mental attitude themselves. It also requires some courage on the teacher's part, since the students are autonomous agents with regard to this process – 'messy individuals', as Nussbaum might say. Teachers will not always be able to predict the direction in which the discussion will go or the emphasis students will place on a particular topic. This novelty and lack of predictability is part of the playfulness of PinS, but it can also be unnerving, especially for the teacher who comes to the lesson with the intention to cover particular curriculum topics in a particular way. However, as Maxine Greene (2000: 51, 52) has suggested, one of our interests as teachers ought to be 'in creating a civilization that can tolerate the potency of desire, the thrust of diverse energies, the vitality of play, and the intention to transform', which opens the possibility of bringing into being 'something that goes beyond a present situation'. Given that the literature on play and games attests to the benefits of a playful attitude in the classroom, it is well worth facing the challenges of accommodating the experimental and hopefully transformative nature of playful engagement with philosophical ideas in the PinS classroom.

Notes

1 The methodology is known as 'Philosophy in Schools' (hereafter 'PinS') in Australia.
2 Barbara Weber's work on PinS is exceptional in this context for its emphasis on the role of emotions, play and creativity in the PinS classroom.
3 Matthews notes his concern with Piagetian theory in this regard, given that it discounts children's non-conforming convictions and what Piaget called 'romancing' or inventing an answer in which one does not really believe. Matthews argues that the philosophically interesting comments a child makes are more likely to explore conceptual connections or conceptual jokes than to express settled convictions (Matthews, 1980: 39).
4 Humour is explained in the literature by three major theories, associated with notions of superiority, incongruity or relief (Smuts, 2014).
5 For example, with reference to play, Winnicott argues that 'play is in fact neither a matter of inner psychic reality nor a matter of external reality' (Winnicott, 1971: 112); Laura Praglin (2006) addresses the notion of the 'in-between' in the work of D. W. Winnicott and Martin Buber.
6 See the following section for an articulation of both processes.
7 Indirection is a phenomenon that applies to friendship as well as to art, both of which are ideally engaged in for their own sake and in both whatever is achieved by engagement occurs indirectly since these activities require a particular, non-instrumental kind of intentionality (Lynch, 2005: 100).
8 NSW (New South Wales) Department of Education Professional Learning and Leadership Development: Quality Teaching in NSW Public Schools: www.det.nsw.edu.au/proflearn/areas/qt/resources.htm, accessed 10 December 2014.
9 However, as noted above, Piaget has been criticized for a focus on conformity in children's convictions, rather than on their attempts at conceptual exploration and playfulness. See note 3 above.

References

Bateson, G. (1973) *Steps to an Ecology of Mind*, London: Granada Publishing.
Cam, P. (1995) *Thinking Together: Philosophical Inquiry for the Classroom*, Alexandria, NSW: Hale and Iremonger.
Cam, P. (2006) *Twenty Thinking Tools*, Camberwell: ACER Press.
Creasey, G. L., Jarvis, P. A. and Berk, L. (1998) 'Play and social competence', in Saracho, O. N. and Spodek, B. (eds) *Multiple Perspectives on Play in Early Childhood Education*, Albany, NY: State University of New York Press, 116–43.
Csikszentmihalyi, M. (1975) *Beyond Boredom and Anxiety*, San Francisco: Jossey-Bass Inc.
Csikszentmihalyi, M. and Bennett, S. (1971) 'An exploratory model of play', *American Anthropologist*, New Series, 73(1), 45–58.

Dewey, J. (1977 [1910]) *How We Think*, Mineola, NY: Dover Publications.

Erikson, E. H. (1963) *Childhood and Society*, New York: W. W. Norton and Company.

Fleer, M. (2010) *Early Learning and Development: Cultural-historical Concepts in Play*, Cambridge: Cambridge University Press.

Garvey, C. (1997) *Play*, Cambridge, MA: Harvard University Press.

Greene, M. (2000) *Releasing the Imagination: Essays on Education, the Arts, and Social Change*, New York: Jossey-Bass.

Huizinga, J. (1955 [1938]) *Homo Ludens: A Study of the Play Element in Culture*, Boston: Beacon Press.

Isenberg, J. and Quisenberry, N. (1988) 'Play: A necessity for all children – A position paper', Olney, MD: Association for Childhood Education International.

Kant, I. (1952 [1790]) *Critique of Judgement*, transl. Meredith, J. C., Oxford: Clarendon Press.

Lipman, M., Sharp, A. M. and Oscanyan, F. S. (1980) *Philosophy in the Classroom*, 2nd edn, Philadelphia: Temple University Press.

Lynch, S. (2005) *Philosophy and Friendship*, Edinburgh: Edinburgh University Press.

Matthews, G. B. (1980) *Philosophy and the Young Child*, Cambridge, MA: Harvard University Press.

Mead, G. H. (1962 [1934]) *Mind, Self and Society: From the Standpoint of a Social Behaviorist*, ed. C. W. Morris, Chicago: University of Chicago Press.

NSW Department of Education Professional Learning and Leadership Development (n.d.) Quality Teaching Resources, www.det.nsw.edu.au/proflearn/areas/qt/resources.htm, accessed 10 December 2014.

Nussbaum, M. C. (2006) 'Winnicott on surprises of the self', *Massachusetts Review (The Messy Self)*, 47(2), 375–93.

Piaget, J. (1962 [1951]) *Play, Dreams and Imitation in Childhood*, New York: W. W. Norton and Company.

Piaget, J. (1965) *The Moral Judgement of the Child*, New York: The Free Press.

Plato (1961) 'Theatetus', *The Collected Dialogues*, Bollingen Series LXXI, ed. Hamilton, E. and Cairns, H., Princeton, NJ: Princeton University Press.

Praglin, L. (2006) 'The nature of the 'in-between' in D. W. Winnicott's concept of transitional space and in Martin Buber's *das Zwischenmenschliche*', *Universitas*, 2(2), 1–9.

Simmel, G. (1950 [1910]) *The Sociology of Georg Simmel*, transl. Wolff, K. H., New York: The Free Press.

Smith, R. (2011) 'The play of Socratic dialogue', *Journal of Philosophy of Education*, 45(2), 221–33.

Smuts, A. (2014) 'Humor', *International Encyclopedia of Philosophy*, www.iep.utm.edu/humor/, accessed 27 September 2014.

Vygotsky, L. (1978) *Mind in Society: The Development of Higher Psychological Processes*, Cambridge, MA: Harvard University Press.

Wagner, J. and Brooks, R. (1978) *The Bunyip of Berkeley's Creek*, Melbourne: Penguin Australia.

Weber, B. (2011) 'Childhood, philosophy and play: Friedrich Schiller and the interface between reason, passion and sensation', *Journal of Philosophy of Education*, 45(2), 235–50.

Winnicott, D. W. (1971) *Playing and Reality*, Middlesex: Penguin Books.

Wohlwend, K. E. (ed.) (2011) *Literacy, Play and Globalization: Converging Imaginaries in Children's Critical and Cultural Performances*, London and New York: Routledge.

14 Entangled in the midst of it
A diffractive expression of an ethics for playwork

Wendy Russell

> Something's happening. Try as we might to gain an observer's remove, that's where we find ourselves: in the midst of it. There's happening doing. This is where philosophical thinking must begin: immediately in the middle.
>
> (Massumi, 2011: 1)

> Not even a moment exists on its own. 'This' and 'that', 'here' and 'now', don't pre-exist what happens but come alive with each meeting.... Meeting each moment, being alive to the possibilities of becoming, is an ethical call, an invitation that is written into the very matter of all being and becoming.
>
> (Barad, 2007: 396)

Introduction

Playworkers in the UK work with school-aged children to support their play. The practice is underpinned by a set of principles that establish playwork's professional and ethical framework (PPSG, 2005). These principles create a number of contradictions for practice that have an ethical dimension, and this chapter offers a modest exploration of this that seeks to reconfigure taken-for-granted assumptions that have become common-sense truths. It is modest in the sense that it marks an experimental and initial playing with ideas that are different for the author: philosophy as an activity in the midst of it (Massumi, 2011). It is offered as an 'expression': not a reproduction of an already existing state of affairs to be accurately communicated, more an immanent, mutual deterritorialization of the gap between content and form of expression. This is itself an ethical act:

> There is indeed an ethics of expression.... It is a basically pragmatic question of how one performatively contributes to the stretch of expression in the world – or conversely prolongs its capture.... Where expression stretches, potential determinately emerges into something new. Expression's tensing is by nature creative.... To tend the stretch of expression, to foster and inflect it rather than trying to own it, is to enter the stream, contributing to its probings: this is co-creative, an aesthetic endeavor. It is also an ethical endeavor, since it is to ally oneself with change: for an ethics of emergence.
>
> (Massumi, 2002: xxii)

In this spirit of modest and ethical expression, then, the chapter opens by placing the Playwork Principles in the midst of their historical context, noting the shift towards prescription and technical standards for practice alongside an enduring sense of dissent and recalcitrance within playwork as a heterogeneous community of practice. Implicit in this 'minoritarian becoming-playworker' (adapting Braidotti, 2012) is an appreciation of the nature and value of children's play that resists dominant, totalizing, developmentalist and instrumental narratives (Lester and Russell, 2013). Such an appreciation is evident in playwork practice (Lester et al., 2014; Russell, 2013) but is articulated infrequently. A different 'cut' on childhood and play that decentres playwork's focus on the psychological subject – and particularly on the material discursive practice of 'intervention' – is offered here as a contribution to the 'stretch of expression', given the mutual implication of epistemology, ontology and ethics (Barad, 2007).

Following this, the chapter critiques the notion of the autonomous rational agent implicit in the Playwork Principles' understanding of both play and playwork so as to reconfigure playwork as relational, affective and affecting, embodied, situated and not reducible to representations in language. What is attempted here is a diffractive reading of texts through each other (a 'mash-up', perhaps, or an ongoing game of Donna Haraway's [1994] cat's cradle) of the work of Karen Barad and Rosi Braidotti, with a sprinkling of Judith Butler, in order to offer an alternative posthuman, nomadic and relational ethics that acknowledges the complexities of the emergent, ongoing and intra-active co-production of play space in which playworkers are already directly implicated.

Playwork as 'becoming-minoritarian' practice: the entanglement of knowledge, being and ethics

Although playworkers in the UK work in a range of contexts, its best-known theorists hail mainly from the adventure playground movement (Brown, 2003; Else, 2014; Hughes, 2006, 2012; PPSG, 2005). This has played its part in the development of an ethos that places high value on self-organised outdoor play with easy access to a range of indeterminate materials, tools and the elements (Russell, 2013). Adventure playgrounds were introduced to the UK by Lady Allen of Hurtwood following her visit to the junk playground in Emdrup, Copenhagen in 1948 and were largely welcomed by the authorities as an effective response to a post-war rise in delinquency among working-class boys (Cranwell, 2007). Although permissiveness and democracy, even anarchy, were at the heart of the adventure playground endeavour, Kozlovsky (2008) suggests this was aimed ultimately at meeting policy's instrumental goals. Out of anarchy and freedom would come an understanding of democracy and citizenship. In the 1960s and 1970s, the work attracted a significant number of people sympathetic to the civil liberties movements, and playwork was at that time often closely allied to radical community development, community arts and youth work (Cranwell, 2007), with many playworkers being 'a mixture of hippy idealists, anarcho-punks and grass-roots community activists with strong libertarian and left-wing beliefs' (Conway, 2005: 2).

In the ensuing decades, shifts in the socio-political landscape raised a number of challenges to the original permissive, adventurous and democratic ethos. In particular, the introduction of health and safety legislation, registration and inspection regimes and the marketization of public services contributed to the development of externally derived prescriptions and standards (Lester and Russell 2013; Shier 1984). Playwork's institutions tried to tread the path between protecting this ethos and retaining some control over the development of such standards that have now become an accepted aspect of the work (Russell, 2013).

These technical standards (for example, National Occupational Standards, quality assurance schemes, risk assessment forms, registration guidelines) mark a significant shift away from the experimentation, unpredictability, anarchy and freedoms of early adventure playground pioneers (Allen, 1968; Benjamin, 1961, 1974; Hughes, 1975), leading some to mourn the loss of a movement, although the idea of 'play' (as a synecdoche encompassing children's play and adult support for it) as 'a dissenting presence that had the capability to invalidate dominant norms, needs and values ... remains strong' (Cranwell, 2007: 62).

What can be seen here is a dialectic playing out between playwork as a social practice with shared internal goods (MacIntyre, 2007) and an increasing focus on technical skills and instrumental outcomes led by playwork's institutions in the name of recognition and status. Playwork's 'dissenting presence', or its recalcitrance (Battram and Russell, 2002), might be understood as an attempt by a social practice to curb the potential for institutions to corrupt its value base (MacIntyre, 2007). The tension remains and is played out in the endless rounds of meetings where official articulations – playwork's 'professing' – are revised, reworded and repackaged in attempts to resolve contradictions both within the practice and between the practice and its institutions. This exercise, however, is doomed to failure: the ineffable qualities of the playwork approach cannot be fixed in time or contained absolutely by representation in this technical manner, as there will always be something that exceeds it, that cannot be articulated in the limits of language.

It perhaps needs to be stressed, however, that this dialectic is by no means a static binary or negative opposition. A Lefebvrian perspective (Lefebvre, 2009) sees dialectics as the basis for perpetual change, ceaseless becoming, through the entanglements of a triad of social practice (from Marx), language and thought (from Hegel) and a Dionysian playfulness/creativity (from Nietzsche) (Schmid, 2008). Rather than the binary negation of essentialist Hegelian dialectics critiqued by Deleuze (2001), such a position can connect with his affirmative 'difference-in-itself'. This requires a nomadic rather than a fixed codifying approach, open to difference, deterritorializing the measured, striated spaces of totalizing certainties (Deuchars, 2011).

This always-becoming dialectical triad is cut here with Barad's (2007) entanglement of epistemology, ontology and ethics. Contrary to Levinas' (1989) argument that ethics is first philosophy prior to epistemology and ontology, Barad (2007: 185) argues that none is prior:

> Practices of knowing and being are not isolable; they are mutually implicated. We don't obtain knowledge by standing outside the world; we know because we are *of* the world.... The separation of epistemology from ontology is a reverberation of a metaphysics that assumes an inherent difference between human and nonhuman, subject and object, mind and body, matter and discourse ... what we need is something like an *ethico-onto-epistem-ology* – an appreciation of the intertwining of ethics, knowing and being – since each intra-action matters.

We have fallen into the common-sense belief that there are fixed and pre-existing realities that can be first discovered and then mirrored faithfully in language. Both these assumptions have been challenged through Barad's (2007) theory of agential realism, developed from the radical challenge to traditional epistemology brought by Niels Bohr's work on quantum physics. These ideas are complex and profound and cannot be adequately summarized here without inevitable oversimplification if not misrepresentation. Nevertheless, key concepts can be used as tropes (as Baradian apparatuses perhaps) to offer up a different way of configuring what we know about children's play and playwork, or rather, to offer up *difference itself as a way of configuring them*. In a shift of optical metaphor, rather than seeking to *reflect* accurately and objectively a pre-existing and concrete reality, 'setting up worries about copy and original and the search for the authentic and the really real' (Haraway, 1997, cited in Barad, 2007: 71), a *diffractive* analysis offers 'a mapping of interference.... A diffraction pattern does not map where differences appear, but rather maps where the effects of difference appear' (Haraway, 1992: 300). For Barad, the diffraction apparatuses in physics not only reveal the effect of changes that occur when a wave hits an obstacle or slit, they also reveal the entangled structure of phenomena:

> 'Things' don't pre-exist.... Matter is ... not to be understood as a property of things but, like discursive practices, must be understood in more dynamic and productive terms – in terms of intra-activity.
>
> (Barad, 2007: 150)

Barad coins the term 'intra-action' to extend the notion of interaction (which assumes pre-existing agencies) in order to emphasise how agencies emerge through the process of intra-action. This concept is revisited later in the chapter.

Representationalism assumes the knower to be apart from that which is known. The play scholar can define and categorize play as something that exists out there independently of their observation, and that can be accurately represented in language. Defining play requires that its boundaries are fixed and identifiable, that there is a clear separation between play and not-play. The generic concept can then be broken down into smaller bounded and identifiable categories (locomotor play, social play, rough and tumble, for example) with attendant benefits. A performative approach, however, sees 'thinking, observing, and theorizing as practices of engagement with, and as part of, the world in which we have our being' (Barad, 2007: 133). Defining and categorizing are boundary-making practices that have material effects. Furthermore, a posthumanist performative approach not only challenges the ability of language to reflect a reality awaiting discovery, it also challenges the anthropocentric arrogance that humans are somehow apart from nature, an assumption implicit in nature–culture and subject–object binaries; it also pays attention to material, non-human bodies, in the ongoing becoming of the world. Knowledge and meaning are enacted as material discursive practices that determine what can and cannot be said about play and about the relationship of playworkers to playing (or non-playing) children. Knowledge thereby becomes intimately entangled with practice; our current ways of thinking and speaking about play enact an agential cut that closes down other ways of thinking and therefore acting: 'discursive practices are specific material (re)configurings of the world through which the determination of boundaries, properties, and meanings is differentially enacted' (Barad, 2007: 149).

Given all of this, dissent and recalcitrance are important features of playwork ethics, together with an openness to difference (in terms of the otherness of other humans and non-humans, and also of a constant state of becoming). They represent a form of 'becoming minoritarian' practice that seeks to 'escape from "majoritarian" norms, subject positions, and habits of mind and practice' (Lenz-Taguchi, 2012: 267), the agential cuts that produce habitual material discursive practice. This is ethical because it disturbs the hegemonic, common-sense, totalizing material discursive practices that have emerged from the marketized, New Public Management focus on performance indicators, outcomes and technical standards that is now the norm in public service (Banks, 2004; Dahlberg and Moss, 2008), together with the dominance of psychology in the twentieth century and the increasing reach of its gaze in the lives of children (Rose, 1999a). A nomadic, relational ethics reconfigures the internalized, individuated, rational moral agent and pays attention to the forces, desires and entanglements of human, non-human and more-than-human becoming-players that affect and are affected by each other in ways that seek to bring about yet-to-be conditions (Braidotti, 2012). The different diffractive cut on children's play and playwork offered here opens up ethical possibilities for knowing and being, for a different ethics – or an ethics of difference – for playwork.

Playwork's recalcitrance is seen less in grand gestures of major politics and more in everyday 'minor' acts that carry a hope for a better today rather than some final future utopian project (Horton and Kraftl, 2009; Rose, 1999b): moments of nonsense and playfulness that can emerge in spaces where conditions are supportive. These rarely find their way into 'serious' texts about playwork, but have begun to emerge in the virtual spaces of social media. Playwork practice based largely on tacit knowledge, intuitions, hunches and an 'ineffable knack' (Heron, 1996) intersects with external pressures to categorize and codify play into a thing to be provided for its assumed instrumental and future-focused benefits.

Such an ethical stance can be argued for any work with people, but it is particularly salient for those who work with children at play, given both the otherness of children and the notion that play itself can be seen as a Deleuzian line of flight from the dominant adult orderings of time and space (Lester, 2013), where such a line of flight 'does not mean to flee but to re-create or act against dominant systems of thought and social conditions' (Deuchars, 2011: 5).

Apollo and Dionysus at play

Most playworkers, particularly those in open access[1] settings, are funded through the public purse and so need to justify their work in the language of whatever social problem concerns governments at that time. In this endeavour, Apollo rules in the playground. The majoritarian material discursive practice that sees play as a mechanism for learning skills needed later in adult life privileges a pre-existing, stable and separate Cartesian mind over a Dionysian body that requires disciplining. Particular forms of playing are valued over others for their perceived effectiveness in developing the desired skills and healthy bodies (Lester and Russell, 2013). Locomotor play becomes valuable in terms of preventing obesity (Alexander et al., 2014). Pretend play is valued for its role in the development of social cognition and skills (Lillard et al., 2011). Even the category 'risky play' is psychologized so it is no longer irrational, unruly impulsivity in search of high excitement and arousal, rather it is a need that helps children develop risk assessment skills (Lester and Russell, 2014).

Nowhere is the Apollonian child more evident than in the 'return-to-nature' movement that is a current focus of play advocates and environmental organizations alike.[2] The research agenda, and subsequent benefit claims, focus again on the development of disembodied cognitive capacities, including pro-environmental attitudes, mental health and emotion regulation, scientific learning and environmental knowledge (Gill, 2011). The author of the psycho-pathologizing concept of 'nature deficit disorder' (Louv, 2005) encapsulates this in his blog post entitled 'Want your children to get into Harvard? Tell 'em to go outside!' (Louv, 2011).

In all of this, play is seen unproblematically as a force for good, with singular causal links being made between particular forms of play and desired, predominantly cognitive, skills. Play becomes reified, even commodified, into something to be provided by (well-meaning) adults as a way of helping children to fulfil their potential (Lester and Russell, 2013) and to ward off our own adult ontological and existential anxieties about the future (Katz, 2008; Kraftl, 2008). Inevitably, this leads to privileging some forms of play over others, particularly over the Dionysian forms of playing that may elicit adult anxiety or offence (Sutton-Smith, 1997) and that are not necessarily inherently 'good'.

What this illustrates is the entanglement of epistemology, ontology and ethics through majoritarian material discursive practices. They have become so pervasive that they are understood as common sense. It is argued here that ethical playwork has a responsibility to disturb these understandings in order to offer a minoritarian, diffractive cut (Lester *et al.*, 2014): not another fixed position in opposition, rather an openness to what might be different.

These two forms of future-focused, utopian territorialization of children's play (Bauman, 2003; Lester and Russell, 2013) – that is, its instrumentalization in social policy (and therefore public funding) and its rational, Apollonian bias – create ethical paradoxes for playworkers discernible in the assumptions underpinning the Playwork Principle as a code of ethics, and so it is to an examination of these that we now turn.

Decentring the human subject in the Playwork Principles as a code of ethics

Codes of professional ethics are generally public statements that profess a service ideal. As such, their intention is to fulfil a number of functions including protecting service users, giving credence and professional status, giving guidance to practitioners, and helping to create and maintain professional identity (Banks, 2004). Such codes will always be problematic because of the tensions between prescription and professional judgement, and between universal principles and the particular in everyday situated practice.

The service ideal articulated in the Playwork Principles asserts that the broader the range of opportunities available for children to play, the better for their development. However, the instrumentalization and rationalization of play that underpin the justification of public funding for playwork are directly countered by statements intended to minimize the 'adulteration' of play, understood as the pollution of children's ludic habitat with adult desires. This is particularly apparent in the definition of play as

> a process that is freely chosen, personally directed and intrinsically motivated. That is, children and young people determine and control the content and intent of their play, by following their own instincts, ideas and interests, in their own way for their own reasons.
>
> (PPSG, 2005)

Such characteristics, or equivalents, can be found in much of the literature on play, for example, Burghardt (2005), Caillois (2001), Garvey (1977) and Huizinga (1955). They are problematic epistemologically, ontologically and ethically. Of particular relevance here is the assumption of an autonomous subject exercising rational agency over both human and non-human others from which they are ontologically discrete. Such an individualist conception of the subject can be challenged at a pragmatic level: everyday experience shows that compromise and negotiation are key features of playing with both human and non-human others, tempering absolute freedom of choice and direction. Barad's (2007) work reveals the full extent of the entangled nature of matter (human and non-human bodies). Agency is not something that someone possesses, 'agencies do not precede, but rather emerge through, their intra-action' (Barad, 2007: 33). She elaborates:

> Intra-actions are nonarbitrary, nondeterministic causal enactments through which matter-in-the-process-of-becoming is iteratively enfolded into its ongoing differential materialization. Such a dynamics is not marked by an exterior parameter called time, nor does it take place in a container called space. Rather, iterative intra-actions are the dynamics through which temporality and spatiality are produced and iteratively reconfigured.
>
> (Barad, 2007: 179)

At the risk of over-simplifying her work, what this does is radically reconfigure understandings of the ways in which space and time are produced. Human bodies are entangled with other human and non-human bodies. A diffractive figuration of these entanglements (as meaning making and as material discursive practice) focuses less on fixed boundaries between play and not-play, this play and that play, good play and bad play, and more on the dynamic flows and forces of those entanglements and the possibility of becoming-different. As an affirmative figuration it focuses less on children's needs to play in particular ways that are beneficial for their development – a positioning as lack – and more on the Deleuzian-Spinozan idea of *conatus*. This as 'an affirmative, non-intentional intensity, producing connections ... neither a 'want' nor 'lack' but the effort of an individual entity to persevere in its own existence ... determined by its capacity to affect and be affected' (Parr, 2010: 266), in terms of seeking to enhance capacities for joyful existence and avoiding connections that reduce that capacity. A state of playfulness may be seen as one of vitality; this is not merely 'fun' but a state of positive affect that enlivens things for the time of playing. As Lester (2013: 136–7) states:

> Deterritorialisation holds the most promise for self-ordering and 'joy'; it is a desire to seek out leakages in the constraining molar system and establish molecular *lines of flight* away from the plane of organisation. The contention here is that playing may be seen as such a movement away from order, stability and predictability. It is the process of being a child becoming different and open to what it not yet is.... Playing may be seen as desiring to affect and be affected by creating uncertainty and disturbance, and to play with the relationship between disequilibrium and balance.

'Play-spaces' therefore do not pre-exist independently of their production, but emerge through the intra-actions of bodies, affects, histories, material and symbolic objects and so on. Space becomes relational, dynamic and always in the making: '[e]vents and things do not occupy particular positions in space and time; rather, space, time and matter are iteratively produced and performed'

(Barad, 2007: 393). Such a reconfiguration also requires a rethinking of intervention and adulteration, key apparatuses of playwork. The Playwork Principles state:

> Playworkers choose an intervention style that enables children and young people to extend their play. All playworker intervention must balance risk with the developmental benefit and well-being of children.

Illustrative of the other statements that make up the Playwork Principles, this shows how they rest on assumptions that are deontological, utilitarian and teleological: universal assumptions of an autonomous rational agent and of the right actions to take, either according to professional duties or according to a form of felicific calculus that assumes particular outcomes from particular actions. Yet, as with the impossibility of the freely choosing child, playworkers are not apart from but a part of what happens, they are already in the midst of it, already implicated. If spaces are produced through entangled intra-actions, then there can be no single cause and effect of isolated actions that are currently described as interventions.

This raises questions about the playworker as an ethical subject: if there are no singular causes or no individual agents of change, where does responsibility lie? Barad suggests that if responsibility does not lie with individuals alone, this means that responsibility is even greater than if it did: 'entanglements are ... irreducible relations of responsibility'. She continues:

> Responsibility is not an obligation that the subject chooses ... [it] is not a calculation to be performed. It is a relation always already integral to the world's ongoing intra-active becoming and not-becoming.
>
> (Barad, 2010: 265)

Concluding thoughts: towards a playwork ethics of emergence

The key point to be drawn from the discussion so far is that ethics, in this cut, is not about autonomous moral agents but first and foremost about relations. It is an 'ethics of passion that aims at joy and not destruction' (Braidotti, 2012: 175) and at a collective well-being. In this sense it aligns with other poststructuralist philosophies that address politics and power. It is a nomadic ethics of emergence that requires continual questioning of majoritarian and habitual material discursive practices that can have the effect of overcoding and colonizing children's desires (Lester and Russell, 2013).

Embedded in such an ethics is the relation to the other. Responsibility to the other acknowledges an affirmative difference, appreciating children's 'otherness' from adults and resisting the desire to 'know' them in terms of our own worldview, thereby turning them into versions of the same (Levinas, 1969). As Braidotti (2012: 172) argues:

Otherness is approached as the expression of a productive limit, or generative threshold, which calls for an always already compromised set of negotiations. Nomadic theory prefers to look for the ways in which Otherness prompts, mobilizes, and allows for flows of affirmation of values and forces which are not yet sustained by the current conditions.

The chapter closes with some tentative suggestions for what might be called dispositions for an ethics for playwork. These are adapted from Rushing's (2010) analysis of Judith Butler's ethics. They are not offered as essential characteristics of an ideal playworker, given what has been said here about moral agents. Butler makes the case for developing a subjectivity that is at ease with vulnerability, rather than the overriding thrust towards invincibility, mastery, supremacy. In applying Butler's interpretation of Levinas to playwork, the relation with children *precedes* being a playworker; playworker subjectivities are produced through these relationships in an ongoing state of becoming. In this sense, they are performative.

The dispositions proposed for an ethics of playwork are: openness; playfulness; humility; and patience/restraint as a disposition of *not*-doing that can guard against the totalizing and essentializing that policy often assumes and requires.

Openness is about being comfortable with not knowing, in terms of both children and playwork colleagues as others and in terms of play's unpredictability and spontaneity. 'Openness to others is an expression of the nomadic relational structure of the subject and a precondition for the creation of ethical bonds' (Braidotti, 2012: 174).

Playfulness does not mean forever playing the clown. It does mean being open to turning situations on their head, accepting moments of nonsense that arise, and bringing a playful disposition to situations that may be conflictual, if appropriate. It means not taking play too seriously, as it is far too important for that.

Humility requires an uncertainty regarding our selves, given that categories (for example, woman, playworker) seek to essentialize and smooth away difference, a form of violence in the Levinasian sense. In the spirit of a nomadic ethics, this unsettles any core idea of identity, freeing us to be unknown to ourselves and to live at the edge of our own limits of knowledge. In terms of relationships with children, and especially children at play, 'we work in a field of not knowing' (Sturrock *et al.*, 2004: 33).

Patience and restraint involves not demanding that the other explain or define themselves in a way we can understand. It is perhaps a disposition of *not* doing, of waiting and seeing. This is not to be confused with doing nothing, particularly in terms of discussions regarding intervention and adulteration in playwork. It requires a mindfulness and openness to the unknown and to uncertainty, perhaps even a sense of wonder at what may emerge rather than anxiety at what might happen. 'The ethical subject is an embodied sensibility, which responds to its proximal relationship to the other through a mode of wonderment' (Barad, 2007: 391).

Given all that has been said, it should go without saying that these dispositions are interdependent and interrelated, applying to relations both with the children and with other human and non-human bodies. Cultivating these dispositions may support the conditions for a radical ethics of transformation that pays attention to the forces and values of relations: the capacity to affect and be affected.

Acknowledgements

Thanks go to the playworkers involved in both research projects and to colleagues, particularly Stuart Lester for continually stretching my horizons and introducing me to new ways of seeing. Some sections of the chapter are taken from Russell (2013).

Notes

1 The term 'open access' refers to play projects where the children are in principle free to come and go, in contrast to out-of-school settings where caregivers pay for childcare and the children stay until collected. In practice, the boundaries are not quite so clear-cut, as some open access setting offer formal childcare or children are told by their caregivers to attend the setting until collected.
2 For a detailed discussion of this, see Stuart Lester's chapter in this book.

References

Alexander, S., Frohlich, K. and Fusco, C. (2014) 'Active play may be lots of fun, but it's certainly not frivolous: The emergence of active play as a health practice in Canadian public health', *Sociology of Health and Illness*, 36(8), 1188–1204.
Allen, M. (1968) *Planning for Play*, London: Thames and Hudson.
Banks, S. (2004) *Ethics, Accountability and the Social Professions*, Basingstoke: Palgrave Macmillan.
Barad, K. (2007) *Meeting the Universe Halfway: Quantum Physics and the Entanglement of Matter and Meaning*, London: Duke University Press.
Barad, K. (2010) 'Quantum entanglements and hauntological relations of inheritance: Dis/continuities, spacetime enfoldings, and justice-to-come', *Derrida Today*, 3(2), 240–68.
Battram, A. and Russell, W. (2002) 'The edge of recalcitrance: Playwork, order and chaos', paper presented at Play Wales conference 'Spirit of adventure play is alive and kicking', Cardiff, June.
Bauman, Z. (2003) 'Utopia with no topos', *History of the Human Sciences*, 16(1), 11–25.
Benjamin, J. (1961) *In Search of Adventure: A Study of the Junk Playground*, London: National Council of Social Service.
Benjamin, J. (1974) *Grounds for Play*, London: Bedford Square Press.
Braidotti, R. (2012) 'Nomadic ethics', in Smith, D. W. and Somers-Hall, H. (eds) *The Cambridge Companion to Deleuze*, Cambridge: Cambridge University Press, 170–97.
Brown, F. (2003) 'Compound flexibility: The role of playwork in child development', in Brown, F. (ed.) *Playwork Theory and Practice*, Buckingham: Open University Press, 51–65.

Burghardt, G. M. (2005) *The Genesis of Animal Play: Testing the Limits*, Cambridge, MA: MIT Press.

Caillois, R. (2001 [1961]) *Man, Play and Games*, transl. Barash, M., Urbana, IL and Chicago: University of Illinois Press.

Conway, M. (2005) 'From guerrilla playwork to the centre of government policy on play?' presented at 'PlayEd 2005: What is the future for playwork? The 17th Play and Human Development meeting', Ely, 1–2 March.

Cranwell, K. (2007) 'Adventure playgrounds and the community in London (1948–70)', in Russell, W., Handscomb, B. and Fitzpatrick, J. (eds) *Playwork Voices: In Celebration of Bob Hughes and Gordon Sturrock*, London: London Centre for Playwork Education and Training, 62–73.

Dahlberg, G. and Moss, P. (2008) 'Beyond quality in early childhood education and care – languages of evaluation', *CESifo DICE Report, Journal for Institutional Comparisons*, 6(2), 21–8.

Deleuze, G. (2001 [1968]) *Difference and Repetition*, transl. Patton, P., London: Continuum.

Deuchars, R. (2011) 'Creating lines of flight and activating resistance: Deleuze and Guattari's war machine', *AntePodium*, available at www.victoria.ac.nz/atp/articles/pdf/Deuchars-2011.pdf (accessed 27 August 2014).

Else, P. (2014) *Making Sense of Play: Supporting Children in their Play*, Maidenhead: Open University Press.

Garvey, C. (1977) *Play*, London: Fontana.

Gill, T. (2011) *Children and Nature: A Quasi-systematic Review of the Empirical Evidence*, London: Greater London Authority.

Haraway, D. (1992) 'The promises of monsters: A regenerative politics for inappropriate/d others', in Grossberg, L., Nelson, C. and Treichler, P. (eds) *Cultural Studies*, Abingdon: Routledge, 295–337.

Haraway, D. (1994) 'A game of cat's cradle: Science studies, feminist theory, cultural studies', *Configurations*, 2(1), 59–71.

Haraway, D. (1997) *Modest_Witness@Second_Millennium, FemaleMan©_Meets_OncoMouse™: Feminism and Technoscience*, London: Routledge.

Heron, J. (1996) *Co-operative Inquiry: Research into the Human Condition*, London: Sage.

Horton, J. and Kraftl, P. (2009) 'Small acts, kind words and "not too much fuss": Implicit activisms', *Emotion, Space and Society*, 2: 14–23.

Hughes, B. (1975) *Notes for Adventure Playground Workers*, London: Children and Youth Action Group.

Hughes, B. (2006) *Play Types: Speculations and Possibilities*, London: London Centre for Playwork Education and Training.

Hughes, B. (2012) *Evolutionary Playwork and Reflective Analytic Practice*, 2nd edn, London: Routledge.

Huizinga, J. (1955) *Homo Ludens: A Study of the Play Element in Culture*, Boston: Beacon Press.

Katz, C. (2008) 'Childhood as spectacle: Relays of anxiety and the reconfiguration of the child', *Cultural Geographies*, 15(1), 5–17.

Kozlovsky, R. (2008) 'Adventure playgrounds and postwar reconstruction', in Gutman, M. and de Coninck-Smith, N. (eds) *Designing Modern Childhoods: History, Space, and the Material Culture of Children; An International Reader*, Newark, NJ: Rutgers University Press, 171–90.

Kraftl, P. (2008) 'Young people, hope, and childhood-hope', *Space and Culture*, 11(2), 81–92.

Lefebvre, H. (2009 [1940]) *Dialectical Materialism*, Minneapolis: University of Minnesota Press.

Lenz-Taguchi, H. (2012) 'A diffractive and Deleuzian approach to analysing interview data', *Feminist Theory*, 13(3), 265–81.

Lester, S. (2013) 'Playing in a Deuleuzian playground', in Ryall, E., Russell, W. and MacLean, M. (eds) *Philosophy of Play*, London: Routledge, 130–40.

Lester, S. and Russell, W. (2013) 'Utopian visions of childhood and play in English social policy', in Parker, A. and Vinson, D. (eds) *Youth Sport, Physical Activity and Play: Policy, Intervention and Participation*, London: Routledge, 40–52.

Lester, S. and Russell, W. (2014) 'Turning the world upside down: Playing as the deliberate creation of uncertainty', *Children*, 1: 241–60.

Lester, S., Fitzpatrick, J. and Russell, W. (2014) *Co-creating an Adventure Playground (CAP): Reading Playwork Stories, Practices and Artefacts*, Gloucester: University of Gloucestershire.

Levinas, E. (1969) *Totality and Infinity: An Essay on Exteriority*, transl. Lingis, A., Pittsburgh: Duquesne University Press.

Levinas, E. (1989) 'Ethics as first philosophy', in Hand, S. (ed.) *The Levinas Reader*, Oxford: Blackwell, 75–87.

Lillard, A., Pinkham, A. M. and Smith, E. (2011) 'Pretend play and cognitive development', in Goswami, U. (ed.) *Handbook of Cognitive Development*, 2nd edn, London: Blackwell, 285–311.

Louv, R. (2005) *Last Child in the Woods: Saving our Children from Nature Deficit Disorder*, Chapel Hill, NC: Algonquin.

Louv, R. (2011) 'Want your kids to get into Harvard? Tell 'em to go outside!' *The New Nature Movement*, blogpost, 25 August, available at: http://blog.childrenandnature.org/2011/08/25/want-your-kids-to-get-into-harvard-tell-em-to-go-outside/ (accessed 28 August 2014).

MacIntyre, A. (2007 [1981]) *After Virtue: A Study in Moral Theory*, 3rd edn, Notre Dame, IN: Notre Dame Press.

Massumi, B. (2002) *A Shock to Thought: Expression After Deleuze and Guattari*, London: Routledge.

Massumi, B. (2011) *Semblance and Event: Activist Philosophy and the Occurrent Arts*, Cambridge, MA: MIT Press.

Parr, A. (ed.) (2010) *The Deleuze Dictionary*, 2nd edn, Edinburgh: Edinburgh University Press.

PPSG (Playwork Principles Scrutiny Group) (2005) *The Play Principles*, Cardiff: PPSG.

Rose, N. (1999a) *Governing the Soul: The Shaping of the Private Self*, 2nd edn, London: Routledge.

Rose, N. (1999b) *Powers of Freedom: Reframing Political Thought*, Cambridge: Cambridge University Press.

Rushing, S. (2010) 'Preparing for politics: Judith Butler's ethical dispositions', *Contemporary Political Theory*, 9(3), 284–303.

Russell, W. (2013) *The Dialectics of Playwork: A Conceptual and Ethnographic Study of Playwork using Cultural Historical Activity Theory*, PhD thesis, University of Gloucestershire.

Schmid, C. (2008) 'Henri Lefebvre's theory of the production of space: Towards a three-dimensional dialectic', in Goonewardena, K., Kipfer, S., Milgrom, R. and Schmid, C.

(eds) *Space, Difference and Everyday Life: Reading Henri Lefebvre*, Abingdon: Routledge, 27–45.

Shier, H. (1984) *Adventure Playgrounds: An Introduction*, London: National Playing Fields Association.

Sturrock, G., Russell, W. and Else, P. (2004) *Towards Ludogogy: The Art of Being and Becoming through Play*, Sheffield: Ludemos Associates.

Sutton-Smith, B. (1997) *The Ambiguity of Play*, Cambridge, MA: Harvard University Press.

15 'Excess is truly the key'
Community, flow and the play of control in the picture books of Thomas King

Helene Staveley

- Coyote wants people to play baseball with her, so she sings her special song and dances her special dance. But when Christopher Columbus and his gangster clowns arrive, taking away her animal and human friends to sell across the water, Coyote only sees potential baseball players. Coyote's mischief catalyzes the trauma of First Contact in *A Coyote Columbus Story* (1992).
- Coyote wants to sing to Moon with everyone else, but his singing voice is awful. So Coyote offends Moon, and she hides at the bottom of the lake, darkening the world and endangering the people. When Coyote does sing, Moon rises so high to escape his song that her light is barely enough to see by. Because of Coyote the world's inhabitants lose their intimacy with Moon in *Coyote Sings to the Moon* (1998).
- Coyote adores his golden clothes until Raven praises Bear's rich suit. In a fashion frenzy Coyote collects every suit of clothes in the forest. The animals wear the humans' clothes while their own are missing. By the time all garments return to their owners, Coyote has caused permanent silence between animals and humans in *Coyote's New Suit* (2004).
- A human child disguised as a reindeer disrupts Coyote's solstice plans. Returning her to her natural habitat, Coyote and his friends journey to a wonderland of big-box stores where dreams come true for anyone with cash or credit to spend. In *A Coyote Solstice Tale* (2008) Coyote plots to acquire the peace and goodwill that lurk in Costco's aisles.

These are the scenarios of Thomas King's Coyote picture-book tetralogy for children. They are madcap yarns that fuse contemporary lifestyles with ancient narratives about a creator of the world whose lust for fun continually threatens the world she/he[1] created. These complex narratives are energized by attitudes around play and game, and they address complex child users[2] and complex adult users who know exactly why Coyote wants to play, but also recognize the consequences of her play. In these four picture-books, play and game can promote but also disrupt the communitas and flow that Victor Turner (1982) and Richard Schechner (2002) discuss. King's narratives establish game and play cultures as potentially utopian: should the right conditions exist, play could resolve all discord. Within the game, the community can release its regular critical self-scrutiny and enjoy the flow of play. But godgames, discussed in more detail below, are also pervasive in King's tetralogy, where they transform play into ambivalent systems of bafflement and frustration: the godgame is a utopia for the god who designs it, but a misery for her player-subjects. King's godgame narratives for children engage in narrative play to explore the limits of responsibility while mirroring the excesses of consumer frenzy.

The playing field: King, Coyote and narratives for children

King's picture-book tetralogy achieves playfulness partly by depicting games and play events within the narrative. Designing the narrative around play-experiences and extending playfulness from the narrative world toward the user's world is a way to model transformative play. Coyote is both trickster and creator in many native North American cultures,[3] and to some extent she/he 'is' play and game even while she also complicates them. As a character King's Coyote brings together such troubling elements as dedication to pleasure coupled with self-absorption, or a strong investment in playful existence linked with refusal of responsibility. Embodying the extremes of the play drive, Coyote unsettles established binaries by fusing them, as Arnold E. Davidson, Priscilla Waldron and Jennifer Andrews observe: 'Coyote, in fact, works against the black and white moral structure of imperialist ideology. She is both good and bad, creator and disrupter' (Davidson, Walton and Andrews, 2003: 80). Coyote's desire to play occasions the narratives of each of King's four picture-books for children; her play-drive is integral to plot and character, and the paired visual and linguistic media of the narratives are also playful, engaging users intellectually.

Children's ability to use their own voices is severely embattled, making it all the more important to heed John Wall's call 'to understand children's agency and to welcome children's voices and participation' in human culture and cultural production (Wall, 2013: 34). While the picture-book format indicates that King is addressing his Coyote narratives to a base of child users,[4] the 'childness' of these users derives from King's own personal construction of what constitutes childhood, as is true for any adult producer of children's books, films, games, toys and so on. Judging from the playful way these four texts presume a child user who is fluent in play and in the narrative cultures of native North Americans, King may understand children as agents-in-process who need to learn and want to participate, but also as Coyote-like in their 'unruliness, passion and disorder' (Wall, 2013: 34). Literary theorist Mark Shackleton observes that

> Traditional Native American trickster tales often have a didactic function. Although the trickster himself usually gains little from experience, the listening audience is intended to learn not to do as the trickster did. Likewise, King's Coyote has learned nothing from negative experience, and at the end of the story she is still planning to fix up the world. The storyteller

anxiously looks at the sky waiting for more falling objects, because with Coyote fixing things, 'nobody in this world is safe'.

(Shackleton, 2013: 189; King, 1993b is quoted)

Somewhat like Coyote, the child-surrogate protagonist and player-god of King's tetralogy, the implied child user of King's text is a potential force for chaos who can experience the consequences of unleashing it by engaging with Coyote's narrative.

King's lusory attitude

As a writer, King, who self-identifies as Cherokee and Canadian, stands among numerous tensions. Born in the US of a Cherokee father and German-Greek mother, King is a Professor Emeritus of Canada's University of Guelph, where he taught literature and creative writing. He is widely known for his creative work, which includes novels, short stories, essays and his tetralogy for children as well as a comic radio series, films and television episodes. His writing is consistently funny and satirical, taking aim at cherished illusions about the dominance of the European settler-invader cultures. In 2014 King won Canada's coveted Governor-General's Award in the Adult Fiction category. He delivered the prestigious Massey Lectures in 2003, the first (and so far only) time a First Nations person has been invited to do so. These five humourous and provocative lectures, *The Truth About Stories* (2003), interrogate the stereotype of North American aboriginal peoples as a failing race doomed to extinction. Far from losing Darwin's survival of the fittest contest, King asserts, the Americas' natives are thriving in ways that confound racist stereotypes. While he recognizes that First Nations people have experienced terrible injustices, King's writing privileges their resourcefulness, resilience, craftiness and skill.

While these are survivor traits, they are also hallmarks of player agency, so they are central to King's project to alter the position of First Nations culture on the Western stage. This agenda informs or even constitutes what Bernard Suits (1978) might call King's 'lusory attitude' – his willingness to engage in more complicated rather than less complicated means and rules because the additional complication transforms the activity into a game. King's narratives subversively presume their readers are intimately familiar with aboriginal narrative strategies – that is, his implied readers are the native inhabitants of the Americas (see Fee and Flick, 1999) rather than the settler-invaders of the Americas. King's subversive strategy deflates false Eurocentric perceptions about the culture of aboriginal American people while accentuating the critical richness and sophistication of First Nations cultural practices. It also reveals fundamental spiritual differences between two cultures. Where Judaeo-Christian religions are characterized by human guilt about falls into experience, there are no similar guilty falls in First Nations spirituality, and no expulsion from the Garden has taken place (King, 2012). The qualitative differences between these world-views seem particularly relevant in King's tetralogy for children, which plays with ideas about responsibility. A player-god who is unhaunted by shameful banishment from the Garden and who is unbound by a saviour's self-sacrifice does not share mainstream Judeo-Christian conceptions of responsibility, and her understandings of play, agency and consequences will not be mainstream either.

King's books for children work as what Mihai Spariosu (1997) terms the literature of irenic play. Irenic literature can, Spariosu claims, 'become a playground suitable for the creation and imaginative enactment of human values that are often incommensurable with those embraced by the community out of which the literary work arises'. Irenic play offers this potential 'precisely because it is a form of play, that is, an *as if* mode of activity and being, in which the world of actuality and that of the imaginary become interwoven and create an intermediary world separate from, yet contingent upon, the other two' (Spariosu 1997: 29). Kimberley Reynolds uses similar terms when she argues that 'children's books have the potential to influence the future' (2007: 15), as

> [t]he stories we give children are blueprints for living in culture as it exists, but they are also where *alternative* ways of living are often piloted in recognition of the fact that children will not just inherit the future, but need to participate in shaping it.
>
> (Ibid. 14; Reynolds' italics)

Using the Coyote narratives that King provides in these four books means experiencing a category of perception that resists normative Eurocentricity and the spiritual freight of guilt and shame; in this version of human experience, play is powerfully creative, building community, but also destructive, shattering both beneficial and detrimental norms. King's child-surrogate protagonist Coyote models the desire to participate and the unruliness of King's imagined child-user, but she also confronts that child-user with the consequences of resisting an education in responsibility.

King, Coyote and godgames

Coyote is willing to disrupt the structural integrity of the communities she has built, and this positions her as a casual version of the *magister ludi* or 'game master': the 'god' who plays godgames. R. Rawdon Wilson (1990) uses the term *magister ludi* to mean a more or less omnipotent game maker who, like a puppeteer, plays with people for his own amusement without respect for their well-being or autonomy. Examples include Oberon and Prospero from Shakespeare's plays and the Duke in *Don Quixote*, each of whom delights in constructing a system of illusions around his players and watching them blunder through the trap. Wilson describes godgames as 'cognitive labyrinths:' 'the successive decisions of the entrapped character may seem to follow a labyrinthine pattern of illusion, choice, and impasse' (Wilson, 1990: 150, 151). For Wilson,

> The world of the gamewright, the god, ... entraps, and thus confronts or plays against, the character-players' worlds. In attempting to play free, the character-players seek their own statement, rationalization, and freedom. If a fictional world is axiologically defined as a set of values, or psychologically as the interiority of the subject, then a godgame constitutes, among other things, a clash of hostile worldhoods.
>
> (Wilson, 1990: 165)

Both godgames and tricksters are emblematic of 'deep play' in which the stakes of play are dangerously high, and of 'dark play' which can critically endanger the lives and well-beings of players (Schechner, 2002: 118–19). Even in light versions it is imperative for player-character to play their way out of the game: Oberon's arbitrary wish to help the human lovers still brings all four to the brink of death before he lifts their enchantment. The irenic potential of godgames speaks less of harmonious healing for the player-community than of a manifest Nietszchean will to power. Thus Coyote herself, who in King's work tends to generate godgames almost spontaneously, complicates King's serious lusory goal of using narrative to cause critical cultural change.

King's Coyote is consistently lazy, so the absurd labyrinths she instigates seem more haphazard than those discussed by Wilson, which are wrought by calculating *magisters ludi*. As Shackleton points out, King's trickster is '*both* culture hero/creator figure *and* buffoon' (ibid., 188; Shackleton's emphasis). King's Coyote is attracted to excess, accumulation, and pleasure; as trickster she embodies paradox, deceit, and flux; her presence brings radical instability to both ends of this spectrum; and she is never in control of her volatile godgames. She/he causes two of the four godgames in King's tetralogy, and 'is played by' the other two, which are designed by Raven – another trickster – and by Moon. Coyote's participation escalates the mischief of Raven's and Moon's godgames. King is equally interested in how the trickster can be tricked as in the effects of excessive trickster play.

Communitas, flow and Coyote

King's Coyote rarely sets out to play maliciously. Still, her godgames effect a clash of worldhoods. They address a heterogeneous collective of players who respect the network of relationships that sustains them, and who willingly cooperate with other players as well as with arbitrary rules and structures so that the game can exist; but the godgames she plays threaten these fragile networks. King scholars agree that his texts function as 'comic warning[s] against the dangers of excessive consumerism' (Shackleton, 2013: 190), and excessive consumerism appears in King's work as an exotic and perverse flow of value that attracts Coyote. Coyote's games disrupt the immanent community of play, rupturing communitas and transforming flow.

Performance theorist Richard Schechner understands communitas and flow as important elements of play. Communitas, for him, is 'A feeling of solidarity, usually short-lived, generated during ritual' (Schechner, 2002: 62). Such rituals can include religious services as well as concerts, sports events and so on. Victor Turner defines communitas as

> the liberation of human capacities of cognition, affect, volition, creativity, etc., from the normative constraints incumbent upon occupying a sequence of social statuses, enacting a multiplicity of social roles, and being acutely conscious of membership in some corporate group such as a family, lineage, clan, tribe, nation, etc., or of affiliation with some pervasive social category such as a class, caste, sex, or age-division.
>
> (Turner, 1982: 44)

Spariosu elaborates that

> because a liminal event reveals 'a model of human society as a homogenous, unstructured communitas, whose boundaries are ideally coterminous with the human species' ... [therefore] communitas no less than liminality is often regarded as dangerous by the powers-that-be who preside over established structure.
>
> (Spariosu, 1997: 69; Turner is quoted)

A solidarity that confounds norms, communitas is volatile and potentially transformative.

Communitas is prevalent in King's narratives, which explore the social significance of relationships and responsibility. In *Columbus*, for example, the human beings enjoy playing baseball with Coyote, their creator, culture hero and buffoon, because, as a playful activity, baseball suppresses arbitrary divisions such as the division between human beings and Coyote, forming a game community. But Coyote 'acts as if she has no relations' when she makes it unpleasant for others to play by changing the game to favour herself. The phrase 'all my relations' relates directly to community, as King explains:

> 'All my relations' is at first a reminder of who we are and of our relationship with both our family and our relatives. It also reminds us of the extended relationship we share with all human beings. But the relationships that Native people see go further, the web of kinship extending to the animals, to the birds, to the fish, to the plants, to all the animate and inanimate forms that can be seen or imagined. More than that, 'all my relations' is an encouragement for us to accept the responsibilities we have within this universal family by living our lives in a harmonious and moral manner (a common admonishment is to say of someone that they act as if they have no relations).
>
> (King quoted in Wolf, 2012:100)

King describes an extant, reliable network of relationships. Coyote herself is embedded in it right along with the people, animals, birds and fish, as are other gods and powers. In the tetralogy, experiencing delight in the extraordinariness of the network is one way to experience communitas. While a variant of the phrase 'all my relations' appears only in the first book, *A Coyote Columbus Story*, all four books emphasize community by using collective nouns that emphasize group identity: 'friends', 'humans', 'animals'. Even proper names such as Beaver, Moose, Otter and Bear connote group as much as individual identity. The books are concerned with how relationships withstand chaos and disruption, and all four of these narratives are cautionary in presuming that Coyote's network of 'relations' is disrupted by her behaviour.

Playing with Coyote nevertheless builds communitas between her and her human being friends because she plays with them as equals. But the clowns in *Columbus* barely notice she exists, let alone seeing her as an equal or superior, so they disregard Coyote's pleasant communitas of play. Throughout *Columbus* 'human beings' is a term that refers exclusively to Coyote's human friends, that is, North American natives. (Coyote has animal friends too.) Columbus and the other clowns are not Coyote's friends and they visit from a distant place, so they are not human beings. When Coyote observes of Columbus and his gang that 'They act as if they've got no relations' (1992, n.p.) she uses a phrase against their poor behaviour that in the past has also been used against hers. Her comment, which dwells on the clowns' blindness to the play-value of her idyllic game-based communitas, indicates that her world-view and lusory attitude are incommensurate with theirs.

Literary theorist Doris Wolf notes that Kent Monkman's illustrations in *Columbus* establish the appeal of Coyote's attractive community (Wolf, 2012: 103). Monkman's inspired images also depict the trouble with Columbus and his crew. Monkman's illustrations more than King's text identify the invaders as gangster clowns, hyperbolizing King's depiction of their shared stressful 'community activities': displaying weapons prominently, searching, being angry, collecting 'valuables' and exhibiting bad manners. When Cartier *et al.* arrive later dressed as priestly clowns, their garb confirms that, somewhere distant from Coyote's home, a perverse community exists that is founded on dark play. Clown attire is the uniform of Europe's dark communitas, the hostile obverse of Coyote's resilient communitas of play.

For Schechner, flow is best described by Mihaly Csikszentmihalyi as 'what people felt when their consciousness of the outside world disappeared and they merged with what they were doing'. 'Players in flow may be aware of their actions, but not of the awareness itself', writes Schechner; '[a]t the same time, flow can be an extreme self-awareness where the player has total control over the play act. These two aspects of flow, apparently contrasting, are essentially the same. In each case, the boundary between the interior psychological self and the performed activity dissolves' (2002: 88). Gadamer notes, 'the attraction of a game, the fascination it exerts, consists precisely in the fact that the game masters the players', and also 'play does not have its being in the player's consciousness or attitude, but on the contrary play draws him into its dominion and fills him with its spirit. The player experiences the game as a reality that surpasses him' (quoted in Feezell, 2013: 26). Just as the clowns are obsessed with and subsumed in the search for plentiful commodities, so Coyote and her human being friends – a category that emphatically excludes all clown-beings – value being subsumed in positive or neutral game-flow.

The flow of game motivates King's Coyote to play. In *Coyote Sings to the Moon*, singing becomes the metaphor for flow. Old Woman sings to Moon every night in the simplest terms: '"Moon, Moon, full Moon" ..., "Moon, Moon, half Moon" ..., "Moon, Moon, crescent Moon"' (King, 1998, n.p.). The regularity of the song, the link it establishes between Moon and the inhabitants of the world below, the repetitive simplicity of the song and its loving attention to Moon's shifting quality: all are suggestive of flow. In the story, the animals convey the compelling nature of the ritual song. They are drawn to listen to Old Woman's 'beautiful voice' and enrich it with the 'livelier beat', 'cool percussion' and 'doo-wop' lyrics that beavers, turtles, frogs and ducks provide: the creatures, Moon and Old Woman become the song. Coyote is already hurt when he arrives late, on the third page-spread, because nobody has told him of this gentle nightly community celebration. His outraged vanity registers as a defence against being excluded from this pleasant ritual and its production of communitas as flow.

King's lusory flair

King's narrative style itself is aimed at generating experiences of communitas and flow. His narrator's voice is conversational, casual and teasing, promoting a sense of intimacy between the implied teller of the tale-in-print and its ideal real-world child user. *A Coyote Columbus Story* uses an intimate address to communicate the patently outrageous:

> It was Coyote who fixed up this world, you know. She is the one who did it. She made rainbows and flowers and clouds and rivers. And she made prune juice and afternoon naps and toe-nail polish and commercials. Some of these things were pretty good, and some of these things were foolish. But what she loved to do best was to play ball.
>
> (1992: n.p.)

Some of Coyote's creations belong to an ancient, pre-human world and some are distinctly twentieth-century; because she loves baseball, a game invented by Americans in the mid-nineteenth century, she invents beavers, turtles, and humans to play baseball with her; and for the same reason she also randomly invents or summons Christopher Columbus, who 'discovered' the Americas in 1492.

The narrative voice of *A Coyote Solstice Tale* (2009) intensifies the sense of flow by telling the story in verse, adding rhythm and rhyme to the mix. Here King appropriates Christmas song conventions to satirize consumerist Christmases. Specifically at issue is 'Rudolph the Red-nosed Reindeer', the song that explains the disguise worn by the unnamed human girl who invades Coyote's space. Wearing sticks on her head and a red ball on her nose, she announces that she is escaping her unpleasant home and seeking friendship and harmony. Cross-dressed as an animal and pop-culture hero while she addresses Coyote, an animal/god and culture hero, across his threshold, the little girl disrupts and transforms the trickster's plans and transgresses the angry, eons-long silence between humans and animals (discussed below).

The experiences of communitas and flow that Coyote was to share with his animal friends during this winter solstice celebration does, in the end, proceed as planned. Near the end, Coyote's posse eats together, relaxes together, and sings and prays together at dawn; then each returns to his home. The simple value of this celebration is heightened by the group's excursion to return the little girl to her natural habitat. Coyote's friends share a unifying experience by walking together through the forest to take the girl home, an extraordinary mission of interspecies fellowship and restitution. Reaching the mall that lurks near their wilderness, Coyote's friends are 'huddled together/As rough herds of humans rushed by/Their arms filled with brightly wrapped boxes/And murderous looks in their eyes' (King, 2008: n.p.). Coyote, however, is enthralled by the mall's perverse spectacle of consumer flow and moves to participate in it; he plunders its treasures to give to his friends but learns he cannot give without paying first, and he has neither money nor credit. His friends wait patiently on the sidelines, commenting silently on Coyote's desire to join and master every flow that he sees, no matter how problematic. The girl leaves gracefully, requesting and receiving permission to visit Coyote again, and the group returns to Coyote's house to enjoy the celebration they had planned.

King's rhyming poetry in *Solstice* has a Seussian beat and casual diction. Its resemblance to a Christmas song generates comfortable and uncomfortable frictions between the solstice and Christmas. While Coyote's godgame in this narrative is benign and simple, restricted as it is to providing a space and food for the group's enjoyment while they spend time together through the night, at the end of it he is dangerously reflective:

And Coyote ...
Well, he sat on the porch in his rocker
And he rocked as he tried to recall
If goodwill and peace could be purchased
For credit or cash at the mall.

Probably, thought Coyote, as he smiled and closed his eyes.
That place had everything.

(King, 2008: n.p.)

Chaos is clearly in store in the near future when Coyote goes to confirm his intuition. Wolf reads King's story-worlds as able to sustain disharmony as well as harmony, even when disfigured by Coyote's mischief and disrupted by the incursions of clowns. Positive flow is always attended by negative flow, but the playful flow that reaches out of this text towards its users has ambivalent potential. The world within the text is fixed and unchanging, the world outside it is open-ended and free.

Out-of-control controllers and volatile value

Narrative godgames are by nature elaborate, intense and explosive. They are portals to chaos and excess, and the gods that design these open-ended games are not in full control. In *Coyote's New Suit*, Coyote is played by a godgame that brings widespread, ongoing damage. Coyote adores his outfit of golden fur, but Raven, bored, points out the attractiveness of other animals' clothes, inciting Coyote to engage in a masquerade. He takes Bear's suit of clothes, set aside while swimming, and wears it to the grocery store, to the ball game, to the bingo; then he forgets it in his closet, and repeats with other suits as often as Raven suggests. Raven tells the nude animals that human beings leave clothes on clotheslines for anyone to use, so the distraught creatures help themselves, and the humans are left with no clothes. Raven suggests a yard sale of the surplus animal clothes in Coyote's closet, which the humans buy; but the foment of forced cross-dressing – animals in human clothes, humans in animal clothes – erupts in conflict. Furious, animals and humans stop speaking to each other, and Raven is delighted. Her dark play instigates multiple thefts; it prevents all thieves from recognizing their part in the crime wave; but it also conceals her own role behind a mask of helpfulness. Worse still, the end repeats the beginning. Coyote has not escaped the labyrinth of Raven's game to see it for what it is, so he succumbs when she tempts him to steal Bear's suit again.

Raven's dark godgame targets Coyote and is the most pernicious of the four because the fictions that sustain it remain intact as the narrative closes. The damage she causes is permanent and threatens to self-perpetuate; the played players remain caught up in the arbitrary hostility rather than critically changing the damaged culture. In *Coyote Sings to the Moon*, Moon's godgame is simpler but also devastating. Outraged by Coyote's disrespect, Moon abdicates her normal role and leaves the world in darkness. Distressed by the disappearance of the being they venerate, the animals and Old Woman seek Moon to no avail. In the dark that he has caused, Coyote trips and slips repeatedly, but all his relations are also punished unjustly by being deprived of their beloved Moon. Johnny Wales' illustrations emphasize Moon's self-indulgence: her retreat beneath the lake is a spa, complete with beach towels, beach umbrellas and personalized pillows, and Moon wears sunglasses and plays chess as a means of ignoring the community that implores her to return. Eventually Coyote's song chases Moon back into the sky, but now her light is distant and her relationship with earth wanes. Worse, her godgame is defeated while his win-condition is met, for Coyote is tasked with singing to Moon every night to keep her out of the lake.

Contrasting with Raven's and Moon's godgames, both strong in structure because they invade and shape reality, both of Coyote's godgames are oddly permeable, being invaded by incompatible games. In *Columbus*, Coyote alters reality to suit her game, magicking set after set of playmates to her side to play baseball. The most disastrous set of playmates is Columbus' crew of clowns. They refuse to play Coyote's game, preferring their pointless capitalist practice of accumulating resources whose use- and exchange-value Coyote does not recognize. Frustrated, Columbus plans to sell Coyote's former playmates, her human being friends, across the water. King writes, 'When Coyote hears this bad idea, she starts to laugh. Who would buy human beings, she says, and she laughs some more. She laughs so hard she has to hold her nose on her face with both hands' (King, 1992: n.p.). The reason for her hilarity is unclear. She considers human beings unmarketable, but is it because each is priceless, or because each is valueless? Monkman's illustrations depict the human beings furiously glaring at Coyote. Is it because she has mortally offended them, or because she is laughing too hard to help them? King's language and Monkman's illustrations both refuse to resolve the ambiguities. Coyote is once again left without playmates until, trying to fix the problem she caused, she summons Cartier and his crew. Their clownish garb signals that they too are obsessed with nefarious capitalist games, but forgetting what has just happened, Coyote again invites the new clowns to play ball with her. Her baseball game leads to the escalating vortex of discord and misery that is First Contact.

The solstice game in *Solstice*, on the other hand, is part ritual; it is an opportunity for Coyote and his friends to celebrate a significant event together by engaging in simple communal activities, or possibly sacred games, such as preparing and eating food, talking, singing, and praying together. Such activities are not rare, but they are intrinsically pleasurable and easy to repeat, attaining gamefulness because they celebrate the extraordinary circumstance of the solstice. Moreover, these activities are not competitive, so they produce neither winners nor losers and circumvent Coyote's desire to be the best and only winner all the time. There is little to control here beyond keeping all members of the group happy and moving through the sequence of gameful acts. But a little girl in a reindeer outfit disrupts these small important solstice games. Coyote's comical shock at the girl's transgressions becomes zestful enthusiasm when he in turn invades 'her' space, the shopping mall that, in the logic of the book, is the home that the girl temporarily escaped. The mall is a nightmare vision of perverse communitas and empty flow. A herd of mindless people 'bumping and pushing/Attempting to find a cashier' (n.p.) during their distinctive 'game' of Christmas shopping stands in for Coyote's quiet friends and their quiet solstice games. But Coyote is entranced by the exotic spectacle and must join it. And so while the girl's transgression may begin to end the silence between animals and humans, it also opens the door to what could be Coyote's most dangerous game: playing peace and goodwill as marketable commodities. As the mall cashier confides and he already knows, 'Excess is truly the key' (King, 2008: n.p.). With Coyote at play, a proliferation of goodwill and peace will lead to terrible perversions.

In *Solstice* the desire to play is still in full force at the end and escalation seems imminent, just as in *Columbus, Moon*, and *New Suit*. In the earlier books

Coyote's refusal to understand his responsibility for harming all of her relations threatens future disasters, and now his eagerness to enter the game of capitalism seems no different. Here the harm he has achieved seems minimal, tempered by his emerging friendship with the little girl, a rapprochement between hostile camps. But Coyote is still attracted to excess, accumulation and pleasure, the foundations of the capitalism that mystifies and fascinates him. Coyote's games expose his lusory community to consumer capitalism and therefore fail to realize their potential as transformers of culture. An amiable, playful intimacy between narrator and user unites them in a conspiracy to assess the flaws of Coyote's games and invites the child-user to engage in the lusory critical thinking that can lead to cultural change.

Conclusion

King's books in their language and images construct play and game to be compelling transformational practices with utopian potential. The temporal hodgepodge, the atmosphere established in the vivid illustrations, the persistent references to games and play activities throughout the tetralogy, the teasing diction: all construct an essentially playful world and existence in which innocence and experience can co-exist free from mainstream concerns about guilt and shame, just as Coyote refuses responsibility along with guilt and shame. As the protagonist of children's books, Coyote volatilizes cultural ethics. On the one hand her presence gestures toward an idyllic play-world that does not recognize such arbitrary binaries as those associated with culture or gender differentiation. On the other it gestures toward a distinct cosmology never marked by a fall from blessed innocence to guilty experience (see King, 2003, 2012). This looks something like what children's narratives always seem to desire: a perpetual state of innocence-as-playfulness without the taint of guilt, shame, stigma, experience. Although she has seen her games and important parts of her world irremediably diminished, often by her own actions, Coyote picks herself back up and continues to live through game. It is no wonder that the worlds King narrates for children are so compelling. They figure a god at play, forever making and breaking, forever playing and being played, the field wide open before her to mark as she will, with no prospect of ever being held to account for her love of play.

Notes

1. King's Coyote is sometimes female, as in *A Coyote Columbus Story*, but sometimes male. Shackleton (2012) and Davidson *et al.* (2003), discussed below, illuminate issues of gender and King's Coyote. I choose to presume a female Coyote for most of this chapter, using masculine pronouns for Coyote only where King's texts demand them.
2. While it is conventional to discuss 'readers' and texts, or players and games, I prefer the term 'user'. Children, especially those who do not read independently, often use books and narratives in unexpected ways, which may not involve 'reading'.

3 There are multiple trickster deities in Native American cultures, including Raven and Nanabush.
4 King published 'A Coyote Columbus' in a collection of stories for adults after publishing it as an illustrated book for children, so it is not clear whether it was written specifically for child users. To the best of my knowledge the other three books in the tetralogy were all written for children.

References

Davidson, A. L., Walton, P. and Andrews, J. (2003) *Border Crossings: Thomas King's Cultural Inversions*, Toronto, Buffalo and London: University of Toronto Press.

Fee, M. and Flick, J. (1999) 'Coyote pedagogy: Knowing where the borders are in Thomas King's *Green Grass, Running Water*', *Canadian Literature*, Summer–Autumn, 161–2.

Feezell, R. (2013) 'A pluralist conception of play', in Ryall, E., Russell, W. and MacLean, M. (eds) *The Philosophy of Play*, London and New York: Routledge.

King, T. (1992) *A Coyote Columbus Story*, illustrated by Monkman, K., Toronto, Vancouver and Berkeley: Groundwood.

King, T. (1993a) *Green Grass, Running Water*, Toronto: HarperPerennial.

King, T. (1993b) *One Good Story, That One*, Toronto: HarperPerennial.

King, T. (1998) *Coyote Sings to the Moon*, Toronto: Key Porter Kids.

King, T. (2003) *The Truth About Stories: A Native Narrative*, Toronto: House of Anansi Press.

King, T. (2004) *Coyote's New Suit*, Toronto: Key Porter Kids.

King, T. (2008) *A Coyote Solstice Tale*, Toronto, Vancouver and Berkeley: Groundwood.

King, T. (2012) *The Inconvenient Indian: A Curious Account of Native People in North America*, Toronto: Doubleday Canada.

Reynolds, K. (2007) *Radical Children's Literature: Future Visions and Aesthetic Transformations in Juvenile Literature*, New York: Palgrave Macmillan.

Schechner, R. (2002) *Performance Studies: An Introduction*, London and New York: Routledge.

Shackleton, M. (2012) ' "Have I Got Stories" and "Coyote Was There": Thomas King's use of trickster figures and the transformation of traditional materials', in Gruber, E. (ed.) *Thomas King: Works and Impact*, Rochester, NY: Camden House.

Spariosu, M. (1997) *The Wreath of Wild Olive: Play, Liminality, and the Study of Literature*, Albany: State University of New York Press.

Suits, B. (1978) *The Grasshopper: Games, Life and Utopia*, Toronto and Buffalo: University of Toronto Press.

Turner, V. (1982) *From Ritual to Theatre: The Human Seriousness of Play*, New York: PAJ Publications.

Wall, J. (2013) ' "All the world's a stage": Childhood and the play of being', in Ryall, E., Russell, W. and MacLean, M. (eds) *The Philosophy of Play*, London and New York: Routledge.

Wilson, R. R. (1990) *In Palamedes' Shadow: Explorations in Play, Game, and Narrative Theory*, Boston: Northeastern University Press.

Wolf, D. (2012) ' "All My Relations": Thomas King's Coyote tetralogy for kids', in Gruber, E. (ed.) *Thomas King: Works and Impact*, Rochester, NY: Camden House.

Index

absorption 13, 14, 86, 91, 128, 128, 141, 146, 149, 173, 206
abstract art 155, 156
accommodation 182, 184, 188, 189
Achilles 111, 112, 117
adulteration 197, 199, 200
adventure playgrounds 66, 192, 193, 201, 202, 203, 204
aesthetics 3, 6, 8, 31, 58, 65, 72, 74–84, 87, 88, 89, 90, 92, 101, 168, 169, 191; agency aesthetic 75, 81; conflict aesthetic 75, 77, 78, 81; curiosity aesthetic 77, 80, 81; decision aesthetic 75, 80, 81; imaginative aesthetic 76, 77, 81, 82; learning aesthetic 76, 77, 80; problem aesthetic 76, 77, 80, 81; reward aesthetic 78, 80, 81; social aesthetic 76, 81; systems aesthetic 76, 80; uncertainty aesthetic 76, 79, 81, 82; victory aesthetic 75, 77, 78, 80, 81; voluntary aesthetic 78, 81
affect/affectivity 61, 63, 81, 83, 125, 155, 192, 210
agency 55, 61, 62, 63, 64, 75, 81, 197, 198, 206, 207, 208
agential realism 61, 64, 194
agon see play, *agon*
alea see play, *alea*
alienation 2, 59
Allen, M. 192, 193, 201
alterity 2, 8, 9
amor fati 99
Ancient Greece 20, 40, 110
anxiety 84, 86, 189, 196, 200, 202
Arendt, H. 42, 44, 45, 50, 51, 52
arete 117, 118
Aristotle 19, 26
art 14, 71, 72, 73, 74, 75, 83, 84–94, 98, 99, 101, 144, 152, 153, 154, 155, 156, 158, 159, 160, 161, 162, 163n1, 166–76, 189n7; as metaphor 73
artist 155, 166–76
Assassin's Creed® 152–5, 159, 161, 163n1
assemblage 61, 63
assimilation 182, 184
authentic 101, 162, 163n1, 166, 175, 194
authenticity 162, 175
autotelic 4, 8, 101, 157

Bakhtin, M. 3
Barad, K. 60, 61, 62, 63, 64, 64n1, 65, 191, 192, 193, 194, 195, 197, 198, 199, 200, 201
Bateman, C. 156, 157, 163n3, 163n6
Bateson, G. 2, 9, 39, 40, 124, 134, 180, 189
Baudrillard, J. 35, 40
becoming 55, 98, 99, 143, 191, 192, 193, 195, 198, 199, 200
behaviour 42, 43, 44, 48, 49, 58, 62, 90–1, 92, 127, 128–9, 136, 142, 145, 149, 182, 185
being 14, 95–100, 126, 143, 147, 152, 154, 158, 181, 191, 192–6, 208
being and nothingness 103
Bencivenga, E. 1, 8, 9
Bey, H. 2, 3, 9
binaries 195, 206, 216
Bodyspacemotionthings 84–94
Borden, I. 142, 143, 150
Boykin, J. 130–1
Braidotti, R. 54, 60, 61, 63, 64, 65, 192, 195, 199, 200, 201
Brentano, F. 96, 97
built environment 136–51
Butler, J. 192, 200

Index

Caillois, R. 7, 31, 37, 40, 42, 45–7, 50, 52n3, 52n4, 78–9, 80, 81, 123, 125, 126–9, 131, 132, 133, 134n4, 197, 202
carnival 17, 29, 133
carnivalesque 2, 89, 142
Cartesian 55, 56, 61, 139, 196
catastrophe 32, 84, 89–90, 91
chaos 171, 207, 211, 213, 214
cheating 50, 111, 112, 113, 116
chess 31, 45, 49, 51, 52n2, 131, 214
child/children/childhood 3, 5, 6, 7, 8, 14, 27, 31, 32, 33, 36, 37, 38, 39, 53–61, 63, 64, 80, 81, 86, 88, 97–9, 114, 117, 124, 126–7, 128, 132, 133, 167–8, 169, 172, 173–4, 179–81, 184–8, 189n3, 189n9, 191–201, 201n1, 205–8, 212, 216, 217n4
children's play *see* play
Christianity 29
citizenship 192
commercial space 144, 149
communitas 7, 8, 148, 205, 209–12, 213, 215
community 8, 16–18, 20, 21, 96, 101–2, 146–7, 149, 150, 181, 185–6, 192–3, 206, 208, 209, 210–12, 216
Community of Inquiry (CoI) 79, 182, 184, 186, 187, 188
competition 14, 29, 37, 38, 51, 74, 78, 80, 110, 112–18, 126, 127, 132, 175n2, 181, 187
conatus 198
conceived space *see* space
consciousness 14, 24, 96, 136, 139, 145, 149, 162, 172, 211
constitutive rules *see* rules
consumerism 209
control 5, 55, 62, 79, 112, 115, 127, 128, 130–3, 145, 193, 209, 211, 214, 215
conversation 180, 182, 212
cosmology 95, 97, 98, 103, 216
Costikyan, G. 75–7, 78, 79, 81, 82
counterexile 22
Coyote 8, 205–17
Crawford, C. 7–6, 78, 79, 80, 82
creativity 17, 22, 58, 98, 102, 133, 175, 180, 181, 187, 189n2, 193, 210
Csikszentmihalyi, M. 85, 93, 146, 147, 150, 182, 183, 186, 188, 189, 211

dance/dancing 29, 33–4, 38, 108–9, 114, 126, 138, 172, 205
dark games 27–39
dark play *see* play
de Certeau, M. 136
death 16, 19, 33, 100, 101, 109, 115–16, 117
deep play *see* play
Deleuze, G. 53, 54, 59, 60, 61, 63, 193
delight 101–2, 208, 211
Derrida, J. 104n11
desire 59, 63, 101, 123–4, 131, 189, 195, 197, 198, 199
desire lines 143
destruction 51, 126–7, 159–62, 199
deterritorialization 191
dialectic, dialectics 18, 20, 103, 114, 143, 145, 150, 160, 181, 193
dialogue 1, 136, 141, 170, 181, 187
dialogue-play *see* play
difference 193–5, 199, 200
diffraction 194
disavowal 72, 79
discipline 31, 54, 127, 128, 131
Discipline & Punish (Foucault) 85, 144
discourse 24, 35–6, 58, 60, 61, 131, 133, 194
disorder 2, 85, 126, 181, 188, 206; Games of 17, 92; Nature Deficit Disorder 196
disposition 5, 8, 43, 200–1
disturbance 126–7, 198
dualism 37, 54
Dunphy, E. (*Only a Game*) 130

earth 19–20, 24, 26, 56, 100, 154, 157–8, 159–62, 163n11, 214
education 15, 55, 58, 179–89
embodiment 136–49, 183
emergence 56, 191, 199
emotion 21, 23, 24, 79, 80, 81, 82, 101, 172, 173–4, 189n2
enframing 3, 5
enjoyment 34, 36, 78, 81, 101, 182, 183, 186, 188
Enlightenment 25, 55
entanglements 61, 62, 193, 195, 198, 199
epistemology 1, 5, 15, 60, 72, 192, 193–4, 196, 197
Eros 100
essence 54, 61, 73, 102, 159, 174, 175
ethical responsibilities 191, 197–200
ethics 54, 63, 64, 116, 171, 179ff
event 35, 62, 138, 147
evil 5, 6, 16, 37, 39, 42–52
evil play *see* play
excess 7, 8, 86, 112, 115–16, 126, 129, 205–9, 214, 215, 216

220   Index

exile 5, 13, 18, 20–6
existence 55, 95, 97, 99–100, 102–3, 124, 140, 143, 173–4, 206

fair play 15, 49, 110
fiction 2, 7, 14, 24, 25, 71, 72, 73, 74, 76, 102, 156–7, 163n3, 207, 209
Fink, E. 6, 95–104
First Nations 207–16
fleetingness 2
Flow (Csikszentmihalyi) 17, 137, 147, 149, 150, 183, 205, 209, 211–14, 215
flow/flows 7, 56, 61, 63, 136, 142, 149, 172, 174, 183, 198, 200, 206, 209, 212, 213
football 38, 46, 49, 115, 116, 118, 124, 129, 130
for-itself 2, 4, 8
Foucault, M. 84, 85–6, 91, 92, 144, 175
frame 2–5, 33, 116, 123, 133–4, 154, 171, 180, 183, 187
freedom 2, 4, 5, 6, 7, 8, 18, 19, 21, 22, 55, 56, 62, 79, 84, 85, 86, 91, 92, 98–9, 102, 136, 137, 166–7, 169–71, 173–5, 180, 182, 192, 193, 197, 209
Freud, S. 173–4
From Ritual to Theatre (Turner) 26, 151, 217
Frow, J. 3–4, 6
fun 7, 8, 27, 34, 36, 37, 39, 76–7, 124, 133, 180, 186, 198, 205
fundamental phenomena 95, 100
Funkenmariechen 29, 38

Gadamer, H.-G. 5, 9, 96, 104n11, 105, 172, 173, 174, 176, 211
game 2, 3, 4, 6, 13, 14, 17, 27, 29, 30, 31, 32, 33, 35, 36, 37, 38, 42–52, 71–82, 85, 90, 98, 99, 107–18, 124, 126, 128–31, 133, 146, 152–63, 169, 180, 184–9, 205–16
'Game Game, The' (Midgley) 3, 9, 83, 128, 135
game-playing *see* play, game-playing
game-world 7, 152, 158, 162
games design 72, 74–8, 80, 153, 156, 157, 160–1
games studies 72–9, 152
godgames 8, 206, 208–9, 213–14, 216
Goffman, E. 3
governance 6, 84–8, 90–2
Grasshopper, The (Suits) 9, 52, 83, 217
Griffin, B. 130

Groos, K. 104n19
Gros, F. 9
grotesque 27, 31, 39
Guattari, F. 54, 59, 60, 61
Guillén, C. 22, 23

habitus 156
happiness 101–3
harm/harmlessness 27, 34, 36, 39, 45–6, 47, 50–2, 216
health 123, 131, 133–4, 196
Hegel, G. 102, 193
Heidegger, M. 7, 95, 96, 104n11, 152–63, 163n1, 163n11
Hell 16, 34, 175
Heraclitus 15, 96, 97–8, 99
Hölderlin, F. 153, 158, 174
Homer 7, 15, 24, 107–18
Homo Ludens (Huizinga) 9, 13, 26, 34, 40, 52, 86, 93, 118, 123–34, 160, 164, 176, 190, 202
Huizinga, J. 2, 5, 7, 13–15, 18, 34, 35, 48, 49, 50, 52n1, 85, 118, 123, 124–5, 128, 131, 133, 159–60, 166, 167, 168, 169, 182, 187, 197
humour 35, 180, 189n4, 207
Husserl, E. 95, 96, 103n4, 104n11, 104n12

idealism 38, 96
idealized play *see* play
identity 31, 38, 58, 62, 125, 127, 131, 147, 149, 150, 184, 197, 200, 211
Iliad (Homer) 15, 107, 110, 111
ilinx see play, ilinx
imagination 5, 22, 24–6, 32, 58, 104n11, 127, 128, 130, 133, 161, 168, 173, 181, 183, 184, 187
immanence 60
imperialism 29
improvisation 46, 126, 132, 137–8
individuality 63, 181, 188
Ingold, T. 56, 61, 62, 63, 143
in-itself 166, 174, 193
innocence 5, 14, 33, 54, 57, 58, 60, 98, 99, 216
instrumental 7, 72, 115, 123, 124, 131, 132, 133, 150, 189n7, 192, 193, 196, 197
intention 2, 20, 48, 49, 51, 54, 91, 92, 115, 182, 189, 189n7, 198
interlocutor 186
interrogative space 87
interstices 2, 7, 25, 133

intervention 85, 86, 87, 90, 91, 145, 192, 199, 200
intra-action 61, 62, 63, 64, 194, 198, 199
intra-activity 61, 194
intrinsic 57, 60, 98, 99, 100, 102, 113, 115, 167, 168, 174, 175, 197, 215
irrational play *see* play, irrational
ir/rationality 14, 58, 181, 187
Islam 16

Jaspers, K. 96
joy 7, 13, 20, 23, 25, 34, 36, 53, 63, 78, 81, 101, 112, 113, 123, 125, 127, 128, 130, 133, 167, 169, 179, 182, 183, 184, 186, 188, 198, 199, 206, 210, 213
Juul, J. 42, 46, 47, 50, 51, 52n4, 74

kalokagathia 117
Kant, I. 6, 42–5, 47, 48, 50, 55, 56, 61, 64n1, 166, 167, 168–9, 171, 175n3, 176n5, 182
kindergarten 58
King, T. 8, 205–17
Koster, R. 76–7

laughter 27, 33, 34, 35, 36, 39, 113, 117, 167
learning 58, 76–7, 80, 150, 179, 185, 186, 196
Lefebvre, H. 7, 136–44, 149, 150, 193
Lévinas, E. 96, 104n11, 193, 199, 200
liberation 25, 180, 210
liminality 2, 4, 5, 13–20, 23, 24, 25, 210; liminoid 17–18
Lin, Y. 38–9
lines of flight 198
lived space *see* space
love 22, 34, 43, 89, 100, 101, 109, 110, 111, 139, 212, 216
ludeme 159
ludic 5, 13, 15, 17–25, 86, 89, 92, 109, 110, 111, 112, 113, 117, 126, 197
ludigenic 84, 87, 90, 92
ludus 7, 46, 125–34, 154
ludus–paidia continuum 131–3
lusory attitude 4, 5, 207, 211
lust 7, 126, 127, 128, 129, 131, 132, 133, 205

McGonigal, J. 77, 78, 80, 81
MacIntyre, A. 193
magic circle 2, 3, 5, 7, 48, 85, 160
magister ludi 208

majoritarian 195, 196, 199
make-believe 45, 71, 72, 73, 78, 87
make-believe play *see* play
Malaby, T. 78, 79, 81
Malone, T.W. 77, 80
Man, Play and Games (Caillois) 40, 45, 52, 82, 125, 134, 202
Maradona, D. 129
martial play 27
Marx, K. 193
Massumi, B. 61, 191
material-discursive practice 61
matter 60–2, 64, 191, 194, 197, 198
mediation 104n20, 161
Merleau-Ponty, M. 96, 103n8
metaphor 2, 3, 5, 17, 81, 82, 97, 98, 99, 101, 104n16, 109, 116, 136, 160, 194, 212
metaphysics 7, 8, 19, 55, 99, 104n14, 194
Metaphysics of Morals, Groundwork of (Kant) 55, 176
Midgley, M. 3, 71, 72, 82, 128, 129, 130, 131
military training 27, 31
mimesis 2, 24, 104n20, 155
mimetic play *see* play, mimesis
mimicry 2, 3, 38
mimicry see play, *mimicry* 2, 3, 38
minoritarian 192, 195, 197
mockery 2, 3
molar 198
molecular 198
moments 3, 4, 8, 63, 129, 132, 133, 137, 142, 143, 144, 149, 195, 200
Monty Python 31, 39
moral development 184, 185–6
moral(s), morality 5, 6, 7, 8, 35, 37, 42–5, 47, 52, 53, 58, 63, 64, 98, 107, 117, 127, 155, 171, 172, 179, 181, 182, 184, 185–7, 195, 199, 200, 206, 210
Morris, R. 6, 84–93
movement 7, 29, 31, 59, 64, 85, 90, 98, 99, 103, 103n9, 123, 125, 129, 136, 138–42, 144, 145, 146, 148, 149, 153, 167, 172, 175, 198
movement, intellectual or social 29, 30, 57, 58, 59, 60, 61, 63, 95, 96, 192, 193, 196

narrative 8, 23, 27, 61, 76, 80, 130, 159, 192, 205–13, 214, 216, 216n2
Native American cultures 8, 206, 207, 210, 211, 217n3
natural playground 53, 58, 59

222 *Index*

nature 5, 6, 53–64, 100, 140, 159, 162, 195, 196
nature–culture dualism 54, 61, 62, 63, 195
'nature deficit disorder' 196
Nietzsche, F. 5, 15, 33–4, 36, 39, 97–8, 104n14, 142, 166, 167, 169, 175, 193
nomadic ethics 192, 193, 195, 199, 200
Nomadic Ethics (Braidotti) 65, 201
nonseriousness 7, 107, 108, 114–15, 117

objectivity 61
Odysseus 108, 109, 110, 113, 114, 115, 116
Odyssey (Homer) 107, 108, 109, 110, 111, 113, 115, 116, 118
ontology 5, 7, 8, 60, 63, 95, 97, 98, 99, 101–3, 103n8, 147, 150, 192, 193–4, 196
'ordinary life' 13, 16, 102, 160, 166, 173, 175
Ortega y Gasset, J. 96, 103n9
Other, the/an 35, 55, 57, 64, 127, 185, 186, 188, 195, 196, 197, 199–200

Paidia 7, 125–34
paradox 1, 2, 6, 7, 8, 25, 34, 44, 101, 123, 133, 166, 170–1, 180, 197, 209
parkour 29, 38, 137
Patočka, J. 96, 103n6
Patroclos 110–11, 112, 113, 116, 117, 118
peak 139, 140–1, 149
Penelope 109–10, 111, 115
perceived space *see* space
performance 3, 4, 6, 8, 104n18, 123, 127, 136, 138, 142, 144, 147, 209
phenomenological 3, 6, 39, 79, 95–6, 97, 100, 103n3, 103n7, 103n9, 124, 125, 130, 143, 152
phenomenology 7, 33, 35, 37, 39, 96–7, 103n3, 103n7, 103n8, 104n11, 104n12
philosophical anthropology 95, 99, 100, 102, 104n16
Philosophy for Children 179
Philosophy in Schools (PinS) 8, 179–89, 189n1, 189n2
physical activity 123–4, 133
Plato 15, 16, 21, 24, 102, 125, 181
play: aesthetic 84, 87, 88, 89, 90, 92; *agon* 2, 5, 14, 15, 18, 20, 29, 35, 37, 38, 80, 113, 123, 125, 126, 128, 130, 131, 132; *alea* 52, 125, 126, 128, 130; chaos 171, 207, 211, 213, 214; children's play 5, 7, 8, 27, 31, 32, 37, 58, 81, 86, 98–9, 114, 126, 128, 132, 133, 169, 180, 185, 192–8, 200, 206; competitive play 7, 14, 50, 74, 75, 80, 107–18, 127, 132, 148, 175n2, 215; cosmic play 97–9; dark play 27, 36–9, 209, 211, 214; deep play 209; dialogue-play 181, 187; evil play 5, 37, 42–52; Free play 6, 21, 168; game-playing 3, 6, 20–2, 27, 31, 32, 38, 72, 74–5, 76, 78, 85, 86, 90, 102, 128–9, 133, 152, 184–6, 192, 205–16; idealized play 5, 6, 27, 34, 38, 51, 58, 160; *ilinx* 38, 80, 125, 126, 128, 130; improvised play 138, 144, 149–50; irenic play 25, 26, 208, 209; irrational play 11, 14, 58, 196; make-believe play 45, 72, 87; as meaningful experience 58; as metaphor 97, 99, 101; metaphysics of 7, 8; mimesis 2, 104n20; *mimicry* 125, 126, 128, 130, 154, 155; narrative play 76, 80, 205, 206, 214; original play 14; play-as-autonomous 5, 47, 48, 52n2, 86, 87, 101, 124–5, 131; play as subject 4–5, 6, 7, 8; play fighting 2; play of animals 2, 14, 100, 104n16, 167, 205; play of gods 8, 20, 100, 104n16, 110, 206, 207, 208–9, 213, 214, 216; play spirit 98, 111, 112, 113, 166, 169, 174–5; play-thing 74, 102; play-world 6, 49, 101, 102, 133, 152–64, 216; as progress 58, 127; rough and tumble play 2, 195; sacred play 160; speculative play 102, 103; structural analysis of 97, 101–2
playful disturbance 126–7, 198
playful engagement 2, 32, 87, 88, 138, 139, 144, 146, 148, 150, 179, 182, 183, 184, 187, 188–9
playfulness 3, 8, 14, 123, 124, 133, 181, 182–3, 188, 189n9, 193, 195, 198, 200, 206, 216
playground 20, 21, 53, 58, 59, 73, 84, 85, 86, 87, 88, 90, 92, 125, 160, 168, 192, 193, 196, 208
playspace (*Spielraum*) 167
playwork 8, 191–7, 199, 200
Playwork Principles 192, 197, 199
pleasure 13, 27, 32, 36, 39, 46, 78, 81, 123, 126, 128, 130, 133, 167, 168, 169, 170, 179, 186, 206, 209, 216
politics 24, 53, 171, 195, 199
posthuman 60–4, 192, 195
postmodern 5, 17, 35

power 15, 18, 20–2, 24–6, 27, 33, 64, 100, 126, 131, 144, 158, 161, 173, 174, 199, 208, 209, 210, 211
practice-as-research 7, 136, 138
production of space 136, 137, 141
Production of Space (Lefebvre) 142
prop theory 72–4

Rawls, J. 87, 90, 114
real world 4, 5, 7, 8, 47, 152, 154, 159, 174, 182, 212
realism 54, 61, 64, 96, 194
recalcitrance 192, 193, 195
re/enact(ment) 6, 18, 20, 29, 56, 57, 59, 61, 62, 64, 141, 144, 187, 195, 198, 208, 210
reflective equilibrium 107, 113, 116
regulatory rules *see* rules, regulatory
Regulier, C. 139
relational ethics 192, 195
repetition 139, 140, 142, 144, 145, 146
representation 31, 32, 39, 53, 61, 52, 71, 72, 73, 99, 104n18, 104n20, 128, 142, 155, 168, 192, 193, 194
representational space 141, 142, 143
representations of space 141, 143
resistance 2, 5, 6, 8, 141, 142, 148, 149
rhetoric 53, 58, 59
rhythms 63, 136, 137, 139–40, 141–5, 147, 149, 150, 172; cyclical rhythms 139–40, 145, 146, 149; intra-ordinary 144, 146; linear rhythms 139–40, 144, 145, 147, 149
Rhythmanalysis (Lefebvre) 136, 137, 139, 142, 143, 144, 149
rhythmic interruption 136, 150
ritual 17, 30, 35, 81, 104, 160, 162, 210, 212, 215
Rousseau, J.-J. 55, 57, 58
rule-bound 2, 42, 45, 46, 47, 48, 123, 138, 181, 184, 185
rule-breaking/rule-violation 1, 49
rule-governed play 45, 176n4
rules: constitutive 2, 4, 48, 49, 87, 89, 90, 91, 92, 130; eligibility 4; optimizing 87, 91, 92; regulatory 2, 4, 90, 91; structured 2, 166, 167, 169, 175

Sartre, J.-P. 96, 104n11
Schechner, R. 37, 146, 205, 209, 210, 211
schema 141, 171, 184, 185
Schütz, A. 96, 103n7
scouting 30, 31, 32

Searle, J. 48, 90
self-realization 55, 125, 127, 129
seriousness/nonseriousness/overseriousness 2, 3, 7, 13, 15, 17, 18, 19, 107, 108, 114, 115, 117, 183
skateboarding 137, 142, 150n2
sociability 182
Socrates 16, 24, 181
space: production of 136, 137, 141, 142; conceived space 145; lived space 141, 144; perceived space 142, 144
Spariosu, M. 4, 5, 13, 15, 24, 208, 210
spatial practice 136, 138, 141, 142, 143, 144, 145, 150
spectator 102, 113, 117, 118, 129, 170
Spinoza, B. 198
spoilsport 50
spontaneity 200
sport 2, 7, 14, 15, 27, 29, 30, 38, 50, 80, 107–18, 123–4, 125, 126, 127, 129, 131, 132, 133, 146, 155, 169, 172, 173, 210
Sterne, L. 27
subject 4, 5, 6, 9, 57, 59, 63, 74, 85, 96, 141, 168, 170, 171, 172, 173, 194, 195, 197, 199, 200, 206
subjecthood 4, 5, 7
subjectivity 4, 5, 63, 200
subversion 3, 4, 145
Suits, B. 4, 48–9, 78, 81, 129, 207
Sutton-Smith, B. 2, 17, 37, 58, 79, 124, 146, 147, 196
symbol 2, 4, 6, 95, 97, 100, 102, 103n3, 104n20, 110, 116, 142, 145, 184

technology 59
Temporary Autonomous Zone (TAZ) 2, 3
Tetris 155, 156
the 'in-between' 16, 19, 21, 180, 189n5
theology 15, 16
thinking skills 183, 184
Thus Spoke Zarathustra (Nietzsche) 33–4, 36, 97
time 3, 7, 13, 17, 18, 23, 45, 48, 57, 58, 59, 62, 63, 64, 95, 104n13, 125, 136, 140, 144, 145, 147, 152, 153, 155, 156, 162, 163n1, 166, 167, 172, 173, 174, 175, 182, 193, 196, 198
training 27, 29, 31, 32, 33, 38, 127, 144
transformation 25, 125, 137, 201, 216
trickster 8, 206, 209, 213, 217n3
Truth 3, 8, 9, 24, 34, 55, 79, 124, 153, 155, 156, 163, 191
Turner, V. 17–18, 146, 148, 205, 210

understanding 2, 6, 8, 17, 22, 37, 39, 53, 55, 58, 61, 63, 64, 71, 72, 73, 74, 80, 84, 89, 95, 99, 101, 107, 113, 123, 137, 139, 141, 149, 159, 162, 164n13, 168, 186, 188, 192, 197, 198, 208
urban 7, 29, 136–7, 144
urban space and capital 136, 144
utopia(n) 5, 13, 14, 15, 18, 20, 21, 22, 23, 24, 25, 26, 57, 59, 195, 197, 205, 206, 216

van Creveld, M. 35
vertigo 80, 126
video games 74, 156
violence 14, 31, 32, 34, 38, 54, 57, 110, 112, 115, 117, 139, 159, 200
virtuality 171
volition 85, 86, 87, 210

Walton, K. 71–4
war 5–6, 8, 14, 15, 22, 27–39, 107, 108, 109, 111, 112, 115, 116, 117, 157, 160, 161, 169
war games 35–8
will to power 25, 33, 209
winning 51, 112, 126
wisdom 112, 181
Wittgenstein, L. 20, 71, 72, 82
work 3, 5, 7, 8, 13, 17–18, 20, 29, 31, 59, 73, 78, 97, 100, 101, 130, 136, 143, 144, 152, 159, 161, 163n1, 182, 183–4, 191–201
world-decay 7, 152, 154, 155, 157, 162
world-withdrawal 7, 152, 155, 156, 157, 162, 163n1
worlding 7, 154, 156–7, 162–3, 163n1